Women at Work

Women at Work

INTERVIEWS FROM
the PARIS REVIEW

WITH A PREFACE BY

Ottessa Moshfegh

AND ILLUSTRATIONS BY

Joana Avillez

PARIS REVIEW EDITIONS

New York

Paris Review Editions
544 West 27th Street, New York 10001

Copyright © 2017 by The Paris Review
All rights reserved.

ISBN 978-0-692-93484-5

Printed by the Sheridan Press in Hanover, Pa.

First Edition

1 3 5 7 9 10 8 6 4 2

Designed by Jonathan D. Lippincott

Contents

Preface

In a letter to his parents, George Plimpton once described *The Paris Review* interview as "an essay in dialogue on technique." As you will see from this volume, technique is always the main topic—how a writer begins to write, to think of herself as a writer; what struggles she meets; if and how she overcomes them. But thanks to the unusual method invented by Plimpton and the other founders of the *Review* in the early fifties, and still in use today, the conversation is never limited to a discussion of craft or structure. The dialogues turn into stories of their own.

What is the *Paris Review* method? First, the interviewer studies the writer's books. Then the interviewer and subject meet and, in most cases, meet again, and often again. Sometimes one session is enough, but the process can also last months or years (even if the published version is seamlessly presented as the work of a single afternoon). There are no deadlines. Sometimes an interview ends only with the writer's death, as is the case in my own favorite from this collection: Marguerite Yourcenar's. Whenever possible, the author is encouraged to revise, cut, rearrange, and add to her own words. As a result, some of the voices in this book sound edited, literary, written rather than spoken. Others are more casual, such as Isak Dinesen's, whose interview is presented as a three-act play, with the baroness as an almost fictional character—"Slim, straight, chic, she is dressed in black, with long black gloves and a black Parisian hat that comes forward to shadow her remarkable eyes that are lighter in color at the top than at the bottom." The interviewer also captures her perfectly couched attitude toward being investigated as an author: "Read it," Dinesen says ("smiling mischievously") about "The Deluge at Norderney." "Read it, and you'll see how it's written." But even a cagey or blasé answer is revealing in its own way, since it suggests how the writer wished to be seen and, often, what she wished to hide.

So much of the writing life is mundane. Buying printer ink and paper, doing dishes, arranging the pens in the cup, smoke breaks on the phone, taking baths or going for walks or sitting blankly on the couch wondering if the day will end before one makes a discovery or decision. These habits of day-to-day tedium are what can't be seen on the surface of a writer's face when we meet her at a book signing—the time and effort spent living in her own head. Writing is a lonesome art. That's why it requires another person in the room—like an interviewer—to bring her hours of labor to life. In some of these interviews, I feel the awe and sadness of someone looking back at the life she had—past tense. It may still be brimming with passion and purpose, but she is not on the brink of it anymore. In other interviews, the creative process is still in flux, and the writer is in the midst of growth. Sometimes both things are true. Joan Didion says about *A Book of Common Prayer*, "I wrote it around 1975, so [my daughter] would have been nine, but I was already anticipating separation and actually working through that ahead of time. So novels are also about things you're afraid you can't deal with." I love moments like this, proof that while one's published work is meant to stand certain and immovable, the consciousness behind it is in flux, developing personally alongside the work. That for me is the deep attraction of the interviews in this volume. They capture the movement of a self over time, always in contact with another person, from out of the depths and into the light.

The writers in this book all identify as female, although—as one would expect of any dozen women whose careers span more than a century—that fact means very different things from interview to interview. One near constant is the question of the feminist movement and the writer's responsibility to the cause. Sometimes the reaction is defensive. Simone de Beauvoir: "I've shown women as they are, as divided human beings, and not as they ought to be." Sometimes it's downright hostile. My hero Yourcenar: "I have a horror of such movements, because I think that an intelligent woman is worth an intelligent man—if you can find any—and that a stupid woman is every bit as boring as her male counterpart. Human wickedness is almost equally distributed between the two sexes." The travel writer Jan Morris, born James Humphrey Morris, speaks honestly and (to me) surprisingly about the advantages of traveling as a woman in the late twentieth century (having transitioned in 1964): "The relationship between women, between one woman and another, is a much closer one than the relationship between men. Wherever a woman travels in the world she's got a few million friends waiting to help her."

But because these *Paris Review* interviews are "essays in dialogue," not actual essays or fixed portraits, it is misleading to quote them the way I have just done. Each interview is the record, however distilled, of a conversation, with gambits tried and thrown away, attitudes adopted and discarded. Even set down for posterity, they capture the serendipity of talk, the way another person brings perspective into a room where before there was only intensity and solitude. At their best, the interviews retain the lightness and irresponsibility of those candid conversations we remember all our lives because they allowed us to wander into unsuspected truths about ourselves. Each writer is allowed her evasions, even her gaffs, but to point them out does an injustice to the living thing that is trembling beneath the surface of these words—a whole person laying bare what she can of herself and her writing. One has to read them to understand.

Ottessa Moshfegh

Women at Work

Dorothy Parker

THE ART OF FICTION NO. 13

Interviewed by Marion Capron

At the time of this interview, Mrs. Parker was living in a midtown New York hotel. She shared her small apartment with a youthful poodle that had the run of the place and had caused it to look, as Mrs. Parker said apologetically, somewhat "Hogarthian": newspapers spread about the floor, picked lamb chops here and there, and a rubber doll—its throat torn from ear to ear—which Mrs. Parker lobbed left-handed from her chair into corners of the room for the poodle to retrieve—as it did, never tiring of the opportunity. The room was sparsely decorated, its one overpowering fixture being a large dog portrait, not of the poodle, but of a sheepdog owned by the author Philip Wylie, and painted by his wife. The portrait indicated a dog of such size that if it were real would have dwarfed Mrs. Parker, who was a small woman, her voice gentle, her tone often apologetic, but occasionally, given the opportunity to comment on matters she felt strongly about, she spoke almost harshly, and her sentences were punctuated with observations phrased with lethal force. Hers was still the wit that made her a legend as a member of the Round Table of the Algonquin—a humor whose particular quality seemed a coupling of brilliant social commentary with a mind of devastating inventiveness. She seemed able to produce the well-turned phrase for any occasion. A friend remembered sitting next to her at the theater when the news was announced of the death of the stolid Calvin Coolidge. "How can they tell?" whispered Mrs. Parker.

Readers of this interview, however, will find that Mrs. Parker had only contempt for the eager reception accorded her wit. "Why, it got so bad," she had said bitterly, "that they began to laugh before I opened my mouth." And she had a similar attitude toward her value as a serious writer. But Mrs. Parker was her own worst critic. Her three books of poetry may have established her reputation as a master of light verse, but her short stories were essentially serious in tone—serious in that they reflected her own life, which was in many ways an unhappy one—and also serious in their intention. Franklin P. Adams described them in an introduction to her work: "Nobody can write such ironic things unless he has a deep sense of injustice—injustice to those members of the race who are the victims of the stupid, the pretentious and the hypocritical."

INTERVIEWER

Your first job was on *Vogue*, wasn't it? How did you go about getting hired, and why *Vogue*?

After my father died there wasn't any money. I had to work, you see, and Mr. Crowninshield, God rest his soul, paid twelve dollars for a small verse of mine and gave me a job at ten dollars a week. Well, I thought I was Edith Sitwell. I lived in a boarding house at 103rd and Broadway, paying eight dollars a week for my room and two meals, breakfast and dinner. Thorne Smith was there, and another man. We used to sit around in the evening and talk. There was no money, but, Jesus, we had fun.

INTERVIEWER

What kind of work did you do at *Vogue*?

PARKER

I wrote captions. "This little pink dress will win you a beau," that sort of thing. Funny, they were plain women working at *Vogue*, not chic. They were decent, nice women—the nicest women I ever met—but they had no business on such a magazine. They wore funny little bonnets and in the pages of their magazine they virginized the models from tough babes into exquisite little loves. Now the editors are what they should be: all chic and worldly; most of the models are out of the mind of a Bram Stoker, and as for the caption writers—my old job—they're recommending mink covers at seventy-five dollars apiece for the wooden ends of golf clubs "—for the friend who has everything." Civilization is coming to an end, you understand.

INTERVIEWER

Why did you change to *Vanity Fair*?

Mr. Crowninshield wanted me to. Mr. Sherwood and Mr. Benchley—we always called each other by our last names—were there. Our office was across from the Hippodrome. The midgets would come out and frighten Mr. Sherwood. He was about seven feet tall and they were always sneaking up behind him and asking him how the weather was up there. "Walk down the street with me," he'd ask, and Mr. Benchley and I would leave our jobs and guide him down the street. I can't tell you, we had more fun. Both Mr. Benchley and I subscribed to two undertaking magazines: *The Casket* and *Sunnyside*. Steel yourself: *Sunnyside* had a joke column called "From Grave to Gay." I cut a picture out of one of them, in color, of how and where to inject embalming fluid, and had it hung over my desk until Mr. Crowninshield asked me if I could possibly take it down. Mr. Crowninshield was a lovely man, but puzzled. I must say we behaved extremely badly. Albert Lee, one of the editors, had a map over his desk with little flags on it to show where our troops were fighting during the First World War. Every day he would get the news and move the flags around. I was married, my husband was overseas, and since I didn't have anything better to do I'd get up half an hour early and go down and change his flags. Later on, Lee would come in, look at his map, and he'd get very serious about spies— shout, and spend his morning moving his little pins back into position.

INTERVIEWER

How long did you stay at *Vanity Fair*?

Four years. I'd taken over the drama criticism from P. G. Wodehouse. Then I fixed three plays—one of them *Caesar's Wife*, with Billie Burke in it—and as a result I was fired.

You *fixed* three plays?

Well, panned. The plays closed and the producers, who were the big boys—Dillingham, Ziegfeld, and Belasco—didn't like it, you know. *Vanity Fair* was a magazine of no opinion, but I had opinions. So I was fired. And Mr. Sherwood and Mr. Benchley resigned their jobs. It was all right for Mr. Sherwood, but Mr. Benchley had a family—two children. It was the greatest act of friendship I'd known. Mr. Benchley did a sign, "Contributions for Miss Billie Burke," and on our way out we left it in the hall of *Vanity Fair*. We behaved very badly. We made ourselves discharge chevrons and wore them.

Where did you all go after *Vanity Fair*?

Mr. Sherwood became the motion-picture critic for the old *Life*. Mr. Benchley did the drama reviews. He and I had an office so tiny that an inch smaller and it would have been adultery. We had *Parkbench* for a cable address, but no one ever sent us one. It was so long ago—before you were a gleam in someone's eyes—that I doubt there *was* a cable.

It's a popular supposition that there was much more communication between writers in the twenties. The Round Table discussions in the Algonquin, for example.

PARKER

I wasn't there very often—it cost too much. Others went. Kaufman was there. I guess he was sort of funny. Mr. Benchley and Mr. Sherwood went when they had a nickel. Franklin P. Adams, whose column was widely read by people who wanted to write, would sit in occasionally. And Harold Ross, the *New Yorker* editor. He was a professional lunatic, but I don't know if he was a great man. He had a profound ignorance. On one of Mr. Benchley's manuscripts he wrote in the margin opposite *Andromache*, "Who he?" Mr. Benchley wrote back, "You keep out of this." The only one with stature who came to the Round Table was Heywood Broun.

INTERVIEWER

What was it about the twenties that inspired people like yourself and Broun?

PARKER

Gertrude Stein did us the most harm when she said, "You're all a lost generation." That got around to certain people and we all said, Whee! We're lost. Perhaps it suddenly brought to us the sense of change. Or irresponsibility. But don't forget that, though the people in the twenties seemed like flops, they weren't. Fitzgerald, the rest of them, reckless as they were, drinkers as they were, they worked damn hard and all the time.

Did the "lost generation" attitude you speak of have a detrimental effect on your own work?

Silly of me to blame it on dates, but so it happened to be. Dammit, it *was* the "twenties" and we had to be smarty. I *wanted* to be cute. That's the terrible thing. I should have had more sense.

And during this time you were writing poems?

My verses. I cannot say poems. Like everybody was then, I was following in the exquisite footsteps of Miss Millay, unhappily in my own horrible sneakers. My verses are no damn good. Let's face it, honey, my verse is terribly dated—as anything once fashionable is dreadful now. I gave it up, knowing it wasn't getting any better, but nobody seemed to notice my magnificent gesture.

Do you think your verse writing has been of any benefit to your prose?

Franklin P. Adams once gave me a book of French verse forms and told me to copy their design, that by copying them I would get precision in prose. The men you imitate in verse influence your prose, and what I got out of it was precision, all I realize I've ever had in prose writing.

How did you get started in writing?

I fell into writing, I suppose, being one of those awful children who wrote verses. I went to a convent in New York—the Blessed Sacrament. Convents do the same things progressive schools do, only they don't know it. They don't teach you how to read; you have to find out for yourself. At my convent we *did* have a textbook, one that devoted a page and a half to Adelaide Anne Procter; but we couldn't read Dickens; he was vulgar, you know. But I read him and Thackeray, and I'm the one woman you'll ever know who's read every word of Charles Reade, the author of *The Cloister and the Hearth*. But as for helping me in the outside world, the convent taught me only that if you spit on a pencil eraser it will erase ink. And I remember the smell of oilcloth, the smell of nuns' garb. I was fired from there, finally, for a lot of things, among them my insistence that the Immaculate Conception was spontaneous combustion.

Have you ever drawn from those years for story material?

All those writers who write about their childhood! Gentle God, if I wrote about mine you wouldn't sit in the same room with me.

What, then, would you say is the source of most of your work?

Need of money, dear.

And besides that?

It's easier to write about those you hate—just as it's easier to criticize a bad play or a bad book.

What about "Big Blonde" (1929)? Where did the idea for that come from?

I knew a lady—a friend of mine who went through holy hell. Just say I knew a woman once. The purpose of the writer is to say what he feels and sees. To those who write fantasies—the Misses Baldwin, Ferber, Norris—I am not at home.

That's not showing much respect for your fellow women, at least not the writers.

As artists they're not, but as providers they're oil wells; they gush. Norris said she never wrote a story unless it was fun to do. I understand Ferber whistles at her typewriter. And there was that poor sucker

Flaubert rolling around on his floor for three days looking for the right word. I'm a feminist, and God knows I'm loyal to my sex, and you must remember that from my very early days, when this city was scarcely safe from buffaloes, I was in the struggle for equal rights for women. But when we paraded through the catcalls of men and when we chained ourselves to lampposts to try to get our equality—dear child, we didn't foresee *those* female writers. Or Clare Boothe Luce, or Perle Mesta, or Oveta Culp Hobby.

INTERVIEWER

You have an extensive reputation as a wit. Has this interfered, do you think, with your acceptance as a serious writer?

PARKER

I don't want to be classed as a humorist. It makes me feel guilty. I've never read a good tough quotable female humorist, and I never was one myself. I couldn't do it. A smartcracker they called me, and that makes me sick and unhappy. There's a hell of a distance between wisecracking and wit. Wit has truth in it; wisecracking is simply calisthenics with words. I didn't mind so much when they were good, but for a long time anything that was called a crack was attributed to me—and then they got the shaggy dogs.

INTERVIEWER

How about satire?

Ah, satire. That's another matter. They're the big
boys. If I'd been called a satirist there'd be no living with me. But by "satirist" I mean those boys in
the other centuries. The people we call satirists now
are those who make cracks at topical topics and consider themselves satirists—creatures like George
S. Kaufman and such who don't even know what
satire is. Lord knows, a writer should show his times,
but not show them in wisecracks. Their stuff is not
satire; it's as dull as yesterday's newspaper. Successful satire has got to be pretty good the day after
tomorrow.

INTERVIEWER

And how about contemporary humorists? Do you
feel about them as you do about satirists?

PARKER

You get to a certain age and only the tired writers
are funny. I read my verses now and I ain't funny.
I haven't been funny for twenty years. But anyway there aren't any humorists anymore, except for
Perelman. There's no need for them. Perelman must
be very lonely.

INTERVIEWER

Why is there no need for the humorist?

PARKER

It's a question of supply and demand. If we needed
them, we'd have them. The new crop of would-be
humorists doesn't count. They're like the would-be
satirists. They write about topical topics. Not like

Thurber and Mr. Benchley. Those two were damn well-read and, though I hate the word, they were cultured. What sets them apart is that they both had a point of view to express. That is important to all good writing. It's the difference between Paddy Chayefsky, who just puts down lines, and Clifford Odets, who in his early plays not only sees but has a point of view. The writer must be aware of life around him. Carson McCullers is good, or she used to be, but now she's withdrawn from life and writes about freaks. Her characters are grotesques.

INTERVIEWER

Speaking of Chayefsky and McCullers, do you read much of your own or the present generation of writers?

PARKER

I will say of the writers of today that some of them, thank God, have the sense to adapt to their times. Mailer's *The Naked and the Dead* is a great book. And I thought William Styron's *Lie Down in Darkness* an extraordinary thing. The start of it took your heart and flung it over there. He writes like a god. But for most of my reading I go back to the old ones—for comfort. As you get older you go much farther back. I read *Vanity Fair* about a dozen times a year. I was a woman of eleven when I first read it—the thrill of that line "George, who was laying on his face, dead, with a bullet through his heart." Sometimes I read, as an elegant friend of mine calls them, "who-did-its." I love Sherlock Holmes. My life is so untidy and he's so neat. But as for living novelists, I suppose E. M. Forster is the best, not knowing what that is, but at least he's a semifinalist, wouldn't you think?

Somerset Maugham once said to me, "We have a novelist over here, E. M. Forster, though I don't suppose he's familiar to you." Well, I could have kicked him. Did he think I carried a papoose on my back? Why, I'd go on my hands and knees to get to Forster. He once wrote something I've always remembered: "If I had to choose between betraying my country and betraying my friend I hope I should have the guts to betray my country." Now doesn't that make the Fifth Amendment look like a bum?

INTERVIEWER

Could I ask you some technical questions? How do you actually write out a story? Do you write out a draft and then go over it or what?

PARKER

It takes me six months to do a story. I think it out and then write it sentence by sentence—no first draft. I can't write five words but that I change seven.

INTERVIEWER

How do you name your characters?

PARKER

The telephone book and from the obituary columns.

INTERVIEWER

Do you keep a notebook?

PARKER

I tried to keep one, but I never could remember where I put the damn thing. I always say I'm going to keep one tomorrow.

How do you get the story down on paper?

I wrote in longhand at first, but I've lost it. I use two fingers on the typewriter. I think it's unkind of you to ask. I know so little about the typewriter that once I bought a new one because I couldn't change the ribbon on the one I had.

INTERVIEWER
You're working on a play now, aren't you?

PARKER
Yes, collaborating with Arnaud d'Usseau. I'd like to do a play more than anything. First night is the most exciting thing in the world. It's wonderful to hear your words spoken. Unhappily, our first play, *The Ladies of the Corridor* (1953), was not a success, but writing that play was the best time I ever had, both for the privilege and the stimulation of working with Mr. d'Usseau and because that play was the only thing I have ever done in which I had great pride.

INTERVIEWER
How about the novel? Have you ever tried that form?

PARKER
I wish to God I could do one, but I haven't got the nerve.

INTERVIEWER
And short stories? Are you still doing them?

I'm trying now to do a story that's purely narrative.
I think narrative stories are the best, though my past
stories make themselves stories by telling themselves
through what people say. I haven't got a visual mind.
I hear things. But I'm not going to do those he-said,
she-said things anymore, they're over, honey, they're
over. I want to do the story that can only be told
in the narrative form, and though they're going to
scream about the rent, I'm going to do it.

Do you think economic security an advantage to
the writer?

Yes. Being in a garret doesn't do you any good unless
you're some sort of a Keats. The people who lived
and wrote well in the twenties were comfortable and
living easy. They were able to find stories and novels,
and good ones, in conflicts that came out of two million dollars a year, not a garret. As for me, I'd like to
have money. And I'd like to be a good writer. These
two can come together, and I hope they will, but if
that's too adorable, I'd rather have money. I hate
almost all rich people, but I think I'd be darling at it.
At the moment, however, I like to think of Maurice
Baring's remark: "If you would know what the Lord
God thinks of money, you have only to look at those
to whom he gives it." I realize that's not much help
when the wolf comes scratching at the door, but it's
a comfort.

What do you think about the artist being supported by the state?

Naturally, when penniless, I think it's superb. I think that the art of the country so immeasurably adds to its prestige that if you want the country to have writers and artists—persons who live precariously in our country—the state must help. I do not think that any kind of artist thrives under charity, by which I mean one person or organization giving him money. Here and there, this and that—that's no good. The difference between the state giving and the individual patron is that one is charity and the other isn't. Charity is murder and you know it. But I do think that if the government supports its artists, they need have no feeling of gratitude—the meanest and most sniveling attribute in the world—or baskets being brought to them, or apple polishing. Working for the state—for Christ's sake, are you grateful to your employers? Let the state see what its artists are trying to do—like France with the Académie Française. The artists are a part of their country and their country should recognize this, so both it and the artists can take pride in their efforts. Now I mean that, my dear.

How about Hollywood as provider for the artist?

Hollywood money isn't money. It's congealed snow, melts in your hand, and there you are. I can't talk about Hollywood. It was a horror to me when I was there and it's a horror to look back on. I can't imagine how I did it. When I got away from it I couldn't even refer to the place by name. "Out there," I called it. You want to know what "out there" means to me? Once I was coming down a street in Beverly Hills and I saw a Cadillac about a block long, and out of the side window was a wonderfully slinky mink, and an arm, and at the end of the arm a hand in a white suede glove wrinkled around the wrist, and in the hand was a bagel with a bite out of it.

INTERVIEWER

Do you think Hollywood destroys the artist's talent?

PARKER

No, no, no. I think nobody on earth writes down. Garbage though they turn out, Hollywood writers aren't writing down. That is their best. If you're going to write, don't pretend to write down. It's going to be the best you can do, and it's the fact that it's the best you can do that kills you. I want so much to write well, though I know I don't, and that I didn't make it. But during and at the end of my life, I will adore those who have.

INTERVIEWER

Then what is it that's the evil in Hollywood?

PARKER

It's the people. Like the director who put his finger in Scott Fitzgerald's face and complained, "Pay you. Why, you ought to pay us." It was terrible about Scott; if you'd seen him you'd have been sick. When he died no one went to the funeral, not a single soul came, or even sent a flower. I said, "Poor son of a bitch," a quote right out of *The Great Gatsby*, and everyone thought it was another wisecrack. But it was said in dead seriousness. Sickening about Scott. And it wasn't only the people, but also the indignity to which your ability was put. There was a picture in which Mr. Benchley had a part. In it Monty Woolley had a scene in which he had to enter a room through a door on which was balanced a bucket of water. He came into the room covered with water and muttered to Mr. Benchley, who had a part in the scene, "Benchley? Benchley of *Harvard*?" "Yes," mumbled Mr. Benchley and he asked, "Woolley? Woolley of *Yale*?"

INTERVIEWER

How about your political views? Have they made any difference to you professionally?

PARKER

Oh, certainly. Though I don't think this "blacklist" business extends to the theater or certain of the magazines, in Hollywood it exists because several gentlemen felt it best to drop names like marbles which bounced back like rubber balls about people they'd seen in the company of what they charmingly called "commies." You can't go back thirty years to Sacco and Vanzetti. I won't do it. Well, well, well, that's the way it is. If all this means something to the good of the movies, I don't know what it is. Sam Goldwyn said, "How'm I gonna do decent pictures when all my good writers are in jail?" Then he added, the infallible Goldwyn, "Don't misunderstand me, they all ought to be hung." Mr. Goldwyn didn't know about "hanged." That's all there is to say. It's not the tragedies that kill us, it's the messes. I can't stand messes. I'm not being a smartcracker. You know I'm not when you meet me—don't you, honey?

(1956)

Isak Dinesen

THE ART OF FICTION NO. 14

Interviewed by Eugene Walter

It was, in a sense, typecasting, when a few years ago a film was planned that would have shown us Garbo playing the role of Isak Dinesen in a screen version of *Out of Africa* (1937)...for the writer is, like the actress, a Mysterious Creature of the North. Isak Dinesen is really the Danish Baroness Karen Christentze Blixen-Finecke and is the daughter of Wilhelm Dinesen, author of a classic nineteenth-century work, *Boganis Jagtbreve* (*Letters from the Hunt*). Baroness Blixen has published under different names in various countries: usually Isak Dinesen, but also Tania Blixen and Karen Blixen. Old friends call her Tanne, Tanya, and Tania. Then there is a delightful novel she preferred not to acknowledge for a while, though any reader with half an eye could guess the baroness hiding behind the second pseudonym, Pierre Andrézel. Literary circles have buzzed with legends about her: she is really a man, he is really a woman, "Isak Dinesen" is really a brother-and-sister collaboration, "Isak Dinesen" came to America in the 1870s, she is really a Parisienne, he lives at Elsinore, she stays mostly in London, she is a nun, he is very hospitable and receives young writers, she is difficult to see and lives as a recluse, she writes in French; no, in English; no, in Danish; she is really—and so the buzzing never stopped.

In 1934 the house of Haas & Smith (later absorbed by Random House) brought out a book called *Seven Gothic Tales*, which Mr. Haas had accepted on first reading. It became a best seller. A favorite among writers and painters, the book was discussed from first appearance as of some permanence.

Outside the canon of modern literature, like an oriole outside a cage of moulting linnets, "Isak Dinesen" offers to her readers the unending satisfaction of the tale told: "And then what happened? ... Well, then ... " Her storyteller's, or ballad maker's, instinct, coupled with an individual style of well-ornamented clarity, led Hemingway, accepting the Nobel Prize, to protest it should have gone to Dinesen.

SCENE ONE

Rome, early summer, 1956. The first dialogue takes place in a sidewalk restaurant in the Piazza Navona, that long space, once flooded, where mock naval battles raged. The twilight is darkening the sky to an iris color; against it the obelisk that stands amidst Bernini's figures seems pale and weightless. At a café table sit Baroness Blixen, her secretary–traveling companion, Clara Svendsen, and the Interviewer. The Baroness is like a personage from one of her own tales. Slim, straight, chic, she is dressed in black, with long black gloves and a black Parisian hat that comes forward to shadow her remarkable eyes, which are lighter in color at the top than at the bottom. Her face is slender and distinguished; around her mouth and eyes play the faint ghosts of smiles, changing constantly. Her voice is pleasing, being soft but with enough force and timbre for one to hear at once that this is a lady with opinions of both grave profundity and of most enchanting frivolity. Her companion, Miss Svendsen, is a fresh-faced young person with a charming smile.

ISAK DINESEN

Interview? Oh, dear ... Well, yes, I suppose so ... but not a list of questions or a third degree, I hope ... I was interviewed a short time ago ... Terrible ...

MISS SVENDSEN

Yes, there was a man who came for a documentary film ... It was like a catechism lesson ...

DINESEN

Couldn't we just talk together as we've been doing, you could write down what you like?

INTERVIEWER

Yes, then you could scratch out some things and scribble in others.

DINESEN

Yes. I ought not to undertake too much. I've been ill for over a year and in a nursing home. I really thought I should die. I planned to die, that is, I made preparations. I expected to.

The doctor in Copenhagen told me: "Tania Blixen is very clever, but the cleverest thing she's ever done is to survive these two operations."

DINESEN

I even planned a last radio talk... I have made a number of radio talks on all kinds of subjects, in Denmark... They seem to enjoy me as a radio speaker there... I planned a talk on how easy it was to die... Not a morbid message, I don't mean that, but a message of, well, cheer... that it was a great and lovely experience to die. But I was too ill, you know, to get it done. Now, after being so long in the nursing home and so ill, I don't feel I do really belong to this life. I am hovering like a seagull. I feel that the world is happy and splendid and goes on but that I'm not part of it. I've come to Rome to try and get into the world again. Oh, look at the sky now!

INTERVIEWER

Do you know Rome well? How long since you've been here?

DINESEN

A few years ago, when I had an audience with the Pope. I first came in 1912 as a young girl, staying with my cousin and best friend, who was married to our Danish ambassador to Rome. We rode in the Borghese gardens then, every day. There were carriages with all the great beauties of the day in them, and one stopped and chatted. It was delightful. Now look at these motors and motor bicycles and noise and rushing about. It's what the young today want, though: speed is the greatest thing for them. But when I think of riding my horse—I always had a horse when I was a girl—I feel that something very precious is lost to them today. Children of my day lived differently. We had little in the way of toys, even in great houses. Modern mechanical playthings, which furnish their own motion, had hardly come into existence. We had simpler toys and had to animate them. My love of marionettes springs from this, I think. I've tried my hand at writing marionette plays. One might, of course, buy a hobbyhorse, but we loved better a knotted stick personally chosen in the woods, which our imagination could turn into Bucephalus or Pegasus. Unlike children of today, who are content from birth to be observers... we were creators. Young people today are not acquainted with the elements or in touch with them. Everything is mechanical and urban: children are raised up without knowing live fire, living water, the earth. Young people want to break with the past, they hate the past, they don't want to even hear of it, and one can partly understand it. The near past to them is nothing but a long history of wars, which to them is without interest. It may be the end of something, of a kind of civilization.

INTERVIEWER

But loathe leads to love: they may be led in a circle back to a tradition. I should be frightened of indifference more.

DINESEN

Perhaps. And I myself, you know, I should like to love what they love. Now, I love jazz. I think it's the only new thing in music in my lifetime. I don't prefer it to the old music, but I enjoy it very much.

Much of your work seems to belong to the last century. For instance, *The Angelic Avengers* (1944).

[*Laughing.*] Oh, that's my illegitimate child! During the German occupation of Denmark I thought I should go mad with boredom and dullness. I wanted so to be amused, to amuse myself, and besides I was short of money, so I went to my publisher in Copenhagen and said, Look here, will you give me an advance on a novel and send me a stenographer to dictate it to? They said they would, and she appeared, and I started dictating. I had no idea at all of what the story would be about when I began. I added a little every day, improvising. It was very baffling to the poor stenographer.

Yes, she was used to business letters, and when she'd type the story from her shorthand notes, she'd put numbers sometimes like "the 2 terrified girls" or "his 1 love."

I'd start one day by saying, "Then Mr. So-and-so entered the room," and the stenographer would cry out, "Oh dear, but he can't! He died yesterday in chapter seventeen." No, I prefer to keep *The Angelic Avengers* my secret.

I loved it, and I remember it had excellent notices.
Did many people guess that you had written it?

A few.

And what about *Winter's Tales* (1942)? That came
out in the midst of the war—how did you get the
book to America?

I went to Stockholm—not in itself an easy thing
to accomplish—and, what was even more difficult,
took the manuscript with me. I went to the American
embassy and asked them if they didn't have planes
going to the United States every day, and if they
couldn't take the manuscript, but they said they only
carried strictly political or diplomatic papers, so
I went to the British embassy and asked them, and
they asked could I supply references in England, and
I could (I had many friends in the cabinet, among
them Anthony Eden), so they cabled to check this,
then said yes they could, which started the manuscript on its way to America.

I'm ashamed of the American embassy. They surely
could have taken it.

Oh, don't be too hard on them. I owe a lot to my
American public. Anyway, with the manuscript I

sent a letter to my American publishers just telling them that everything was in their hands, and that I couldn't communicate with them at all, and I never knew anything of how *Winter's Tales* was received until after the war ended, when suddenly I received dozens of charming letters from American soldiers and sailors all over the world: the book had been put into Armed Services Editions—little paper books to fit a soldier's pocket. I was very touched. They sent me two copies of it; I gave one to the king of Denmark and he was pleased to see that, after all, some voice had spoken from his silent country during that dark time.

INTERVIEWER

And you were saying about your American public?

DINESEN

Yes, I shall never forget that they took me in at once. When I came back from Africa in 1931, after living there since 1914, I had lost all the money I had when I married because the coffee plantation didn't pay, you know; I asked my brother to finance me for two years while I prepared *Seven Gothic Tales*, and I told him that at the end of two years I'd be on my own. When the manuscript was ready, I went to England, and one day at luncheon there was the publisher Huntington, and I said, "Please, I have a manuscript and I wish you'd look at it." He said, "What is it?" and when I replied, "A book of short stories," he threw up his hands and cried, "No!" and I begged, "Won't you even look at it?" and he said, "A book of short stories by an unknown writer? No hope!" Then I sent it to America, and it was taken right away by Robert Haas, who published it, and the general public took it and liked it, and they have always been faithful. No, thank you, no more coffee. I'll have a cigarette.

Publishers everywhere are boneheaded. It's the traditional lament of the author.

DINESEN

The amusing thing is that after the book was published in America, Huntington wrote to Robert Haas praising it and begging for the address of the author, saying he must have the book for England. He had met me as Baroness Blixen, while Mr. Haas and I had never seen one another. Huntington never connected me with Isak Dinesen. Later he did publish the book in England.

INTERVIEWER

That's delightful; it's like something from one of the tales.

DINESEN

How lovely to sit here in the open, but we must be going, I think. Shall we continue our discussion on Sunday? I should like to see the Etruscan things at the Villa Giulia: we might chat a little then. Oh, look at the moon!

INTERVIEWER

Splendid. I'll find a taxi.

SCENE TWO

Rainy, warm Sunday noon. The Etruscan collection in the Villa Giulia is not too crowded because of the weather. The Baroness Blixen is now attired in a suit of reddish-brown wool and a conical ochre-colored straw hat that again shadows her extraordinary eyes. As she strolls through the newly arranged Etruscan figures, pottery, and jewelry, she seems as remote as they from the ordinary gallery goers who are pattering through. She walks slowly, very erect, stopping to gaze lingeringly at those details that please her.

DINESEN

How could they get that blue, do you suppose? Powdered lazuli? Look at that pig! In the north we give a great mythological importance to the pig. He's a kind of minion of the sun. I suppose because his sweet fat helps to keep us warm in the darkest and coldest time. Very intelligent animal ... I love all animals. I have a huge dog in Denmark, an Alsatian; he's enormous. I take him walking. If I survive him, I think I shall get a very small dog—a pug. Though I wonder if it's possible to get a pug now. They used to be very fashionable. Look at the lions on that sarcophagus. How could the Etruscans have known the lion? In Africa it was the animal that I loved the most.

INTERVIEWER

You must have known Africa at its best. What made you decide to go?

DINESEN

When I was a young girl, it was very far from my thoughts to go to Africa, nor did I dream then that an African farm should be the place in which I should be perfectly happy. That goes to prove that God has a greater and finer power of imagination than we have.

But at the time when I was engaged to be married to my cousin Bror Blixen, an uncle of ours went out to Africa big-game hunting and came back all filled with praise of the country. Theodore Roosevelt had been hunting there then, too; East Africa was in the news. So Bror and I made up our minds to try our luck there, and our relations on both sides financed us in buying the farm, which was in the highlands of Kenya, not far from Nairobi. The first day I arrived there, I loved the country and felt at home, even among unfamiliar flowers, trees, and animals, and changing clouds over the Ngong Hills, unlike any clouds I had ever known. East Africa then was really a paradise, what the Red Indians called "happy hunting grounds." I was very keen on shooting in my young days, but my great interest all through my many years in Africa was the African natives of all tribes, in particular the Somali and the Maasai. They were beautiful, noble, fearless, and wise people. Life was not easy running a coffee plantation. Ten thousand acres of farmland, and locusts and drought... and too late we realized that the table land where we were located was really too high for raising coffee successfully. Life out there was, I believe, rather like eighteenth-century England: one might often be hard up for cash, but life was still rich in many ways, with the lovely landscape, dozens of horses and dogs, and a multitude of servants.

INTERVIEWER

I suppose that you began to write seriously there?

DINESEN

No, I really began writing before I went to Africa, but I never once wanted to be a writer. I published a few short stories in literary reviews in Denmark when I was twenty years old, and the reviews encouraged me, but I didn't go on—I don't know, I think I had an intuitive fear of being trapped. Also, when I was quite young, for a while I studied painting at the Danish Royal Academy of Fine Arts; then I went to Paris in 1910 to study with Simon and Menard, but [*chuckles*]...but I did little work. The impact of Paris was too great; I felt it was more important to go about and see pictures, to see Paris, in fact. I painted a little in Africa, portraits of the natives mostly, but every time I'd get to work, someone would come up and say an ox had died or something, and I'd have to go out in the fields. Later, when I knew in my heart I should have to sell the farm and go back to Denmark, I did begin to write. To put my mind to other things I began to write tales. Two of the *Gothic Tales* were written there. But earlier, I learned how to tell tales. For, you see, I had the perfect audience. White people can no longer listen to a tale recited. They fidget or become drowsy. But the natives have an ear still. I told stories constantly to them, all kinds. And all kinds of nonsense. I'd say, "Once there was a man who had an elephant with two heads..." and at once they were eager to hear more. "Oh? Yes, but Memsahib, how did he find it, and how did he manage to feed it?" or whatever. They loved such invention. I delighted my people there by speaking in rhyme for them; they have no rhyme, you know, had never discovered it. I'd say things like "*Wakamba na kula mamba*" ("The Wakamba tribe eats snakes"), which in prose would have infuriated them, but which amused them mightily in rhyme. Afterward they'd say, "Please, Memsahib, talk like rain," so then I knew they had liked it, for rain was very precious to us there. Oh, here's Miss Svendsen. She's Catholic, so she went off today to hear a special cardinal. Now we'll go buy some postcards. Hope there is one of the lions.

SVENDSEN

Good morning.

DINESEN

Clara, you must see the delightful lions; then we'll get some postcards and go for lunch.

[*Postcards are found, a taxi is summoned, umbrellas opened, the party runs for taxi, drives off through the Borghese gardens.*]

SCENE THREE

The Casina Valadier is a fashionable restaurant in the gardens, just above the Piazza del Popolo, and commands a fine view of Rome. After a brief glimpse of the rain-grayed city from the flooded terrace, the party goes into a brocaded room, with considerately shaded girandoles, brightly colored carpets, and pictures.

DINESEN

I'll sit here so I can see everything. [*Lights cigarette.*]

INTERVIEWER

Pleasant place, isn't it?

DINESEN

Yes, very pleasant, and I recognize it. I was here in 1912. Every now and again here in Rome I recognize very vividly a place I've visited then. [*Pause.*] Oh, I shall go mad!

INTERVIEWER

[*Startled.*] What is it?

DINESEN

Look how crooked that picture is! [*Indicates blackened portrait across room.*]

INTERVIEWER

I'll straighten it. [*Goes to it.*]

DINESEN

No, more to the right.

INTERVIEWER

Like this?

DINESEN

That's better.

[*Two solemn gentlemen at table beneath portrait indicate bewilderment.*]

SVENDSEN

It's like that at home. So much traffic passes, and I have always to straighten the pictures.

DINESEN

I live on the North Sea, halfway between Copenhagen and Elsinore.

Perhaps halfway between Shiraz and Atlantis?

...Halfway between that island in *The Tempest* and wherever I am.

[*Waiter takes order; luncheon is served.*]

DINESEN

I'll have a cigarette now. Do you mind if we just stay here for a while? I hate to change once I'm installed in a decor I like. People are always telling me to hurry up or come on and do this or do that. Once when I was sailing around the Cape of Good Hope and there were albatrosses, people kept saying, "Why do you stay on deck? Come on in." They said, "It's time for lunch," and I said, "Damn lunch." I said, "I can eat lunch any day, but I shan't see albatrosses again." Such wingspread!

INTERVIEWER

Tell me about your father.

DINESEN

He was in the French army, as was my grandfather. After the Franco-Prussian War, he went to America and lived with the Plains Indians in the great middle part of your country. He built himself a little hut and named it after a place in Denmark where he had been very happy as a young man—Frydenlund ("Happy Grove"). He hunted animals for their skins and became a fur trader. He sold his skins mostly to the Indians, then used his profits to buy them gifts.

A little community grew up around him, and now Frydenlund is, I believe, the name of a locality in the state of Wisconsin. When he returned to Denmark, he wrote his books. So you see, it was natural for me, his daughter, to go off to Africa and live with the natives and, after, return home to write about it. He also, incidentally, wrote a volume of his war experiences called *Paris Under the Commune*.

INTERVIEWER

And how is it that you write in English?

DINESEN

It was quite natural to do so. I was partly schooled in England after being taught always by governesses at home. Because of that, I lack knowledge of plain facts which are common coinage for others. But those governesses were ambitious: they did teach languages, and one of them put me to translating *The Lady of the Lake* into Danish. Then, in Africa, I had been seeing only English people, really. I had spoken English or Swahili for twenty years. And I read the English poets and English novelists. I prefer the older writers, but I remember when I first read Huxley's *Crome Yellow*, it was like biting into an unknown and refreshing fruit.

INTERVIEWER

Most of your tales are laid in the last century, aren't they? You never write about modern times.

DINESEN

I do, if you consider that the time of our grand-parents, that just-out-of-reach time, is so much a part of us. We absorb so much without being aware. Also, I write about characters who together are the tale. I begin, you see, with a flavor of the tale. Then I find the characters, and they take over. They make the design, I simply permit them their liberty. Now, in modern life and in modern fiction there is a kind of atmosphere and above all an interior movement—inside the characters—which is something else again. I feel that in life and in art people have drawn a little apart in this century. Solitude is now the universal theme. But I write about characters within a design, how they act upon one another. Relation with others is important to me, you see, friendship is precious to me, and I have been blessed with heroic friendships. But time in my tales is flexible. I may begin in the eighteenth century and come right up to World War I. Those times have been sorted out, they are clearly visible. Besides, so many novels that we think are contemporary in subject with their date of publication—think of Dickens or Faulkner or Tolstoy or Turgenev—are really set in an earlier period, a generation or so back. The present is always unsettled, no one has had time to contemplate it in tranquility ... I was a painter before I was a writer ... and a painter never wants the subject right under his nose; he wants to stand back and study a landscape with half-closed eyes.

INTERVIEWER

Have you written poetry?

DINESEN

I did as a young girl.

INTERVIEWER

What is your favorite fruit?

DINESEN

Strawberries.

INTERVIEWER

Do you like monkeys?

DINESEN

Yes, I love them in art: in pictures, in stories, in porcelain, but in life they somehow look so sad. They make me nervous. I like lions and gazelles.

SCENE FOUR

Now we are on the parapets of the central tower of the castle of Sermoneta, perched on a hill amidst a clustering town, about an hour and a half south of Rome. We have crossed a moated drawbridge, climbed a rickety ladder-stair. We have seen remains of fourteenth-century frescoes, and in the tower stronghold seen scrawled phrases and drawings on the wall, fresh as new, from when Napoleonic soldiers were incarcerated here. Now the party comes out, shading their eyes. Below, the Pontine plain stretches green and gold to the sea, bathed in bright afternoon sunlight. We can see tiny figures miles below working amidst the bean fields and the peach orchards.

INTERVIEWER

I think it is curious that practically no critic nor reviewer in either America or England has pointed out the great comic element in your works. I hope we might speak a little of the comic spirit in your tales.

Oh, I'm glad you mentioned that! People are always asking me what is the significance of this or that in the tales—"What does this symbolize? What does that stand for?" And I always have a difficult time making them believe that I intend everything as it's stated. It would be terrible if the explanation of the work were outside the work itself. And I do often intend a comic sense, I love a joke, I love the humorous. The name Isak means "laughter." I often think that what we most need now is a great humorist.

INTERVIEWER

What humorists in the English language please you?

DINESEN

Well, Mark Twain, for example. But then all the writers I admire usually have a vein of comic spirit. Writers of tales always do, at least.

INTERVIEWER

Who are writers of tales that appeal to you, or with whom you feel a kinship?

DINESEN

E. T. A. Hoffmann, Hans Andersen, Barbey d'Aurevilly, la Motte Fouqué, Chamisso, Hemingway, Maupassant, Stendhal, Chekhov, Conrad, Voltaire...

SVENDSEN

Don't forget Melville! She calls me Babo after the character in *Benito Cereno*, when she doesn't refer to me as Sancho Panza.

Heavens, you've read them all!

I am really three thousand years old and have dined with Socrates.

Pardon?

[*Laughing and lighting a cigarette.*] Because I was never told what I must read or what I mustn't read, I did read everything that fell into my hands. I discovered Shakespeare very early in life, and now I feel that life would be nothing without him. One of my new stories is about a company of actors playing *The Tempest*, incidentally. I love some of the Victorian novelists no one reads anymore: Walter Scott, for instance. Oh, and I like Melville very much, and the *Odyssey*, the Norse sagas—have you read the Norse sagas? I love Racine, too.

I remember your observation on the Norse mythology in one of the *Winter's Tales*.* It's very interesting

----

* "And I have wondered, while I read," says the young nobleman in "Sorrow-Acre," "that we have not till now understood how much our Nordic mythology in moral greatness surpasses that of Greece and Rome. If it had not been for the physical beauty of the ancient gods, which has come down to us in marble, no modern mind could hold them worthy of worship. They were mean, capricious and treacherous. The gods of our

to me, incidentally, how you have chosen the tale for your form.

DINESEN

It came naturally to me. My literary friends at home tell me that the heart of my work is not in the idea but in the line of the tale. Something you can tell, like one can tell *Ali Baba and the Forty Thieves* but one could not tell *Anna Karenina*.

INTERVIEWER

I should be most interested to know a little of how you work; for instance, how such a tale as "The Deluge at Norderney" (1934) took shape. It seems so ordered and inevitable, yet on study one is amazed at the design, of the tales within the tale.

DINESEN

[*Smiling mischievously.*] Read it, read it, and you'll see how it's written.

EPILOGUE

For epilogue here, let's append a passage from the Baroness Blixen's Albondocani, *a long series of connected tales still unfinished at the time of the author's death in 1962. This excerpt is from "The Blank Page,"* published in Last Tales *(1957). An old woman who earns her living by storytelling is speaking:*

"With my grandmother," she said, "I went through a hard school. 'Be loyal to the story,' the old hag would

---

Danish forefathers are as much more divine than they as the Druid is nobler than the Augur."

say to me, 'Be eternally and unswervingly loyal to the story.' 'Why must I be that, Grandmother?' I asked her. 'Am I to furnish you with reasons, baggage?' she cried. 'And you mean to be a story-teller! Why, you are to become a story-teller, and I shall give you the reasons! Hear then: Where the story-teller is loyal, eternally and unswervingly loyal to the story, there, in the end, silence will speak. Where the story has been betrayed, silence is but emptiness. But we, the faithful, when we have spoken our last word, will hear the voice of silence. Whether a small snotty lass understands it or not.'

"Who then," she continues, "tells a finer tale than any of us? Silence does. And where does one read a deeper tale than upon the most perfectly printed page of the most precious book? Upon the blank page. When a royal and gallant pen, in the moment of its highest inspiration, has written down its tale with the rarest ink of all—where, then, may one read a still deeper, sweeter, merrier, and more cruel tale than that? Upon the blank page."

(1956)

44

Simone de Beauvoir

THE ART OF FICTION NO. 35

Interviewed by Madeleine Gobeil

Simone de Beauvoir had introduced me to Jean Genet and Jean-Paul Sartre, whom I had interviewed. But she hesitated about being interviewed herself: "Why should we talk about me? Don't you think I've done enough in my three books of memoirs?" It took several letters and conversations to convince her otherwise, and then only on the condition "that it wouldn't be too long."

The interview took place in Miss de Beauvoir's studio on the rue Schœlcher in Montparnasse, a five-minute walk from Sartre's apartment. We worked in a large, sunny room which serves as her study and sitting room. Shelves are crammed with surprisingly uninteresting books. "The best ones," she told me, "are in the hands of my friends and never come back." The tables are covered with colorful objects brought back from her travels, but the only valuable work in the room is a lamp made for her by Giacometti. Scattered throughout the room are dozens of phonograph records, one of the few luxuries that Miss de Beauvoir permits herself.

Apart from her classically featured face, what strikes one about Simone de Beauvoir is her fresh, rosy complexion and her clear blue eyes, extremely young and lively. One gets the impression that she knows and sees everything; this inspires a certain timidity. Her speech is rapid, her manner direct without being brusque, and she is rather smiling and friendly.

INTERVIEWER

For the last seven years you've been writing your memoirs, in which you frequently wonder about your vocation and your profession. I have the impression that it was the loss of religious faith that turned you toward writing.

SIMONE DE BEAUVOIR

It's very hard to review one's past without cheating a little. My desire to write goes far back. I wrote stories at the age of eight, but lots of children do the same. That doesn't really mean they have a vocation for writing. It may be that in my case the vocation was accentuated because I had lost religious faith; it's also true that when I read books that moved me deeply, such as George Eliot's *The Mill on the Floss*, I wanted terribly much to be, like her, someone whose books would be read, whose books would move readers.

INTERVIEWER

Have you been influenced by English literature?

The study of English has been one of my passions ever since childhood. There's a body of children's literature in English far more charming than what exists in French. I loved to read *Alice in Wonderland*, *Peter Pan*, George Eliot, and even Rosamond Lehmann.

INTERVIEWER

Dusty Answer?

DE BEAUVOIR

I had a real passion for that book. And yet it was rather mediocre. The girls of my generation adored it. The author was very young, and every girl recognized herself in Judy. The book was rather clever, even rather subtle. As for me, I envied English university life. I lived at home. I didn't have a room of my own. In fact, I had nothing at all. And though that life wasn't free, it did allow for privacy and seemed to me magnificent. The author had known all the myths of adolescent girls—handsome boys with an air of mystery about them and so on. Later, of course, I read the Brontës and the books of Virginia Woolf: *Orlando*, *Mrs. Dalloway*. I don't care much for *The Waves*, but I'm very, very fond of her book on Elizabeth Barrett Browning.

INTERVIEWER

What about her journal?

DE BEAUVOIR

It interests me less. It's too literary. It's fascinating, but it's foreign to me. She's too concerned with whether she'll be published, with what people will say about her. I liked very much *A Room of One's Own* in which she talks about the situation of women. It's a short essay, but it hits the nail on the head. She explains very well why women can't write. Virginia Woolf is one of the women writers who has interested me most. Have you seen any photos of her? An extraordinarily lonely face ... In a way, she interests me more than Colette. Colette is, after all, very involved in her little love affairs, in household matters, laundry, pets. Virginia Woolf is much broader.

INTERVIEWER

Did you read her books in translation?

DE BEAUVOIR

No, in English. I read English better than I speak it.

INTERVIEWER

What do you think about college and university education for a writer? You yourself were a brilliant student at the Sorbonne and people expected you to have a brilliant career as a teacher.

DE BEAUVOIR

My studies gave me only a very superficial knowledge of philosophy but sharpened my interest in it. I benefited greatly from being a teacher—that is, from being able to spend a great deal of time reading, writing, and educating myself. In those days, teachers didn't have a very heavy program. My studies gave me a solid foundation because in order to pass the state exams you have to explore areas that you wouldn't bother about if you were concerned only with general culture. They provided me with a certain academic method that was useful when I wrote *The Second Sex* (1949) and that has been useful, in general, for all my studies. I mean a way of going through books very quickly, of seeing which works are important, of classifying them, of being able to reject those which are unimportant, of being able to summarize, to browse.

INTERVIEWER

Were you a good teacher?

DE BEAUVOIR

I don't think so, because I was interested only in the bright students and not at all in the others, whereas a good teacher should be interested in everyone. But if you teach philosophy you can't help it. There were always four or five students who did all the talking, and the others didn't care to do anything. I didn't bother about them very much.

INTERVIEWER

You had been writing for ten years before you were published, at the age of thirty-five. Weren't you discouraged?

DE BEAUVOIR

No, because in my time it was unusual to be published when you were very young. Of course, there were one or two examples, such as Radiguet, who was a prodigy. Sartre himself wasn't published until he was about thirty-five, when *Nausea* and *The Wall* were brought out. When my first more or less publishable book was rejected, I was a bit discouraged. And when the first version of *She Came to Stay* (1943) was rejected, it was very unpleasant. Then I thought that I ought to take my time. I knew many examples of writers who were slow in getting started. And people always spoke of the case of Stendhal, who didn't begin to write until he was forty.

INTERVIEWER

Were you influenced by any American writers when you wrote your early novels?

DE BEAUVOIR

In writing *She Came to Stay*, I was certainly influenced by Hemingway insofar as it was he who taught us a certain simplicity of dialogue and the importance of the little things in life.

INTERVIEWER

Do you draw up a very precise plan when you write a novel?

DE BEAUVOIR

I haven't, you know, written a novel in ten years, during which time I've been working on my memoirs. When I wrote *The Mandarins* (1954), for example, I created characters and an atmosphere around a given theme, and little by little the plot took shape. But in general I start writing a novel long before working out the plot.

INTERVIEWER

People say that you have great self-discipline and that you never let a day go by without working. At what time do you start?

I'm always in a hurry to get going, though in general I dislike starting the day. I first have tea and then, at about ten o'clock, I get under way and work until one. Then I see my friends and after that, at five o'clock, I go back to work and continue until nine. I have no difficulty in picking up the thread in the afternoon. When you leave, I'll read the paper or perhaps go shopping. Most often it's a pleasure to work.

INTERVIEWER

When do you see Sartre?

DE BEAUVOIR

Every evening and often at lunchtime. I generally work at his place in the afternoon.

INTERVIEWER

Doesn't it bother you to go from one apartment to another?

DE BEAUVOIR

No. Since I don't write scholarly books, I take all my papers with me and it works out very well.

INTERVIEWER

Do you plunge in immediately?

DE BEAUVOIR

It depends to some extent on what I'm writing. If the work is going well, I spend a quarter or half an hour reading what I wrote the day before, and I make a few corrections. Then I continue from there. In order to pick up the thread I have to read what I've done.

Do your writer friends have the same habits as you?

No, it's quite a personal matter. Genet, for example, works quite differently. He puts in about twelve hours a day for six months when he's working on something and when he has finished he can let six months go by without doing anything. As I said, I work every day except for two or three months of vacation when I travel and generally don't work at all. I read very little during the year, and when I go away I take a big valise full of books, books that I didn't have time to read. But if the trip lasts a month or six weeks, I do feel uncomfortable, particularly if I'm between two books. I get bored if I don't work.

Are your original manuscripts always in longhand? Who deciphers them? Nelson Algren says that he's one of the few people who can read your handwriting.

I don't know how to type, but I do have two typists who manage to decipher what I write. When I work on the last version of a book, I copy the manuscript. I'm very careful. I make a great effort. My writing is fairly legible.

In *The Blood of Others* (1945) and *All Men Are Mortal* (1946) you deal with the problem of time. Were you influenced, in this respect, by Joyce or Faulkner?

No, it was a personal preoccupation. I've always been keenly aware of the passing of time. I've always thought that I was old. Even when I was twelve, I thought it was awful to be thirty. I felt that something was lost. At the same time, I was aware of what I could gain, and certain periods of my life have taught me a great deal. But, in spite of everything, I've always been haunted by the passing of time and by the fact that death keeps closing in on us. For me, the problem of time is linked up with that of death, with the thought that we inevitably draw closer and closer to it, with the horror of decay. It's that, rather than the fact that things disintegrate, that love peters out. That's horrible too, though I personally have never been troubled by it. There's always been great continuity in my life. I've always lived in Paris, more or less in the same neighborhoods. My relationship with Sartre has lasted a very long time. I have very old friends whom I continue to see. So it's not that I've felt that time breaks things up, but rather the fact that I always take my bearings. I mean the fact that I have so many years behind me, so many ahead of me. I count them.

INTERVIEWER

In the second part of your memoirs, you draw a portrait of Sartre at the time he was writing *Nausea*. You picture him as being obsessed by what he calls his "crabs," by anguish. You seem to have been, at the time, the joyous member of the couple. Yet, in your novels you reveal a preoccupation with death that we never find in Sartre.

But remember what he says in *The Words*. That he never felt the imminence of death, whereas his fellow students—for example, Nizan, the author of *Aden, Arabie*—were fascinated by it. In a way, Sartre felt he was immortal. He had staked everything on his literary work and on the hope that his work would survive, whereas for me, owing to the fact that my personal life will disappear, I'm not the least bit concerned about whether my work is likely to last. I've always been deeply aware that the ordinary things of life disappear, one's day-to-day activities, one's impressions, one's past experiences. Sartre thought that life could be caught in a trap of words, and I've always felt that words weren't life itself but a reproduction of life, of something dead, so to speak.

INTERVIEWER

That's precisely the point. Some people claim that you haven't the power to transpose life in your novels. They insinuate that your characters are copied from the people around you.

DE BEAUVOIR

I don't know. What is the imagination? In the long run, it's a matter of attaining a certain degree of generality, of truth about what is, about what one actually lives. Works which aren't based on reality don't interest me unless they're out-and-out extravagant, for example the novels of Alexandre Dumas or of Victor Hugo, which are epics of a kind. But I don't call "made-up" stories works of the imagination but rather works of artifice. If I wanted to defend myself, I could refer to Tolstoy's *War and Peace*, all the characters of which were taken from real life.

Let's go back to your characters. How do you choose their names?

I don't consider that very important. I chose the name Xavière in *She Came to Stay* because I had met only one person who had that name. When I look for names, I use the telephone directory or try to remember the names of former pupils.

To which of your characters are you most attached?

I don't know. I think that I'm interested less in the characters themselves than in their relationships, whether it be a matter of love or friendship. It was the critic Claude Roy who pointed that out.

In every one of your novels we find a female character who is misled by false notions and who is threatened by madness.

Lots of modern women are like that. Women are obliged to play at being what they aren't, to play, for example, at being great courtesans, to fake their personalities. They're on the brink of neurosis. I feel very sympathetic toward women of that type. They interest me more than the well-balanced housewife and mother. There are, of course, women who interest me even more, those who are both true and independent, who work and create.

None of your female characters are immune from love. You like the romantic element.

Love is a great privilege. Real love, which is very rare, enriches the lives of the men and women who experience it.

In your novels, it seems to be the women—I'm thinking of Françoise in *She Came to Stay* and Anne in *The Mandarins*—who experience it most.

The reason is that, despite everything, women give more of themselves in love because most of them don't have much else to absorb them. Perhaps they're also more capable of deep sympathy, which is the basis of love. Perhaps it's also because I can project myself more easily into women than into men. My female characters are much richer than my male characters.

You've never created an independent and really free female character who illustrates in one way or other the thesis of *The Second Sex*. Why?

I've shown women as they are, as divided human beings, and not as they ought to be.

After your long novel, *The Mandarins*, you stopped writing fiction and began to work on your memoirs. Which of these two literary forms do you prefer?

I like both of them. They offer different kinds of satisfaction and disappointment. In writing my memoirs, it's very agreeable to be backed up by reality. On the other hand, when one follows reality from day to day, as I have, there are certain depths, certain kinds of myth and meaning that one disregards. In the novel, however, one can express these horizons, these overtones of daily life, but there's an element of fabrication that is nevertheless disturbing. One should aim at inventing without fabricating. I had been wanting to talk about my childhood and youth for a long time. I had maintained very deep relationships with them, but there was no sign of them in any of my books. Even before writing my first novel, I had a desire to have, as it were, a heart-to-heart talk. It was a very emotional, a very personal need. After *Memoirs of a Dutiful Daughter* (1958) I was unsatisfied, and then I thought of doing something else. But I was unable to. I said to myself, I've fought to be free. What have I done with my freedom, what's become of it? I wrote the sequel that carried me from the age of twenty-one to the present time, from *The Prime of Life* (1960) to *Force of Circumstance* (1963)—

At the meeting of writers in Formentor a few years ago, Carlo Levi described *The Prime of Life* as "the great love story of the century." Sartre appeared for the first time as a human being. You revealed a Sartre who had not been rightly understood, a man very different from the legendary Sartre.

DE BEAUVOIR

I did it intentionally. He didn't want me to write about him. Finally, when he saw that I spoke about him the way I did, he gave me a free hand.

INTERVIEWER

In your opinion, why is it that, despite the reputation he's had for twenty years, Sartre the writer remains misunderstood and is still violently attacked by critics?

DE BEAUVOIR

For political reasons. Sartre is a man who has violently opposed the class into which he was born and which therefore regards him as a traitor. But that's the class which has money, which buys books. Sartre's situation is paradoxical. He's an antibourgeois writer who is read by the bourgeoisie and admired by it as one of its products. The bourgeoisie has a monopoly on culture and thinks that it gave birth to Sartre. At the same time, it hates him because he attacks it.

INTERVIEWER

In an interview with Hemingway in *The Paris Review*, he said, "All you can be sure about in a political-minded writer is that if his work should last you will have to skip the politics when you read it." Of course, you don't agree. Do you still believe in "commitment"?

Hemingway was precisely the type of writer who never wanted to commit himself. I know that he was involved in the Spanish Civil War, but as a journalist. Hemingway was never deeply committed, so he thinks that what is eternal in literature is what isn't dated, isn't committed. I don't agree. In the case of many writers, it's also their political stand which makes me like or dislike them. There aren't many writers of former times whose work was really committed. And although one reads Rousseau's *Social Contract* as eagerly as one reads his *Confessions*, one no longer reads *The New Heloise*.

INTERVIEWER

The heyday of existentialism seems to have been the period from the end of the war to 1952. At the present time, the "new novel" is in fashion; and such writers as Drieu La Rochelle and Roger Nimier.

DE BEAUVOIR

There's certainly a return to the right in France. The new novel itself isn't reactionary, nor are its authors. A sympathizer can say that they want to do away with certain bourgeois conventions. These writers aren't disturbing. In the long run, Gaullism brings us back to Pétainism, and it's only to be expected that a collaborator like La Rochelle and an extreme reactionary like Nimier be held in high esteem again. The bourgeoisie is showing itself again in its true colors—that is, as a reactionary class. Look at the success of Sartre's *The Words*. There are several things to note. It's perhaps—I won't say his best book, but one of his best. At any rate, it's an excellent book, an exciting display of virtuosity, an amazingly written work. At the same time, the reason it has had such success is that it's a book that is not "committed." When the critics say that it's his best book, along with *Nausea*, one should bear in mind that *Nausea* is an early work, a work that is not committed, and that it is more readily accepted by the left and right alike than are his plays. The same thing happened to me with *Memoirs of a Dutiful Daughter*. Bourgeois women were delighted to recognize their own youth in it. The protests began with *The Prime of Life* and continued with *Force of Circumstance*. The break is very clear, very sharp.

INTERVIEWER

The last part of *Force of Circumstance* is devoted to the Algerian War, to which you seem to have reacted in a very personal way.

DE BEAUVOIR

I felt and thought about things in a political way, but I never engaged in political action. The entire last part of *Force of Circumstance* deals with the war. And it seems anachronistic in a France that is no longer concerned with that war.

INTERVIEWER

Didn't you realize that people were bound to forget about it?

I deleted lots of pages from that section. I therefore realized that it would be anachronistic. On the other hand, I absolutely wanted to talk about it, and I'm amazed that people have forgotten it to such a degree. Have you seen the film *La belle vie*, by the young director Robert Enrico? People are stupefied because the film shows the Algerian War. Claude Mauriac wrote in *Le Figaro littéraire*: "Why is it that we're shown parachute troopers on public squares? It's not true to life." But it is true to life. I used to see them every day from Sartre's window at Saint-Germain-des-Prés. People have forgotten. They wanted to forget. They wanted to forget their memories. That's the reason why, contrary to what I expected, I wasn't attacked for what I said about the Algerian War but for what I said about old age and death. As regards the Algerian War, all Frenchmen are now convinced that it never took place, that nobody was tortured, that insofar as there was torture they were always against torture.

At the end of *Force of Circumstance* you say: "As I look back with incredulity at that credulous adolescent, I am astounded to see how I was swindled." This remark seems to have given rise to all kinds of misunderstandings.

People—particularly enemies—have tried to interpret it to mean that my life has been a failure, either because I recognize the fact that I was mistaken on a political level or because I recognize that after all a woman should have had children, et cetera. Anyone who reads my book carefully can see that I say the very opposite, that I don't envy anyone, that I'm perfectly satisfied with what my life has been, that I've kept all my promises and that consequently if I had my life to live over again I wouldn't live it any differently. I've never regretted not having children insofar as what I wanted to do was to write.

Then why "swindled"? When one has an existentialist view of the world, like mine, the paradox of human life is precisely that one tries to *be* and, in the long run, merely exists. It's because of this discrepancy that when you've laid your stake on being—and, in a way, you always do when you make plans, even if you actually know that you can't succeed in being—when you turn around and look back on your life, you see that you've simply existed. In other words, life isn't behind you like a solid thing, like the life of a god (as it is conceived, that is, as something impossible). Your life is simply a human life.

So one might say, as Alain did, and I'm very fond of that remark, Nothing is promised us. In one sense, it's true. In another, it's not. Because a bourgeois boy or girl who is given a certain culture is actually promised things. I think that anyone who had a hard life when he was young won't say in later years that he's been "swindled." But when I say that I've been swindled I'm referring to the seventeen-year-old girl who daydreamed in the country near the hazel bush about what she was going to do later on. I've done everything I wanted to do, writing books, learning about things, but I've been swindled all the same because it's never anything more. There are also Mallarmé's lines about the perfume of sadness that remains in the heart, I forget exactly how they go. I've had what I wanted, and, when all is said and done, what one wanted was always something else. A woman psychoanalyst wrote me a very intelligent letter in which she said that "in the last analysis, desires always go far beyond the object of desire." The fact is that I've had everything I desired, but the "far beyond" which is included in the desire itself is not attained when the desire has been fulfilled. When I was young, I had hopes and a view of life which all cultured people and bourgeois optimists encourage one to have and which my readers accuse me of not encouraging in them. That's what I meant, and I wasn't regretting anything I've done or thought.

INTERVIEWER

Some people think that a longing for God underlies your works.

DE BEAUVOIR

No. Sartre and I have always said that it's not because there's a desire to *be* that this desire corresponds to any reality. It's exactly what Kant said on the intellectual level. The fact that one believes in causalities is no reason to believe that there is a supreme cause. The fact that man has a desire to be does not mean that he can ever attain being or even that being is a possible notion, at any rate the being that is a reflection and at the same time an existence. There is a synthesis of existence and being that is impossible. Sartre and I have always rejected it, and this rejection underlies our thinking. There is an emptiness in man, and even his achievements have this emptiness. That's all. I don't mean that I haven't achieved what

I wanted to achieve but rather that the achievement is never what people think it is. Furthermore, there is a naive or snobbish aspect, because people imagine that if you have succeeded on a social level you must be perfectly satisfied with the human condition in general. But that's not the case.

"I'm swindled" also implies something else—namely, that life has made me discover the world as it is, that is, a world of suffering and oppression, of undernourishment for the majority of people, things that I didn't know when I was young and when I imagined that to discover the world was to discover something beautiful. In that respect, too, I was swindled by bourgeois culture, and that's why I don't want to contribute to the swindling of others and why I say that I was swindled, in short, so that others aren't swindled. It's really also a problem of a social kind. In short, I discovered the unhappiness of the world little by little, then more and more, and finally, above all, I felt it in connection with the Algerian War and when I traveled.

Some critics and readers have felt that you spoke about old age in an unpleasant way.

DE BEAUVOIR
A lot of people didn't like what I said because they want to believe that all periods of life are delightful, that children are innocent, that all newlyweds are happy, that all old people are serene. I've rebelled against such notions all my life, and there's no doubt about the fact that the moment, which for me is not old age but the beginning of old age, represents—

even if one has all the resources one wants, affection, work to be done—represents a change in one's existence, a change that is manifested by the loss of a great number of things. If one isn't sorry to lose them it's because one didn't love them. I think that people who glorify old age or death too readily are people who really don't love life. Of course, in present-day France you have to say that everything's fine, that everything's lovely, including death.

INTERVIEWER

Beckett has keenly felt the swindle of the human condition. Does he interest you more than the other "new novelists"?

DE BEAUVOIR

Certainly. All the playing around with time that one finds in the "new novel" can be found in Faulkner. It was he who taught them how to do it, and in my opinion he's the one who does it best. As for Beckett, his way of emphasizing the dark side of life is very beautiful. However, he's convinced that life is dark and only that. I too am convinced that life is dark, and at the same time I love life. But that conviction seems to have spoiled everything for him. When that's all you can say, there aren't fifty ways of saying it, and I've found that many of his works are merely repetitions of what he said earlier. *Endgame* repeats *Waiting for Godot*, but in a weaker way.

INTERVIEWER

Are there many contemporary French writers who interest you?

Not many. I receive lots of manuscripts, and the annoying thing is that they're almost always bad. At the present time, I'm very excited about Violette Leduc. She was first published in 1946 in *Collection Espoir*, which was edited by Camus. The critics praised her to the skies. Sartre, Genet, and Jouhandeau liked her very much. She never sold. She recently published a great autobiography called *The Bastard*, the beginning of which was published in *Les Temps Modernes*, of which Sartre is editor in chief. I wrote a preface to the book because I thought that she was one of the unappreciated postwar French writers. She's having great success in France at the present time.

INTERVIEWER

And how do you rank yourself among contemporary writers?

DE BEAUVOIR

I don't know. What is it that one evaluates? The noise, the silence, posterity, the number of readers, the absence of readers, the importance at a given time? I think that people will read me for some time. At least, that's what my readers tell me. I've contributed something to the discussion of women's problems. I know I have from the letters I receive. As for the literary *quality* of my work, in the strict sense of the word, I haven't the slightest idea.

—*Translated from the French by Bernard Frechtman*

(1956)

Elizabeth Bishop

THE ART OF POETRY NO. 27

Interviewed by Elizabeth Spires

T he interview took place at Lewis Wharf,
Boston, on the afternoon of June 28, 1978,
three days before Miss Bishop and two
friends were to leave for North Haven, a Maine
island in Penobscot Bay where she summered. Her
living room, on the fourth floor of Lewis Wharf, had
a spectacular view of Boston Harbor; when I arrived,
she immediately took me out on the balcony to point
out such Boston landmarks as Old North Church
in the distance, mentioning that Old Ironsides was
moored nearby.

Her living room was spacious and attractive, with
wide-planked polished floors, a beamed ceiling, two
old brick walls, and one wall of books. Besides some
comfortable modern furniture, the room included a
jacaranda rocker and other old pieces from Brazil,
two paintings by Loren MacIver, a giant horse conch
from Key West, and a Franklin stove with firewood
in a donkey pannier, also from Brazil. The most

conspicuous piece was a large carved figurehead of an unknown beast, openmouthed, with horns and blue eyes, which hung on one wall below the ceiling.

Her study, a smaller room down the hall, was in a state of disorder. Literary magazines, books, and papers were piled everywhere. Photographs of Marianne Moore, Robert Lowell, and other friends hung on the walls; one of Dom Pedro, the last emperor of Brazil, she especially liked to show to her Brazilian visitors. "Most have no idea who he is," she said. "This is after he abdicated and shortly before he died—he looked very sad." Her desk was tucked in a far corner by the only window, also with a north view of the harbor.

At sixty-seven, Miss Bishop was striking, her short, swept-back white hair setting off an unforgettably noble face. She was wearing a black tunic shirt, gold watch and earrings, gray slacks, and flat brown Japanese sandals that made her appear shorter than her actual height: five feet, four inches. Although she looked well and was in high spirits, she complained of having had a recent hay fever attack and declined to have her photograph taken with the wry comment, "Photographers, insurance salesmen, and funeral directors are the worst forms of life."

Seven or eight months later, after reading a profile I had written for the *Vassar Quarterly* (which had been based on this interview) and worrying that she sounded like "the soul of frivolity," she wrote me: "I once admired an interview with Fred Astaire in which he refused to discuss 'the dance,' his partners, or his 'career' and stuck determinedly to *golf*—so I hope that some readers will realize I do think about art once in a while even if babbling along like a very shallow brook ... "

Though Miss Bishop did have the opportunity of correcting those portions of this interview incorporated in the *Vassar Quarterly* article, she never saw it in this form.

INTERVIEWER
Your living room seems to be a wonderful combination of the old and new. Is there a story behind any of the pieces, especially that figurehead? It's quite imposing.

ELIZABETH BISHOP
I lived in an extremely modern house in Brazil. It was very beautiful, and when I finally moved I brought back things I liked best. So it's just a kind of mixture. I really like modern things, but while I was there I acquired so many other things I couldn't bear to give them up. This figurehead is from the São Francisco River. Some are more beautiful; this is a very ugly one.

INTERVIEWER
Is it supposed to ward off evil spirits?

BISHOP
Yes, I think so. They were used for about fifty years on one section, two or three hundred miles, of the river. It's nothing compared to the Amazon but it's the next biggest river in Brazil. This figurehead is primitive folk art. I think I even know who made it. There was a black man who carved twenty or thirty, and it's exactly his style. Some of them are made of much more beautiful wood. There's a famous one called the Red Horse made of jacaranda. It's beautiful, a

great thing like this one, a horse with its mouth open, but for some reason they all just disappeared. I made a weeklong trip on that river in 1967 and didn't see one. The riverboat, a stern wheeler, had been built in 1880—something for the Mississippi, and you can't believe how tiny it was. We splashed along slowly for days and days... a very funny trip.

INTERVIEWER

Did you spend so much of your life traveling because you were looking for a perfect place?

BISHOP

No, I don't think so. I really haven't traveled that much. It just happened that although I wasn't rich I had a very small income from my father, who died when I was eight months old, and it was enough when I got out of college to go places on. And I traveled extremely cheaply. I could get along in Brazil for some years but now I couldn't possibly live on it. But the biographical sketch in the first anthology I was in said, "Oh, she's been to Morocco, Spain, et cetera," and this has been repeated for years even though I haven't been back to any of these places. But I never traveled the way students travel now. Compared to my students, who seem to go to Nepal every Easter vacation, I haven't been anywhere at all.

INTERVIEWER

Well, it always sounds as if you're very adventurous.

BISHOP

I want to do the Upper Amazon. Maybe I will. You start from Peru and go down—

Do you write when you're actually traveling?

Yes, sometimes. It depends. I usually take notes but not always. And I keep a kind of diary. The two trips I've made that I liked best were the Amazon trip and one to the Galápagos Islands three or four years ago ... I'd like very much to go back to Italy again because I haven't seen nearly enough of it. And Sicily. Venice is wonderful. Florence is rather strenuous, I think. I was last there in '64 with my Brazilian friend. We rented a car and did northern Italy for five or six weeks. We didn't go to Rome. I *must* go back. There are so many things I haven't seen yet. I like painting probably better than I like poetry. And I haven't been back to Paris for years. I don't like the prices!

You mentioned earlier that you're leaving for North Haven in several days. Will this be a "working vacation"?

This summer I want to do a lot of work because I really haven't done anything for ages and there are a couple of things I'd like to finish before I die. Two or three poems and two long stories. Maybe three. I sometimes feel that I shouldn't keep going back to this place that I found just by chance through an ad in the *Harvard Crimson*. I should probably go to see some more art, cathedrals, and so on. But I'm so crazy about it that I keep going back. You can see the water, a great expanse of water and fields from the house. Islands are beautiful. Some of them come right up, granite, and then dark firs. North Haven isn't like that exactly, but it's very beautiful. The island is sparsely inhabited and a lot of the people who have homes there are fearfully rich. Probably if it weren't for these people the island would be deserted the way a great many Maine islands are, because the village is very tiny. But the inhabitants almost all work—they're lobstermen but they work as caretakers... The electricity there is rather sketchy. Two summers ago it was one hour on, one hour off. There I was with *two* electric typewriters and I couldn't keep working. There was a cartoon in the grocery store—it's eighteen miles from the mainland—a man in a hardware store saying, "I want an extension cord eighteen miles long!" Last year they did plug into the mainland—they put in cables. But once in a while the power still goes off.

INTERVIEWER

So you compose on the typewriter?

BISHOP

I can write prose on a typewriter. Not poetry. Nobody can read my writing so I write letters on it. And I've finally trained myself so I can write prose on it and then correct a great deal. But for poetry I use a pen. About halfway through sometimes I'll type out a few lines to see how they look.

William Carlos Williams wrote entirely on the typewriter. Robert Lowell printed—he never learned to write. He printed everything.

You've never been as prolific as many of your contemporaries. Do you start a lot of poems and finish very few?

Yes. Alas, yes. I begin lots of things and then I give up on them. The last few years I haven't written as much because of teaching. I'm hoping that now that I'm free and have a Guggenheim I'll do a lot more.

How long did it take you to finish "The Moose" (1972)?

That was funny. I started that *years* ago—twenty years ago, at least—I had a stack of notes, the first two or three stanzas, and the last.

It's such a dreamy poem. It seems to move the way a bus moves.

It was all true. The bus trip took place before I went to Brazil. I went up to visit my aunt. Actually, I was on the wrong bus. I went to the right place but it wasn't the express I was supposed to get. It went roundabout and it was all exactly the way I described it, except that I say "seven relatives." Well, they weren't really relatives, they were various stepsons and so on, but that's the only thing that isn't quite true. I wanted to finish it because I liked it, but I could never seem to get the middle part, to get from one place to the other. And then when I was still living in Cambridge I was asked to give the Phi Beta Kappa poem at Harvard. I was rather pleased and I remembered that I had another unfinished poem. It's about whales and it was written a long time ago, too. I'm afraid I'll never publish it because it looks as if I were just trying to be up-to-date now that whales are a "cause."

INTERVIEWER
But it's finished now?

BISHOP
I think I could finish it very easily. I'm going to take it to Maine with me. I think I'll date it or nobody will believe I started it so long ago. At the time, though, I couldn't find the one about whales—this was in '73 or '74, I think—so I dug out "The Moose" and thought, Maybe I can finish it, and I did. The day of the ceremony for Phi Beta Kappa (which I'd never made in college) we were all sitting on the platform at Sanders Theatre. And the man who had asked me to give the poem leaned across the president and said to me, whispering, "What is the name of your poem?" I said, "'The Moose,' M-o-o-s-e," and he got up and introduced me and said, "Miss Bishop will now read a poem called 'The *Moos*.'" Well, I choked and my hat was too big. And later the newspaper account read, "Miss Bishop read a poem called 'The Moose' and the tassle of her mortarboard swung back and forth over her face like a windshield wiper"!

The Glee Club was behind us and they sang rather badly, I thought, everybody thought. A friend of mine who couldn't come to this occasion but worked in one of the Harvard houses and knew some of the boys in the Glee Club asked one of them when they came back in their red jackets, "Well, how was it?" He said, "Oh, it was all right but we didn't sing well"— which was true—and then he said, "A woman read a poem." My friend said, "How was it?" And he said, "Well, as poems go, it wasn't bad"!

INTERVIEWER

Have you ever had any poems that were gifts? Poems that seemed to write themselves?

BISHOP

Oh, yes. Once in a while it happens. I wanted to write a villanelle all my life but I never could. I'd start them but for some reason I never could finish them. And one day I couldn't believe it—it was like writing a letter.* There was one rhyme I couldn't get that ended in *e-n-t* and a friend of mine, the poet Frank Bidart, came to see me and I said, "Frank, give me a rhyme." He gave me a word offhand and I put it in. But neither he nor I can remember which word it was. But that kind of thing doesn't happen very often. Maybe some poets always write that way. I don't know.

INTERVIEWER

Didn't you used to give Marianne Moore rhymes?

---

* The poem is "One Art" (1976), in *Geography III*.

Yes, when she was doing the La Fontaine transla-
tions. She'd call me up and read me something when
I was in New York—I was in Brazil most of that
time—and say she needed a rhyme. She said that
she admired rhymes and meters very much. It was
hard to tell whether she was pulling your leg or not
sometimes. She was Celtic enough to be somewhat
mysterious about these things.

INTERVIEWER

Critics often talk about your more recent poems
being less formal, more "open," so to speak. They
point out that *Geography III* (1976) has more of "you"
in it, a wide emotional range. Do you agree with
these perceptions?

BISHOP

This is what critics say. I've never written the things
I'd like to write that I've admired all my life. Maybe
one never does. Critics say the most incredible things!

INTERVIEWER

I've been reading a critical book about you that Anne
Stevenson wrote. She said that in your poems nature
was neutral.

BISHOP

Yes, I remember the word *neutral*. I wasn't quite sure
what she meant by that.

INTERVIEWER

I thought she might have meant that if nature is neutral there isn't any guiding spirit or force.

Somebody famous—I can't think who it was—somebody extremely famous was asked if he had one question to ask the Sphinx and get an answer, what would it be? And he said, "Is nature for us or against us?" Well, I've never really thought about it one way or the other. I like the country, the seashore especially, and if I could drive, I'd probably be living in the country. Unfortunately, I've never learned to drive. I bought two cars. At least. I had an MG I adored for some years in Brazil. We lived on top of a mountain peak, and it took an hour to get somewhere where I could practice. And nobody really had time to take an afternoon off and give me driving lessons. So I never got my license. And I *never* would have driven in Rio, anyway. But if you can't drive, you can't live in the country.

INTERVIEWER

Do you have the painting here that your uncle did? The one "about the size of an old-style dollar bill" that you wrote about in "Poem" (1972)?

BISHOP

Oh, sure. Do you want to see it? It's not good enough to hang. Actually, he was my great-uncle. I never met him.

INTERVIEWER

The cows in this really are just one or two brushstrokes!

BISHOP

I exaggerated a little bit. There's a detail in the poem that isn't in the painting. I can't remember what it is now. My uncle did another painting when he was fourteen or fifteen years old that I wrote about in an early poem, "Large Bad Picture" (1946). An aunt who lived in Montreal had both of these and they used to hang in her front hall. I was dying to get them and I went there once and tried to buy them, but she wouldn't sell them to me. She was rather stingy. She died some years ago. I don't know who has the large one now.

INTERVIEWER

When you were showing me your study, I noticed a shadow box hanging in the hall. Is it by Joseph Cornell?

BISHOP

No, I did that one. That's one of my little works. It's about infant mortality in Brazil. It's called *Anjinhos*, which means "little angels." That's what they call the babies and small children who die.

INTERVIEWER

What's the significance of the various objects?

BISHOP

I found the child's sandal on a beach wading east of Rio one Christmas and I finally decided to do something with it. The pacifier was bright red rubber. They sell them in big bottles and jars in drugstores in Brazil. I decided it couldn't be red, so I dyed it black with India ink. A nephew of my Brazilian friend, a very smart young man, came to call while I was doing this. He brought two American rock-and-roll musicians and we talked and talked and talked, and

I never thought to explain in all the time they were there what I was doing. When they left, I thought, My God, they must think I'm a witch or something!

INTERVIEWER

What about the little bowls and skillets filled with rice?

BISHOP

Oh, they're just things children would be playing with. And of course rice and black beans are what Brazilians eat every day.

Cornell is superb. I first saw the *Medici Slot Machine* when I was in college. Oh, I loved it. To think one could have *bought* some of those things then. He was very strange. He got crushes on opera singers and ballet dancers. When I looked at his show in New York two years ago I nearly fainted, because one of my favorite books is a book he liked and used. It's a little book by an English scientist who wrote for children about soap bubbles—*Soap Bubbles: Their Colours and the Forces Which Mold Them*, by Sir C. V. Boys, 1889.

His sister began writing me after she read Octavio Paz's poem for Cornell that I translated. (She doesn't read Spanish.) She sent me a German-French grammar that apparently he meant to do something with and never did. A lot of the pages were folded over and they're all made into star patterns with red ink around them … He lived in what was called Elysian Park. That's an awfully strange address to have.

INTERVIEWER

Until recently you were one of the few American poets who didn't make their living teaching or giving readings. What made you decide to start doing both?

I never wanted to teach in my life. I finally did because I wanted to leave Brazil and I needed the money. Since 1970 I've just been *swamped* with people sending me poems. They start to when they know you're in the country. I used to get them in Brazil, but not so much. They got lost in the mail quite often. I don't believe in teaching poetry at all, but that's what they want one to do. You see so many poems every week, you just lose all sense of judgment.

As for readings, I gave a reading in 1947 at Wellesley College two months after my first book appeared. And I was *sick* for days ahead of time. Oh, it was absurd. And then I did one in Washington in '49 and I was sick again and nobody could hear me. And then I didn't give any for twenty-six years. I don't mind reading now. I've gotten over my shyness a little bit. I think teaching helps. I've noticed that teachers aren't shy. They're rather aggressive. They get to be, finally.

Did you ever take a writing course as a student?

When I went to Vassar I took sixteenth-century, seventeenth-century, and eighteenth-century literature, and then a course in the novel. The kind of courses where you have to do a lot of reading. I don't think I believe in writing courses at all. There weren't any when I was there. There was a poetry-writing course in the evening, but not for credit. A couple of my friends went to it, but I never did.

The word *creative* drives me crazy. I don't like to regard it as therapy. I was in the hospital several years ago and somebody gave me Kenneth Koch's book *Rose, Where Did You Get That Red?* And it's true, children sometimes write wonderful things, paint wonderful pictures, but I think they should be *dis*-couraged. From everything I've read and heard, the number of students in English departments taking literature courses has been falling off enormously. But at the same time the number of people who want to get in the writing classes seems to get bigger and bigger. There are usually two or three being given at Harvard every year. I'd get forty applicants for ten or twelve places. Fifty. It got bigger and bigger. I don't know if they do this to offset practical concerns, or what.

INTERVIEWER

I think people want to be able to say they do something creative like throw pots or write poems.

BISHOP

I just came back in March from reading in North Carolina and Arkansas, and I swear if I see any more handcrafts I'll go mad! I think we should go right straight back to the machine. You can only use so many leather belts, after all. I'm sorry. Maybe you do some of these things.

INTERVIEWER

Do many strangers send you poems?

BISHOP

Yes. It's very hard to know what to do. Sometimes I answer. I had a fan letter the other day, and it was adorable. It was in this childish handwriting. His name was Jimmy Sparks and he was in the sixth grade. He said his class was putting together a booklet of poems and he liked my poems very much—he mentioned three—because they rhymed and because they were about nature. His letter was so cute I did send him a postcard. I think he was supposed to ask me to send a handwritten poem or photograph—schools do this all the time—but he didn't say anything like that, and I'm sure he forgot his mission.

INTERVIEWER

What three poems did he like? "The Sandpiper" (1962)?

BISHOP

Yes, and the one about the mirror and the moon, "Insomnia" (1951), which Marianne Moore said was a cheap love poem.

INTERVIEWER

The one that ends, " ... and you love me"?

BISHOP

Yes. I never liked that. I almost left it out. But last year it was put to music by Elliott Carter along with five other poems of mine* and it sounded much better as a song. Yes, Marianne was very opposed to that one.

INTERVIEWER

Maybe she didn't like the last line.

---

* "Anaphora" (19450, "The Sandpiper," "Argument" (1947), "O Breath" (1949), and "View of the Capitol from the Library of Congress" (1951).

I don't think she ever believed in talking about the emotions much.

Getting back to teaching, did you devise formal assignments when you taught at Harvard? For example, to write a villanelle?

Yes, I made out a whole list of weekly assignments that I gave the class; but every two or three weeks was a free assignment and they could hand in what they wanted. Some classes were so prolific that I'd declare a moratorium. I'd say, "Please, nobody write a poem for two weeks!"

Do you think you can generalize that beginning writers write better in forms than not?

I don't know. We did a sestina—we started one in class by drawing words out of a hat—and I wish I'd never suggested it because it seemed to have *swept* Harvard. Later, in the applications for my class, I'd get dozens of sestinas. The students seemed to think it was my favorite form—which it isn't.

I once tried a sestina about a woman who watches soap operas all day.

Did you watch them in college?

No.

Well, it seemed to be a fad at Harvard. Two or three years ago I taught a course in prose and discovered my students were watching the soap operas every morning and afternoon. I don't know when they studied. So I watched two or three just to see what was going on. They were *boring*. And the advertising! One student wrote a story about an old man who was getting ready to have an old lady to dinner (except she was really a ghost), and he polished a plate till he could see his face in it. It was quite well done, so I read some of it aloud, and said, "But look, this is impossible. You can never see your face in a plate." The whole class, in unison, said, "Joy!" I said, "What? What are you talking about?" Well, it seems there's an ad for Joy soap liquid in which a woman holds up a plate and sees—you know the one? Even so, you can't! I found this very disturbing. TV was *real* and no one had observed that it wasn't. Like when Aristotle was right and no one pointed out, for centuries, that women *don't* have fewer teeth than men.

I had a friend bring me a small TV, black and white, when I was living in Brazil. We gave it to the maid almost immediately because we watched it only when there were things like political speeches, or a revolution coming on. But she loved it. She slept with it in her bed! I think it meant so much to her because she couldn't read. There was a soap opera that year called *The Right to Life*. It changed the whole schedule of Rio society's hours because it was on from eight to nine. The usual dinner hour's eight, so either you had to eat dinner before so that the maid could watch *The Right to Life* or eat much later, when it was over. We ate dinner about ten o'clock finally so that Joanna could watch this thing. I finally decided I had to see it, too. It became a chic thing to do and everybody was talking about it. It was absolutely ghastly! They got the programs from Mexico and dubbed them in Portuguese. They were very corny and always very lurid. Corpses lying in coffins, miracles, nuns, even incest.

I had friends in Belo Horizonte, and the mother and their cook and a grandchild would watch the soap operas, the *novellas*, they're called, every night. The cook would get so excited she'd talk to the screen: "No! No! Don't do that! You know he's a bad man, Doña So-and-so!" They'd get so excited, they'd cry. And I knew of two old ladies, sisters, who got a TV. They'd knit and knit and watch it and cry and one of them would get up and say "Excuse me, I have to go to the bathroom" to the television!

INTERVIEWER
You were living in Brazil, weren't you, when you won the Pulitzer Prize in 1956?

BISHOP
Yes, it was pretty funny. We lived on top of a mountain peak—really way up in the air. I was alone in the house with Maria, the cook. A friend had gone to market. The telephone rang. It was a newsman from the American embassy and he asked me who it

was in English, and of course it was very rare to hear someone speak in English. He said, "Do you know you've won the Pulitzer Prize?" Well, I thought it was a joke. I said, "Oh, come on." And he said, "Don't you hear me?" The telephone connection was very bad and he was shrieking. And I said, "Oh, it can't be." But he said it wasn't a joke. I couldn't make an impression on Maria with this news, but I felt I had to share it, so I hurried down the mountain a half mile or so to the next house, but no one was at home. I thought I should do something to celebrate, have a glass of wine or something. But all I could find in that house, a friend's, were some cookies from America, some awful chocolate cookies—Oreos, I think—so I ended up eating two of those. And that's how I celebrated winning the Pulitzer Prize.

The next day there was a picture in the afternoon paper—they take such things very seriously in Brazil—and the day after that my Brazilian friend went to market again. There was a big covered market with stalls for every kind of comestible, and there was one vegetable man we always went to. He said, "Wasn't that Doña Elizabetchy's picture in the paper yesterday?" She said, "Yes, it was. She won a prize." And he said, "You know, it's amazing! Last week Señora Somebody took a chance on a bicycle and *she* won! My customers are so lucky!" Isn't that marvelous?!

INTERVIEWER
I'd like to talk a little bit about your stories, especially "In the Village" (1953), which I've always admired. Do you see any connection, other than the obvious one of shared subject matter, between your stories and poems? In "method of attack," for example?

They're very closely related. I suspect that some of the stories I've written are actually prose poems and not very good stories. I have four about Nova Scotia. One came out last year in *The Southern Review*. I'm working on a long one now that I hope to finish this summer... "In the Village" was funny. I had made notes for various bits of it and was given too much cortisone—I have very bad asthma from time to time—and you don't need any sleep. You feel wonderful while it's going on, but to get off it is awful. So I couldn't sleep much and I sat up all night in the tropical heat. The story came from a combination of cortisone, I think, and the gin and tonic I drank in the middle of the night. I wrote it in two nights.

INTERVIEWER

That's incredible! It's a long, long story.

BISHOP

Extraordinary. I wish I could do it again but I'll never take cortisone again, if I can possibly avoid it.

INTERVIEWER

I'm always interested in how different poets go about writing about their childhood.

BISHOP

Everybody does. You can't help it, I suppose. You are fearfully observant then. You notice all kinds of things, but there's no way of putting them all together. My memories of some of those days are so much clearer than things that happened in 1950, say. I don't think one should make a cult of writing about childhood, however. I've always tried to avoid it. I find I have written some, I must say. I went to an analyst for a couple of years off and on in the forties, a very nice woman who was especially interested in writers, writers and blacks. She said it was amazing that I would remember things that happened to me when I was two. It's very rare, but apparently writers often do.

INTERVIEWER
Do you know what your earliest memory is?

BISHOP
I think I remember learning to walk. My mother was away and my grandmother was trying to encourage me to walk. It was in Canada and she had lots of plants in the window the way all ladies do there. I can remember this blur of plants and my grandmother holding out her arms. I must have toddled. It seems to me it's a memory. It's very hazy. I told my grandmother years and years later and she said, "Yes, you did learn to walk while your mother was visiting someone." But you walk when you're one, don't you?

I remember my mother taking me for a ride on the swan boats here in Boston. I think I was three then. It was before we went back to Canada. Mother was dressed all in black—widows were in those days. She had a box of mixed peanuts and raisins. There were real swans floating around. I don't think they have them anymore. A swan came up and she fed it and it bit her finger. Maybe she just told me this, but I believed it because she showed me her black kid glove and said, "See." The finger was split. Well, I was thrilled to death! Robert Lowell put those swan boats in two or three of the *Lord Weary's Castle* poems.

INTERVIEWER
Your childhood was difficult, and yet in many of your stories and poems about that time there's a tremendously lyrical quality as well as a great sense of loss and tragedy.

BISHOP
My father died, my mother went crazy when I was four or five years old. My relatives, I think they all felt so sorry for this child that they tried to do their very best. And I think they did. I lived with my grandparents in Nova Scotia. Then I lived with the ones in Worcester, Massachusetts, very briefly, and got terribly sick. This was when I was six and seven. Then I lived with my mother's older sister in Boston. I used to go to Nova Scotia for the summer. When I was twelve or thirteen I was improved enough to go to summer camp at Wellfleet until I went away to school when I was fifteen or sixteen. My aunt was devoted to me and she was awfully nice. She was married and had no children. But my relationship with my relatives—I was always a sort of a guest, and I think I've always felt like that.

INTERVIEWER
Was your adolescence a calmer time?

BISHOP
I was very romantic. I once walked from Nauset Light—I don't think it exists anymore—which is the beginning of the elbow [of Cape Cod], to the

tip, Provincetown, all alone. It took me a night and a day. I went swimming from time to time but at that time the beach was absolutely deserted. There wasn't anything on the back shore, no buildings.

How old would you have been?

Seventeen or eighteen. That's why I'd never go back—because I can't bear to think of the way it is now...I haven't been to Nantucket since—well, I hate to say. My senior year at college I went there for Christmas with my then boyfriend. Nobody knew we were there. It was this wonderful, romantic trip. We went the day after Christmas and stayed for about a week. It was terribly cold but beautiful. We took long walks on the moors. We stayed at a very nice inn and we thought that probably the landlady would throw us out (we were very young and this kind of thing wasn't so common then). We had a bottle of sherry or something innocent like that. On New Year's Eve about ten o'clock there was a knock on the door. It was our landlady with a tray of hot grogs! She came in and we had the loveliest time. She knew the people who ran the museum and they opened it for us. There are a couple of wonderful museums there.

I heard a story that you once spent a night in a tree at Vassar outside Cushing dormitory. Is it true?

Yes, it was me, me and a friend whose name I can't remember. We really were crazy and those trees were wonderful to climb. I used to be a great tree climber. Oh, we probably gave up about three in the morning. How did that ever get around? I can't imagine! We stopped being friends afterward. Well, actually she had invited two boys from West Point for the weekend and I found myself *stuck* with this youth all in—[*her hands draw an imagined cape and uniform in the air*]—the dullest boy! I didn't know what to say! I nearly went mad. I think I sort of dropped the friend at that point...I lived in a great big corner room on the top floor of Cushing and I apparently had registered a little late because I had a roommate whom I had never wanted to have. A strange girl named Constance. I remember her entire side of the room was furnished in Scottie dogs—pillows, pictures, engravings, and photographs. And mine was rather bare. Except that I probably wasn't a good roommate either, because I had a theory at that time that one should write down all one's dreams. That that was the way to write poetry. So I kept a notebook of my dreams and thought if you ate a lot of awful cheese at bedtime you'd have interesting dreams. I went to Vassar with a pot about this big—it did have a cover!—of Roquefort cheese that I kept in the bottom of my bookcase...I think everyone's given to eccentricities at that age. I've heard that at Oxford Auden slept with a revolver under his pillow.

INTERVIEWER

As a young woman, did you have a sense of yourself as a writer?

No, it all just happens without your thinking about it. I never meant to go to Brazil. I never meant doing any of these things. I'm afraid in my life everything has just *happened*.

INTERVIEWER

You like to think there are reasons—

BISHOP

Yes, that people plan ahead, but I'm afraid I really didn't.

INTERVIEWER

But you'd always been interested in writing?

BISHOP

I'd written since I was a child, but when I went to Vassar I was going to be a composer. I'd studied music at Walnut Hill and had a rather good teacher. I'd had a year of counterpoint and I also played the piano. At Vassar you had to perform in public once a month. Well, this terrified me. I really was sick. So I played once and then I gave up the piano because I couldn't bear it. I don't think I'd mind now, but I can't play the piano anymore. Then the next year I switched to English.

It was a very literary class. Mary McCarthy was a year ahead of me. Eleanor Clark was in my class. And Muriel Rukeyser, for freshman year. We started a magazine you may have heard of, *Con Spirito*. I think I was a junior then. There were six or seven of us— Mary, Eleanor Clark and her older sister, my friends Margaret Miller and Frani Blough, and a couple of others. It was during Prohibition and we used to go downtown to a speakeasy and drink wine out of teacups. That was our big vice. Ghastly stuff! Most of us had submitted things to *The Vassar Review* and they'd been turned down. It was very old-fashioned then. We were all rather put out because *we* thought we were good. So we thought, Well, we'll start our own magazine. We thought it would be nice to have it be anonymous, which it was. After its third issue *The Vassar Review* came around and a couple of our editors became editors on it and then they published things by us. But we had a wonderful time doing it while it lasted.

INTERVIEWER

I read in another interview you gave that you had enrolled or were ready to enroll after college in Cornell's medical school.

BISHOP

I think I had all the forms. This was the year after I had graduated from Vassar. But then I discovered I would have to take German and I'd already given up on German once, I thought it was so difficult. And I would have had to take another year of chemistry. I'd already published a few things and I think Marianne [Moore] discouraged me, and I didn't go. I just went off to Europe instead.

INTERVIEWER

Did the Depression have much reality for college students in the thirties?

Everybody was frantic trying to get jobs. All the intellectuals were communist except me. I'm always very perverse so I went in for T. S. Eliot and Anglo-Catholicism. But the spirit was pretty radical. It's funny. The girl who was the biggest radical—she was a year ahead of me—has been married for years and years to one of the heads of Time-Life. I've forgotten his name. He's very famous and couldn't be more conservative. He writes shocking editorials. I can still see her standing outside the library with a tambourine collecting money for this cause and that cause.

INTERVIEWER

Wanting to be a composer, a doctor, or a writer— how do you account for it?

BISHOP

Oh, I was interested in all those things. I'd like to be a painter most, I think. I never really sat down and said to myself, I'm going to be a poet. Never in my life. I'm still surprised that people think I am...I started publishing things in my senior year, I think, and I remember my first check for thirty-five dollars and that was rather an exciting moment. It was from something called *The Magazine*, published in California. They took a poem, they took a story— oh, I wish those poems had never been published! They're terrible! I did show the check to my roommate. I was on the newspaper, the *Miscellany*—and I really was, I don't know, mysterious. On the newspaper board they used to sit around and talk about how they could get published and so on and so on. I'd just hold my tongue. I was embarrassed by it.

And still am. There's nothing more embarrassing than being a poet, really.

It's especially difficult to tell people you're meeting for the first time that that's what you do.

Just last week a friend and I went to visit a wonderful lady I know in Quebec. She's seventy-four or seventy-five. And she didn't say this to me but she said to my friend, Alice, "I'd like to ask my neighbor who has the big house next door to dinner, and she's so nice, but she'd be bound to ask Elizabeth what she does and if Elizabeth said she wrote poetry, the poor woman wouldn't say another word all evening!" This is awful, you know, and I think no matter how modest you think you feel or how minor you think you are, there must be an awful core of ego somewhere for you to set yourself up to write poetry. I've never *felt* it, but it must be there.

In your letter to me, you sounded rather wary of interviewers. Do you feel you've been misrepresented in interviews? For example, that your refusal to appear in all-women poetry anthologies has been misunderstood as a kind of disapproval of the feminist movement?

I've always considered myself a strong feminist. Recently I was interviewed by a reporter from the *Chicago Tribune*. After I talked to the girl for a few minutes, I realized that she wanted to play me off as an "old-fashioned" against Erica Jong, and Adrienne [Rich], whom I like, and other violently feminist people. Which isn't true at all. I finally asked her if she'd ever read any of my poems. Well, it seemed she'd read *one* poem. I didn't see how she could interview me if she didn't know anything about me at all, and I told her so. She was nice enough to print a separate piece in the *Chicago Tribune* apart from the longer article on the others. I had said that I didn't believe in propaganda in poetry. That it rarely worked. What she had me saying was "Miss Bishop does not believe that poetry should convey the poet's personal philosophy." Which made me sound like a complete dumbbell! Where she got that, I don't know. This is why one gets nervous about interviews.

INTERVIEWER

Do you generally agree with anthologists' choices? Do you have any poems that are personal favorites? Ones you'd like to see anthologized that aren't?

BISHOP

I'd rather have—well, anything except "The Fish" (1946)! I've declared a moratorium on that. Anthologists repeat each other so finally a few years ago I said nobody could reprint "The Fish" unless they reprinted three others because I got so sick of it.

INTERVIEWER

One or two more questions. You went to Yaddo several times early in your career. Did you find the atmosphere at an artist's colony helpful to your writing?

I went to Yaddo twice, once in the summer for two weeks, and for several months the winter before I went to Brazil. Mrs. Ames was very much in evidence then. I didn't like it in the summer because of the incessant coming and going, but the winter was rather different. There were only six of us, and just by luck we all liked each other and had a very good time. I wrote one poem, I think, in that whole stretch. The first time I liked the horse races, I'm afraid. In the summer—I think this still goes on—you can walk through the Whitney estate to the tracks. A friend and I used to walk there early in the morning and sit at the track and have coffee and blueberry muffins while they exercised the horses. I loved that. We went to a sale of yearlings in August and that was beautiful. The sale was in a big tent. The grooms had brass dustpans and brooms with brass handles and they'd go around after the little colts and sweep up the manure. That's what I remember best about Yaddo.

INTERVIEWER

It was around the time that you went to Yaddo, wasn't it, that you were consultant in poetry to the Library of Congress? Was that year in Washington more productive than your Yaddo experience?

BISHOP

I've suffered because I've been so shy all my life. A few years later I might have enjoyed it more but at the time I didn't like it much. I hated Washington. There were so many government buildings that looked like Moscow. There was a very nice secretary,

Phyllis Armstrong, who got me through. I think she did most of the work. I'd write something and she'd say, "Oh, no, that isn't official," so then she'd take it and rewrite it in gobbledygook. We used to bet on the horses—Phyllis always bet the daily double. She and I would sit there reading the *Racing Form* and poets would come to call and Phyllis and I would be talking about our bets!

All the "survivors" of that job—a lot of them are dead—were invited to read there recently. There were thirteen of us, unfortunately.

INTERVIEWER

A friend of mine tried to get into that reading and she said it was jammed.

BISHOP

It was *mobbed*! And I don't know why. It couldn't have been a duller, more awful occasion. I think we were supposedly limited to ten minutes. I *stuck* to it. But there's no stopping somebody like James Dickey. Stafford was good. I'd never heard him and never met him. He read one very short poem that really brought tears to my eyes, he read it so beautifully.

I'm not very fond of poetry readings. I'd much rather read the book. I know I'm wrong. I've only been to a few poetry readings I could *bear*. Of course, you're too young to have gone through the Dylan Thomas craze ...

When it was somebody like Cal Lowell or Marianne Moore, it's as if they were my children. I'd get terribly upset. I went to hear Marianne several times and finally I just couldn't go because I'd sit there with tears running down my face. I don't know, it's sort of embarrassing. You're so afraid they'll do something wrong.

Cal thought that the most important thing about readings was the remarks poets made in between the poems. The first time I heard him read was years ago at the New School for Social Research in a small, gray auditorium. It was with Allen Tate and Louise Bogan. Cal was very much younger than anybody else and had published just two books. He read a long, endless poem—I've forgotten its title*—about a Canadian nun in New Brunswick. I've forgotten what the point of the poem is, but it's very, very long and it's quite beautiful, particularly in the beginning. Well, he started, and he read very badly. He kind of droned and everybody was trying to get it. He had gotten about two-thirds of the way through when somebody yelled, "Fire!" There was a small fire in the lobby, nothing much, that was put out in about five minutes and everybody went back to their seats. Poor Cal said, "I think I'd better begin over again," so he read the whole thing all over again! But his reading got much, much better in later years.

INTERVIEWER

He couldn't have done any better than the record the Poetry Center recently put out. It's wonderful. And very funny.

BISHOP

I haven't the courage to hear it.

(1981)

---

* "Mother Marie Therese" in *The Mills of the Kavanaughs*.

Marguerite Yourcenar

THE ART OF FICTION NO. 103

Interviewed by Shusha Guppy

I had an appointment with Marguerite Yourcenar on Saturday, November 14, 1987, at her hotel in Amsterdam. I was told that she had not arrived, that several people had been looking for her, including her driver, and that no one knew where she was. Further telephone calls to her home in Maine and to her publishers in Paris revealed that she had had a slight stroke and was recovering, and that there was no cause for concern. She did not recover, and died on December 18. She was eighty-four.

I had first interviewed her on April 11 in London and later sent her the typescript for corrections. It had come back with a good deal of amendment, carefully written on the text and on separate sheets of paper. I was grateful that she had taken so much trouble over it, but she was still not quite satisfied and wanted to see me again, go through it with me, and make sure that everything was exactly as she intended. I was happily anticipating our meeting in Amsterdam, but it was not to be. The following introduction was written after our meeting in London. I have left it in the present tense.

Marguerite Yourcenar has the ardent imagination and clear, intense blue eyes of her Flemish ancestors. The rich, many colored subtlety of her great novels— *Memoirs of Hadrian* (1951); *The Abyss* (1968); *Alexis* (1929); *Coup de Grâce* (1939); and others—is reminiscent of their intricate tapestries, while her sublime mystical appreciation of nature and its beauty evokes the golden age of landscape painting in the Low Countries. For years she has been considered one of France's most distinguished and original writers; yet it was not until 1981, when she was the first woman ever to "join the immortals" and be elected to the Acadèmie Française in the four hundred years of its existence, that she was discovered by the general public.

Marguerite Yourcenar was born in 1903 into a patrician Franco-Belgian family. (Yourcenar is an anagram of her real name *à particule*, de Crayencour.) Her mother died of puerperal fever shortly after her birth, and she was brought up by her father, a great reader and traveler, who taught her Latin and Greek and read the French classics with her. They lived in various European countries, and she learned English and Italian as well.

She published two volumes of poetry in her teens, "which are frankly *oeuvres de jeunesse* and never to be republished." Her two novellas, *Alexis* and *Coup de Grâce*, appeared in 1929 and 1939 respectively (during which time she lived mostly in Greece) and won her critical acclaim. In 1938 she met Grace Frick in Paris, who later "admirably translated" three of her major books. When the war came in 1939 and she could not return to Greece, she was offered hospitality in the U.S. by Grace Frick, "since she had not the means of living in Paris." To support herself, she took a teaching job at Sarah Lawrence College. She also began to write her masterpiece, *Memoirs of Hadrian*, which was published in 1951.

In 1950 Yourcenar and Frick bought a house on Mount Desert Island, off the coast of Maine, where they lived between long journeys abroad. Grace Frick died in 1979 after a long illness, but Marguerite Yourcenar still lives there, though she continues to travel extensively.

Her latest book, *Two Lives and a Dream* (1987), was published recently in England, and she is now working on *Le Labyrinthe du monde*, completing the autobiographical triptych that began with *Souvenirs pieux* (1974) and *Archives du nord* (1977). She has just written a long essay on Borges—a lecture given recently at Harvard.

Marguerite Yourcenar's intellectual vigor and curiosity are still prodigious, despite age and an open-heart operation two years ago. She has just translated James Baldwin's *The Amen Corner* and Yukio Mishima's *Five Modern Nō Plays* into French, from the original English and Japanese, helped for the latter by her friend J. M. Shisagi, Mishima's executor. She was in London briefly for the publication of *Two Lives and a Dream*, and this interview took place at her hotel in Chelsea. She was elegantly dressed in black and white and spoke an exquisite French, with a markedly patrician accent, in a deep, mellifluous tone.

You have just spent the day in Richmond; was it just to walk in the beautiful park there or for some other reason?

MARGUERITE YOURCENAR

Well, it had to do with the book I am writing at the moment, which is a book built entirely of memories, and in the present chapter I evoke the fourteen months I spent in England when I was twelve and we lived in Richmond. But where exactly I can't recall. I saw dozens of little houses in as many streets, all looking alike, with tiny gardens, but I couldn't tell which one was ours. It was during the first and second years of World War I, which, unlike the Second World War, did not drop from the sky in England— there were no bomb alerts or blitzes. I used to go for long walks in Richmond Park on fine days and to museums in London when it rained. I saw the Elgin Marbles at the British Museum and went to the Victoria and Albert frequently. I used to drop my sweet wrappings in a porcelain dragon there—I bet they're still there!

INTERVIEWER

What is your new book to be called?

YOURCENAR

The French title is *Quoi? L'Eternité*, which is from a poem of Rimbaud's: "*Elle est retrouvée. Quoi? – L'Eternité.*" The book is the third volume of my memoirs. The other two are being translated into Engish at the moment. There are certain words one can't translate literally, and one has to change them.

For example the first volume is called *Souvenirs pieux* in French, and I have translated it as *Dear Departed*, which conveys the same nuance of irony. The second volume is called *Archives du nord*, but "the north" in another language evokes a different image: in England the north refers to Manchester, or even Scotland; in Holland it is the Frisian Islands, which have nothing to do with the north of France. So I have changed it completely, and taken the first line of a Bob Dylan song—"Blowin' in the Wind." I quote the song inside as an epigraph: "How many roads must a man walk down / Before you can call him a man?" It is very beautiful, don't you think? At least it defines well my father's life, and many lives. But to come to the present volume, I don't think *"Quoi? L'Eternité"* would work in English, and we will have to find another title. Among the Elizabethan poets there must be quantities of quotations about eternity, so I think I might find something there.

INTERVIEWER

Let's go back to the beginning. You were very close to your father. He encouraged you to write and he published your first poems. It was a limited edition and I believe is now unobtainable. What do you think of them in retrospect?

YOURCENAR

My father had them published at his own expense—a sort of compliment from him. He shouldn't have done it—they were not much good. I was only sixteen. I liked writing, but I had no literary ambitions. I had all these characters and stories in me, but I had hardly any knowledge of history and none of life to do anything with them. I could say that all my books were conceived by the time I was twenty, although they were not to be written for another thirty or forty years. But perhaps this is true of most writers—the emotional storage is done very early on.

INTERVIEWER

This relates to what you once said, that "books are not life, only its ashes." Do you still believe that?

YOURCENAR

Yes, but books are also a way of learning to feel more acutely. Writing is a way of going to the depth of being.

INTERVIEWER

From your father's death in 1929 to 1939 you only published two novellas, *Alexis* and *Coup de Grâce*, which you said were based on people you knew. Who were they?

YOURCENAR

My father loved an extraordinary woman, exceedingly free in her private life, yet of an almost heroic morality. She chose to remain with her husband though her real attraction was for a man who was Alexis. As for *Coup de Grâce*, I can now tell you that Sophie is very close to me at twenty, and Erick, the young man ardently attached to her own brother whom she falls in love with, was someone I knew, but political problems separated us. Of course one never knows how close fictional characters are to real people. At the beginning of my memoirs I say, *"L'être que j'appelle moi"*—the person I call myself—which means that I don't know who I am. Does one ever?

Next came *Memoirs of Hadrian*, which was immediately hailed as a masterpiece and became a best seller all over the world. Why did you choose the historical novel as a genre?

I have never written a historical novel in my life. I dislike most historical novels. I wrote a monologue about Hadrian's life, as it could have been seen by himself. I can point out that this treatise-monologue was a common literary genre of the period and that others besides Hadrian had done it. Hadrian is a very intelligent man, enriched by all the traditions of his time, while Zeno, the protagonist of *The Abyss* (*L'Œuvre au noir*) is also very intelligent and in advance of his time—indeed of all other epochs too—and is defeated at the end. Nathanaël, the hero of the third panel, *Two Lives and a Dream*, is by contrast a simple, nearly uneducated man who dies at twenty-eight of tuberculosis. He is a sailor at first who becomes shipwrecked off the coast of Maine in America, marries a girl who dies of TB, travels back to England and Holland, marries a second time a woman who turns out to be a thief and a prostitute, and is finally taken up by a wealthy Dutch family. For the first time he comes into contact with culture— listens to music, looks at paintings, lives in luxury. But he keeps a clear head and sharp eyes, because he knows that while he is listening to music in the hospital, opposite his house, men and women are suffering and dying of disease. Eventually he is sent away to an island in the north and dies in peace, surrounded by wild animals and nature. The question is: How far can one go without accepting any culture? The answer is, for Nathanaël, very far, through lucidity of mind and humility of heart.

INTERVIEWER
You met Grace Frick, who later translated *Hadrian*, in 1938. Did you move to the States straight away?

YOURCENAR
At first only for a few months. I was living in Greece then, in Athens. I came to Paris for a visit and the war broke out. I could not go back to Greece and had no money to live in Paris. Grace, with infinite kindness, asked me to come to America for a while. I thought it would be for six months, but there I still am!

INTERVIEWER
What made you choose Mount Desert Island?

YOURCENAR
We had a friend who was a professor of theology at Yale. In 1940 he took a house in Maine while he was on sabbatical, and asked his friends to come and stay. Grace and I went to visit him, and thought that it would be nice to have a house in this still (then) peaceful island. Grace went all over the villages on horseback and became known as "the lady who is looking for a house"! There were luxury houses, sort of chalets for millionaires, or village houses with no facilities, and nothing in between. We finally bought a simple house and modernized it, putting in central heating and a few other amenities. Did you know that Mount Desert was discovered by the French

sailor and explorer Champlain? His ship developed some trouble and he had to stay there for a while to have it repaired. He named it Mount Desert, but alas it is now anything but deserted, and in summer boatloads of tourists pour in from everywhere.

One striking aspect of your work is that nearly all your protagonists have been male homosexuals: Alexis, Erick, Hadrian, Zeno, Mishima. Why is it that you have never created a woman who would be an example of female sexual deviance?

I do not like the word *homosexual*, which I think is dangerous—for it enhances prejudice—and absurd. Say "gay" if you must. Anyway, homosexuality, as you call it, is not the same phenomenon in a man as in a woman. Love for women in a woman is different from love for men in a man. I know a number of "gay" men, but relatively few openly "gay" women. But let us go back to a passage in *Hadrian* where he says that a man who *thinks*, who is engaged upon a philosophical problem or devising a theorem, is neither a man nor a woman, nor even human. He is something else. It is very rare that one could say that about a woman. It does happen, but very seldom; for example, the woman whom my father loved was very sensuous and also, in terms of her times, an "intellectual," but the greatest element of her life was love, especially love for her husband. Even without reaching the high level of someone like Hadrian, one is in the same mental space, and it is unimportant whether one is a man or a woman. Can I say also that love between women interests me less, because I have never met with a great example of it.

But there are writers, like Gertrude Stein and Colette, who have tried to illuminate female homosexuality.

I do not happen to like Colette and Gertrude Stein. The latter is completely foreign to me; Colette, in matters of eroticism, often falls to the level of a Parisian concierge. You look for an example of a woman who is in love with another woman, but *how* is she in love? Is it an ardent passion of a few months? Or a bond of friendship over a long period? Or something in between? When you are in love you're in love—the sex of the beloved does not matter very much. What matters is the feelings, emotions, relationships between people.

Nonetheless, having portrayed Hadrian so eloquently, could you have done something similar on, say, Sappho? And you have been very discreet about your own life, with Grace Frick for example.

We must set Sappho aside, since we know next to nothing about her. As for my own life: There are times when one must reveal certain things, because otherwise things could not be said with verisimilitude. For example, as I said, Sophie's story in *Coup de Grâce* is based on a true incident. But I was always, as they say, "more intellectually oriented" than Sophie.

And I was not raped by a Lithuanian sergeant, nor lodged in a ruined castle! As for my relationship with Grace Frick, I met her when we were both women of a certain age, and it went through different stages: first passionate friendship, then the usual story of two people living and traveling together for the sake of convenience and because they have common literary interests. During the last ten years of her life she was very ill. For the last eight years she couldn't travel and that's why I stayed in Maine during those winters. I tried to help her till the end, but she was no longer the center of my existence, and perhaps had never been. The same is true reciprocally, of course. But what is love? This species of ardor, of warmth, that propels one inexorably toward another being? Why give so much importance to the genitourinary system of people? It does not define a whole being, and it is not even erotically true. What matters, as I said, concerns emotions, relationships. But *whom* you fall in love with depends largely on chance.

INTERVIEWER

Do you think the emphasis on the physical, sexual aspect of love is due partly to psychoanalysis? Perhaps this is what Anna Akhmatova meant when she said Freud ruined literature.

YOURCENAR

Freud turns sexuality into a sort of metaphor, and a metaphor not quite worked out. It seems that he was a great innovator, being the first to speak of sexuality with frankness. But that does not make his theories acceptable. But he did not ruin literature—it was not in his power to do so, since literature is a very great thing. And then no one thinks of Freud in terms of his time and circumstances. He came from a poor, Orthodox Jewish family, living in a little provincial town. Naturally, as a young professor, he was struck by examples of pleasure in Vienna. As a result he saw the world from this double perspective.

INTERVIEWER

It is not so much his pioneering work as a doctor one questions now, but his philosophic-psychological extrapolations.

YOURCENAR

Quite so. He makes a number of extravagant extrapolations, starting from very limited, restricted, and small premises. Hence its attraction for the modern world. But he was the first man to speak about sexuality with sincerity and frankness, when it was still taboo. So everyone was fascinated. But we can now say to him: Thank you for your pioneering effort, but to us it is not a new venture, nor a total discovery. As a great psychologist I prefer Jung. He was sometimes strange, but there was genius in his madness. He was more a poet and had a larger perception of human nature. In his memoirs (*Memories, Dreams, Reflections*) you are often confronted with the mystery of life itself. For example, his mother hatred, so strong that a table breaks itself in two when they are together! A stunning parapsychological episode or a beautiful symbol?

INTERVIEWER

Is it because beyond a certain level the male-female dichotomy is irrelevant to you that you have not

been interested in feminism? What has been your
relationship to the feminist movement of the last few
decades?

YOURCENAR

It does not interest me. I have a horror of such movements, because I think that an intelligent woman is
worth an intelligent man—if you can find any—and
that a stupid woman is every bit as boring as her male
counterpart. Human wickedness is almost equally
distributed between the two sexes.

INTERVIEWER

Is that why you did not wish to be published by
Virago Press in England?

YOURCENAR

I did not want to be published by them—what a
name!—because they publish *only* women. It reminds
one of ladies' compartments in nineteenth-century
trains, or of a ghetto, or simply of those basements
of restaurants where one is confronted by a door
marked *Women* and another marked *Men*. But of
course there are social differences, and geograph-
ical ones. The Muslim woman is somewhat more
restricted. But even there, I have just spent the winter
in Morocco, and when I saw women walking arm in
arm, going to the hammam (public baths)—a place
which is not at all like the Turkish baths one imagines
through Ingres's pictures, and where any minute one
risks one's neck, so slippery it is—well, those women
often seem happier than their Parisian or New Yorker
sisters. They get a lot out of their friendships. There
was a Moghul princess called Jahanara, the daughter

of Sultan Jahan, an admirable poet. I have found too little information concerning her, but she was initiated to Sufism by her brother, the admirable Prince Dara, assassinated in his thirties by his brother, the fanatic Aurangzeb. So you see even Muslim women could achieve eminence despite their circumstances, if they had it in them.

INTERVIEWER

Because Sufism liberates them from the rigid confines of orthodox Islam. There is another Sufi poetess, Rabe'a. She wrote most of her surviving poems with her blood when they opened her veins in a warm bath until she bled to death. At least that's the story. It was a common punishment for heretics then, and Sufis were, on and off, considered heretical.

YOURCENAR

Jahanara was not murdered, but the Sufi master who had initiated her and her brother Dara was finally put to death.

INTERVIEWER

Going back to your work, your book *Fires* (1936) is a series of monologues written from the point of view of women...

YOURCENAR

The impersonal narrator, who writes the small linking sentences, is also evidently a woman, but her reflections on love are genderless. There are three monologues that concern men—Achilles, Patroclus, and Phaedo—and with them we are in the world of *Alexis*. On the other hand Phaedra, Antigone,

Clytemnestra, Sappho, Lena are women, ranging from supreme greatness (Antigone) to vulgarity (Clytemnestra).

You mentioned once that what you wished to do through your work was to revive *le sense du sacré*. It is a common complaint that today we have lost the sense of the sacred—even those who have greatly contributed to this state of affairs complain about it! Will you expand on it a bit more, in relation to your work?

The sacred is the very essence of life. To be aware of the sacred even as I am holding this glass is therefore essential. I mean this glass has a form, which is very beautiful, and which evokes the great mystery of void and plenitude that has haunted the Chinese for centuries. Inside, the glass can serve as a receptacle, for ambrosia or poison. What matters to the Taoists is the void. And glass was invented by someone we don't know. As I say in *The Abyss*, when Zeno is lying down in his monk's cell, the dead are far away and we can't reach them, nor even the living. Who made this table? If we tried to find out how every object around us came into being we would spend our lives doing it. Everything is too far away in the past, or mysteriously too close.

To what do you attribute this loss of the sacred? Is it due, as some maintain, to the development of capitalism and its corollary, consumerism?

Certainly consumerism has a lot to answer for. One lives in a commercialized society against which one *must* struggle. But it is not easy. As soon as one is dealing with the media one becomes their victim. But have we really lost the sense of the sacred? I wonder! Because unfortunately in the past the sacred was intricately mixed with superstition, and people came to consider superstitious even that which was not. For example, peasants believed that it was better to sow the grain at full moon. But they were quite right: that is the moment when the sap rises, drawn by gravitation. What is frightening is the loss of the sacred in human, particularly sexual, relationships, because then no true union is possible.

INTERVIEWER

Perhaps this feeling for the sacred is the reason why you are particularly interested in ecology and conservation?

YOURCENAR

It is most important. The Dutch have kindly elected me to their academy, the Erasmus Institute for the Arts and Letters. Unlike its French counterpart it includes a substantial prize, half of which one has to donate to a charity. I gave mine to the World Wildlife Fund. They protested at first, saying that the institute was for the promotion of the arts and letters, not lions and birds! But I said that I would have to refuse the prize unless I could make my gift, and they accepted. How sincere are the Green and Ecology parties, and how much of it is political posturing, I simply do not know. But something has to be done before it is too late. It is almost too late already, with the acid rain destroying Europe's forests and the defoliation of the tropical forests in South America.

INTERVIEWER

Talking about the academy, you were the first woman in four hundred years to be elected to the French academy. How did it happen? I ask this because traditionally one must make an application and go canvassing with other members. One reads heart-wrenching letters from past candidates, notably Baudelaire, begging the members to vote for them.

YOURCENAR

Poor Baudelaire! He had greatly suffered from the condemnation of some of his poems, *Les Fleurs du mal*, and membership in the academy for him could have been revenge. In my case Jean d'Ormesson wrote asking me if I would object to being nominated, without any visit or other effort on my part. I said no, finding it discourteous to refuse. I was wrong. There are a few serious and interesting academicians; there are also, and always have been, more mediocre choices. Furthermore, the academy, like the *Figaro*, where most academicians do write, represents now a more or less strongly rightist group. I am myself neither rightist nor leftist. I did refuse to wear the academy's uniform—my long black velvet skirt and cape were designed by Saint Laurent. And of course I refused the customary gift of the sword. But I received a Hadrian coin from voluntary contributors.

Since your election to the academy you have become much better known to the general public and lionized by the literary world. Do you mix with the Parisian literary society?

YOURCENAR

I do not know what being "lionized" means, and I dislike all literary worlds, because they represent false values. A few great works and a few great books are important. They are aside and apart from any "world" or "society."

INTERVIEWER

I would like to go back again to the early days and talk about your influences. You have been compared to Gide by many people. Was he an influence? For example, they say that Nathanaël, the hero of your *Two Lives and a Dream*, is named after the one in Gide's *Les nourritures terrestres*. Is that true?

YOURCENAR

I don't like Gide very much. I find him dry and sometimes superficial. I chose Nathanaël because it is a Puritan name, and he is a young Dutch sailor from a Puritan family. Other members of the family are called Lazarus or Eli for the same reason. They are Biblical names and have no connection with Gide's book. We are very far from the state of happy inebriation presented by Gide in the *Nourritures*, and which is no longer possible in our time, in the face of so much madness and chaos.

But *Alexis* has the form of a Gidian *récit* ...

YOURCENAR

A *récit* in the form of a letter is an old literary French form. I have said that the gratitude young writers felt for Gide was, to a large extent, because of his use of classical prose forms. But why choose any one in particular? There are hundreds of great books in different languages by which we all are or should be influenced.

INTERVIEWER

Of course, but there are always certain affinities with various writers. Who are they in your case? Baudelaire, Racine, the Romantics?

YOURCENAR

Baudelaire certainly; and some of the Romantics. The French middle ages much more, and certain poets of the seventeenth century, such as Maynard, "*La belle vieille*," and many, many other poets, French and non-French. Racine up to a point, but he is such a unique case that no one can be compared to him.

INTERVIEWER

Except for Britannicus all his protagonists were women: Phèdre, Bérénice, Athalie, Roxane ...

YOURCENAR

Proust had this idea that Racine's Phèdre could be indentified with a man as well as a woman. But Racine's Phèdre is much more French than Greek: You will see it at once if you compare her to the

Greek Phèdre. Her passionate jealousy is a typical theme of French literature, just as it is in Proust. That is why even in *Phèdre*, Racine *had* to find her a rival, Aricie, who is an insignificant character, like a bridal from a popular dress shop. In other words, love as possession, *against* someone. And that is prodigiously French. Spanish jealousy is quite different: it is real hatred, the despair of someone who has been deprived of his/her food. As for the Anglo-Saxon love, well, there is nothing more beautiful than Shakespeare's sonnets, while German love has produced some wonderful poetry too.

INTERVIEWER

I have this theory that the French do not understand Baudelaire and never have. They speak of his rhetoric, yet he is the least rhetorical of poets. He writes like an Oriental poet—dare I say like a Persian poet?

YOURCENAR

Baudelaire is a sublime poet. But the French don't even understand Hugo, who is also a sublime poet. I have—as Malraux also did—taken titles from Hugo's verses: *Le cerveau noir de Piranèse* (1963), and others. Whenever I am passing by Place Vendôme in Paris I recall Hugo's poem in which he is thinking of Napoleon, wondering if he should prefer *"la courbe d'Annibal, ou l'angle d'Alexandre, au carré de César."* A whole strategy contained in one line of alexandrine! Of course there are times when Hugo is bad and rhetorical—even great poets have their off days—but nonetheless he is prodigious.

INTERVIEWER

Is this what Gide meant when he said: "*Victor Hugo, hélas*"?

YOURCENAR

To have said "*hélas*" is proof of a certain smallness in Gide.

INTERVIEWER

He also rejected Proust's manuscript of *Swann's Way*, saying, "Here is the story of a little boy who can't go to sleep"!

YOURCENAR

We were talking about jealousy: maybe Gide was jealous of Proust; or perhaps he honestly could not like the long and subjective beginning of the *Temps perdu*. He was not, as we are, cognizant of Proust's whole work.

INTERVIEWER

So who was a decisive influence on you in youth?

YOURCENAR

As I said in the preface to *Alexis*, at the time it was Rilke. But this business of influence is a tricky one. One reads thousands of books, of poets, modern and ancient, as one meets thousands of people. What remains of it all is hard to tell.

INTERVIEWER

You mentioned modern poets. Which ones for example?

There is a Swedish poet whom I have never succeeded in introducing to my French friends: Gunnar Ekelöf. He has written three little books called *Divans*, I suppose influenced by Persian poetry. And, of course, Borges, and some of Lorca's poems, and Pessoa, Apollinaire.

INTERVIEWER

Talking about Borges, what about other South American writers, the whole school of magical realism?

YOURCENAR

I don't like them—they are like factory products.

INTERVIEWER

What about the literature of your adopted country, the United States?

YOURCENAR

I'm afraid I haven't read much. I have read a lot of things unconnected with Western literature. At the moment I am reading a huge book by a Moroccan Sufi poet, books on ecology, sagas from Iceland, and so on.

INTERVIEWER

But surely you must have read writers like Henry James, Faulkner, Hemingway, Edith Wharton?

YOURCENAR

Some. There are great moments in Hemingway, for example "The Battler," or, even better, "The Killers," which is a masterpiece of the American short story. It is a tale of revenge in the underworld, and it is excellent. Edith Wharton's short stories seem to me much better than her novels. *Ethan Frome*, for example, is the story of a peasant of New England. In it the protagonist, a woman of the world, puts herself in his place and describes the life of these people in winter, when all the roads are frozen, isolated. It is short and very beautiful. Faulkner brings with him the true horror of the South, the illiteracy and racism of poor whites. As for Henry James, the best definition is the one by Somerset Maugham, when he said that Henry James was an alpinist, equipped to conquer the Himalayas, and walked up Baker Street! Henry James was crushed by his stifling milieu—his sister, his mother, even his brother, who was a genius, but of a more philosophical and professorial kind. James never told his own truth.

INTERVIEWER

You have just translated *The Amen Corner*, and I know that you admire James Baldwin and are a friend of his. What do you think of his work now?

YOURCENAR

Baldwin has written some admirable pages, but he does not have the courage to go to the end of his conclusions. He should have hit much harder. His life has been hard. He was one of nine children in Harlem, poor, a preacher at fifteen, a runaway at eighteen, working as a laborer, first in the army during the war and later in the street, earning barely enough to survive. Somehow he gets to Paris where he manages to get himself incarcerated for the crime of having no fixed address and no profession. He has a drink problem now, but many American writers have had problems with drinking; perhaps it is due to the puritanism which has reigned over the American soul for so long. But at the same time, when the Americans are generous, cordial, intelligent, they are somehow more so than the Europeans. I know at least five or six Americans like that.

INTERVIEWER

You are also interested in Japanese literature and your book on Mishima is considered one of the best essays on him. When did you get involved with Japan?

YOURCENAR

My interest in Japanese literature goes back to when I was about eighteen and first discovered it through certain books. I read Mishima in French when he first appeared and found some of his work very beautiful. Later I saw that a great deal of absurdities were written about him and decided to write my book in order to present a more genuine Mishima. Now they have even made a detestable film of his life. Mrs. Mishima went to Hollywood and tried to stop it, but in vain. Four years ago I started learning Japanese, and after a while with the help of a Japanese friend translated Mishima's *Five Modern Nō Plays* into French. They are beautiful.

INTERVIEWER

Traveling extensively as you do, how do you manage to write? Where do you find so much energy, and what is your work routine?

I write everywhere. I could write here, as I am talking to you. When in Maine or elsewhere, when I am traveling, I write wherever I am or whenever I can. Writing doesn't require too much energy—it is a relaxation, and a joy.

INTERVIEWER

Looking back on your life, do you feel that you have had a "good" life, as the expression goes?

YOURCENAR

I don't know what a "good" life is. But how can one not be sad looking at the world around us at present? But there are also moments when I feel—to use a military expression my father liked—that "it is all counted as leave" (*Tout ça compte dans le congé!*). Happiness sometimes exists.

INTERVIEWER

You are also interested in Sufism, and are planning an essay on Jahanara. What attracts you to it? I am particularly interested because I come from that tradition.

YOURCENAR

It is a philosophy that deals with the divine as the essence of perfection, which is the Friend, and which the Buddhists seek within themselves, knowing that it comes from themselves, that liberation is from within. But I can't say that I am a Buddhist or a Sufi, or a socialist. I don't belong to any doctrine in particular. But there are spiritual affinities.

It seems crass to ask of someone as remarkably youthful and energetic as you are whether you ever think of death?

I think about it all the time. There are moments when I am tempted to believe that there is at least a part of the personality that survives, and others when I don't think so at all. I am tempted to see things as Honda does, in Mishima's last book, the one he finished the day he died. Honda, the principal character, realizes that he has been lucky enough to have loved four people, but that they were all the same person in different forms, in, if you like, successive reincarnations. The fifth time he has made a mistake and the error has cost him dearly. He realizes that the essence of these people is somewhere in the universe and that some day, perhaps in ten thousand years or more, he will find them again, in other forms, without even recognizing them. Of course, reincarnation here is only a word, one of the many possible words to stress a *certain* continuity. Certainly all the physical evidence points to our total annihilation, but if one also considers all the metaphysical *données*, one is tempted to say that it is not as simple as that.

(1988)

Margaret Atwood

THE ART OF FICTION NO. 121

Interviewed by Mary Morris

argaret Atwood was born in Ottawa, Ontario, in 1939. As a child, she lived in the wilderness of northern Quebec and also spent time in Ottawa, Sault Sainte Marie, and Toronto. She was eleven before she attended a full year of school. In high school Atwood began to write poetry inspired by Edgar Allen Poe, and at sixteen she committed herself to a writing career, publishing a collection of poems, *Double Persephone* (1961), six years later.

Her second book of poetry, *The Circle Game* (1964), earned her the Governor General's Award—Canada's highest literary honor—and from that time forward she has been a dominant figure in Canadian letters. In 1972 Atwood sparked a hot debate when she published a controversial critical study of Canadian literature, *Survival: A Thematic Guide to Canadian Literature*. In it she claimed that Canadian literature reflects the submissive as well as survivalist tendencies of the country, born from its being a subordinate ally to the United States, a former colony, and a country with vast stretches of untamed land. Following the publication of this volume, Atwood retreated from Toronto, where she had been working as an editor at the publishing house Anansi, to a farm in Alliston, Ontario, where she began to write full-time.

Atwood has published nineteen collections of poetry—including *The Circle Game, The Journals of Susanna Moodie* (1970), *Power Politics* (1971), *You Are Happy* (1974), *True Stories* (1981), and *Interlunar* (1984)—but she is best known for her novels, which include *Surfacing* (1972), *Lady Oracle* (1976), and *Cat's Eye* (1988). Her most widely read novel is *The Handmaid's Tale* (1986), a chilling account of a puritanical theocracy that won Atwood a second Governor General's Award and was recently made into a motion picture. She is also the author of two children's books, *Up in the Tree* (1978) and *Anna's Pet* (1980), and two collections of short stories, *Dancing Girls* (1977) and *Bluebeard's Egg* (1983). She has edited Oxford anthologies of Canadian verse and Canadian short stories and, with Shannon Ravenel, the 1989 volume of *The Best American Short Stories*.

The question of the status of women has frequently been an issue in Atwood's work, and feminists have seized upon her writing as a product of the movement. Atwood has also made other political and philosophical issues themes in her work, such as Canada's struggle to create an identity and, in recent years, her concern for human rights.

This interview was conducted in a house near Princeton University, where Atwood had gone to give some readings and lectures. In person, Atwood is much as one might expect from reading her work—incisive. For many hours over a period of two days, while teenage boys bounced basketballs and played music outside, people walked in and out, and football games played on the television in the next room, Atwood sat, attentive, answering each question without hesitation. She never strayed from her point, never seemed to tire, and remained, like a narrator from any one of her books, unflappable.

INTERVIEWER

Has the theme of survival always been intrinsic to your work?

MARGARET ATWOOD

I grew up in the north woods of Canada. You had to know certain things about survival. Wilderness survival courses weren't very formalized when I was growing up, but I was taught certain things about what to do if I got lost in the woods. Things were immediate in that way and therefore quite simple. It was part of my life from the beginning.

INTERVIEWER

When did you make the leap from considering survival to be a physical battle to considering it to be an intellectual or political struggle?

ATWOOD

When I started thinking about Canada as a country it became quite evident to me that survival was a national obsession. When I came to the States in the sixties, I felt that nobody knew where Canada was. Their brother may have gone there to fish or something. When I was at Harvard, I was invited as a "foreign student" to a woman's house for an evening for which I was asked to wear "native costume." Unfortunately I'd left my native costume at home and had no snowshoes. So there I was, without native costume with this poor woman and all this food, sitting around waiting for the really exotic foreign students in *their* native costumes to turn up—which they never did because, as everybody knew, foreign students didn't go out at night.

INTERVIEWER

You've written about the theme of foreignness a good deal.

ATWOOD

Foreignness is all around. Only in the heart of the heart of the country, namely the heart of the United States, can you avoid such a thing. In the center of an empire, you can think of your experience as universal. Outside the empire or on the fringes of the empire, you cannot.

INTERVIEWER

In your afterword to *The Journals of Susanna Moodie* you write that if the mental illness of the United States is megalomania, that of Canada is paranoid schizophrenia. Could you say something more about that?

ATWOOD

The United States is big and powerful; Canada is divided and threatened. Maybe I shouldn't have said

"illness." Maybe I should have said "state of mind."
Men often ask me, Why are your female characters
so paranoid? It's not paranoia. It's recognition of
their situation. Equivalently, the United States's feeling that it is big and powerful is not a delusion. It *is*
big and powerful. Possibly, its wish to be even bigger and more powerful is the mentally ill part. Every
Canadian has a complicated relationship with the
United States, whereas Americans think of Canada
as the place where the weather comes from. Compli-
cation is a matter of how you perceive yourself in an
unequal power relationship.

INTERVIEWER

How do you view Canada and its literature within
this political relationship?

ATWOOD

Canada is not an occupied country. It's a dominated
country. Things are more clear-cut in an occupied
country—the heroes and the villains are obvious.
One of the complicating things, of course, is that
the United States will eagerly swallow anything. It's
very welcoming in that way. Canadian writers often
find that they have a better time in the United States
than they do in Canada, because living in Canada is
to some extent like living in a small town. They will
rally around you when you break your leg, but on the
other hand, if you get too big for your britches, well,
they perceive it as exactly that. Alice Munro's book,
which is titled *The Beggar Maid* in the United States,
is called *Who Do You Think You Are?* in Canada...as
in, Who do you think you are, behaving like that—
the prime minister? The U.S. loves success, the

American dream that anybody can be president of the United States or get into *People* magazine. But with Canadians, it's much more likely to be, You know, people might not like it if you did that. There are a lot more snipers in the bushes.

INTERVIEWER

Where have you been treated better as a writer, would you say?

ATWOOD

I suffer more vicious attacks, more personal attacks, in Canada, because that's where I'm from. Families have their most desperate fights among themselves, as we know. However, if you look at per capita sales figures, people recognizing me in the street, of course it's more in Canada. If I sold as many books per capita in the United States as in Canada, I'd be a billionaire.

INTERVIEWER

Is it more difficult for women to get published than men?

ATWOOD

I'm afraid the question is simply too broad. Do we mean, for instance, in North America, or in Ireland, or in Afghanistan? There are categories other than gender. Age, class, and color, for instance. Region. National origin. Previous publication. Sexual orientation. I suppose we could rephrase the question and ask, is it more difficult for a first novelist who is female than for her male counterpart of the same age, class, color, national origin or location, and comparable talent, whatever that may be. Judging from the experience of Latin American female writers—of which there are many, though few are known in translation—the answer would be yes. Women in many countries find it difficult to get published at all—consider the Middle East, for instance. Or black women in South Africa. In fact, they find it difficult to write. Or difficult to become educated. The barriers to women writing are often put in place at a very early age and in very basic ways.

But if we're just talking about, say, North America, obviously commercial publishers want to publish things they can sell. Whether such publishers will publish a given book—whether by a man, woman, or turtle—depends a lot on what they think its reception will be. I don't think there's an overt policy against books by women or an overt quota. Much depends on the book and on the intuition of the publisher. It's true, however, that the majority of books that do appear are still written by men and reviewed by men. Then there's the subject of reviewing. That's where you're most likely to see gender bias, bias of all kinds.

INTERVIEWER

Is it difficult to write from the point of view of a male?

ATWOOD

Most of the "speakers" or narrative points of view in my books are those of women, but I have sometimes used the point of view of a character who is male. Notice I try to avoid saying "the male point of view." I don't believe in the male point of view any more than I believe in the female point of view. There are a good many of both, though it's true that there are some thoughts and attitudes that are unlikely to be held by men on the one hand or women on the other. So when I do use a male character, it's because the story is about something or someone that can't be otherwise conveyed or that would be altered if it were to be conveyed through a female character. For instance, I recently published a story in *Granta* called "Isis in Darkness" (1990). It's about the relationship—the tenuous relationship over the years—between a woman poet and a man who has, I guess, a sort of literary crush on her and how the woman affects the man's life. If I'd told it through the woman herself ... well, you can't tell such stories about romantic infatuation from the point of view of the object of the infatuation without losing the flavor of the emotion. They would just become "who is that creep hanging around outside the balcony" stories.

INTERVIEWER

Can you tell the gender of a writer from reading the text alone?

ATWOOD

Sometimes, certainly, but not always. There's a famous case in England of an Anglican vicar who said he couldn't get anything published. So he wrote under the name of an East Asian woman and got a novel accepted by Virago. There's a certain amount of opinion around that says, for instance, that women can't or shouldn't write from a male point of view and so forth. Men are very sniffy about how they're portrayed by women, but the truth is that most of the really vicious, unpleasant male characters in fiction or theater have been written by men. The ethnic joke principle seems to be at work—it's okay to say a man has smelly feet, no ethics, and bad table manners if the writer is a man, but if it's a woman saying exactly the same thing, then she somehow hates men. The male amour propre is wounded. And if she writes nice male characters, they're seen as "weak" by other men—though if a man puts a man in the kitchen, that's realism. And on and on.

We have fallen very much into the habit of judging books by their covers. "Authenticity" has become a concern. I tend to side with creative freedom. Everyone should write as she or he feels impelled. Then let's judge the results, not the picture of the author on the back flap.

Your question also assumes that "women" are a fixed quantity and that some men are "better" at portraying this quantity than others are. I, however, deny that the quantity is fixed. There is no single, simple, static "women's point of view." Let's just say that good writing of any kind by anyone is surprising, intricate, strong, sinuous. Men who write stereotyped women or treat them like stuffed furniture or sex aids are portraying something—their inner lives, perhaps—and that's interesting to know about up to a point. But it should not be mistaken for life outside the author's head.

INTERVIEWER

How do the activities of writing poetry and writing prose differ for you?

ATWOOD

My theory is that they involve two different areas of the brain, with some overlap. When I am writing fiction, I believe I am much better organized, more methodical—one has to be when writing a novel. Writing poetry is a state of free float.

I have the feeling that you work out problems in your poetry, but that you hold onto the metaphors and dramatize them in your novels.

The genesis of a poem for me is usually a cluster of words. The only good metaphor I can think of is a scientific one: dipping a thread into a supersaturated solution to induce crystal formation. I don't think I solve problems in my poetry; I think I uncover the problems. Then the novel seems a process of working them out. I don't think of it that way at the time—that is, when I'm writing poetry, I don't know I'm going to be led down the path to the next novel. Only after I've finished the novel can I say, Well, this poem was the key. This poem opened the door.

When I'm writing a novel, what comes first is an image, scene, or voice. Something fairly small. Sometimes that seed is contained in a poem I've already written. The structure or design gets worked out in the course of the writing. I couldn't write the other way round, with structure first. It would be too much like paint-by-numbers. As for lines of descent—that is, poem leading to novel—I could point to a number of examples. In my second collection of poems, *The Animals in That Country* (1968), there's a poem called "Progressive Insanities of a Pioneer." That led into the whole collection called *The Journals of Susanna Moodie* and that in turn led into *Surfacing.*

Or, another line of descent, the poems in parts of *True Stories* have obvious affiliations with the novel *Bodily Harm* (1981). It's almost as if the poems open something, like opening a room or a box or a pathway. And then the novel can go in and see what else is in there. I'm not sure this is unique. I expect that many other ambidextrous writers have had the same experience.

Do writers perceive differently than others? Is there anything unique about the writer's eye?

It's all bound up with what sorts of things we have words for. Eskimos, the Inuit, have fifty-two words for snow. Each of those words describes a different kind of snow. In Finnish they have no *he* or *she* words. If you're writing a novel in Finnish, you have to make gender very obvious early on, either by naming the character or by describing a sex-specific activity. But I can't really answer this question because I don't know how "others" observe the world. But judging from the letters I receive, many others recognize at least part of themselves in what I write, though the part recognized varies from person to person, of course. The unique thing about writers is that they write. Therefore they are pickier about words, at least on paper. But everyone "writes" in a way; that is, each person has a "story"—a personal narrative—which is constantly being replayed, revised, taken apart, and put together again. The significant points in this narrative change as a person ages—what may have been tragedy at twenty is seen as comedy or nostalgia at forty. All children "write." (And paint, and sing.) I suppose the real question is why do so many people give it up. Intimidation, I suppose. Fear of not being good. Lack of time.

INTERVIEWER
Do you ever feel struck by the limitations of language?

ATWOOD
All writers feel struck by the limitations of language. All serious writers.

INTERVIEWER
Why is there so much violence in your work? *Bodily Harm* in particular.

ATWOOD
Sometimes people are surprised that a woman would write such things. *Bodily Harm*, for instance, was perceived as some kind of incursion into a world that is supposed to be male. Certainly violence is more a part of my work than it is of Jane Austen's, or George Eliot's. They didn't do it in those days. Charles Dickens wrote about Bill Sikes bludgeoning Nancy to death, getting blood all over everything, but if a woman had written that, nobody would have published it. Actually, I grew up violence free and among people who were extremely civilized in their behavior. When I went out into the wider world, I found violence more shocking than would somebody who was used to it. Also, during the Second World War, although there was not violence in my immediate vicinity, the angst—you know, the anxiety about the war—was ever present. Canada went into the

war in 1939, about two months before I was born. The per capita death rate was high.

Yet you write as if you've lived through violence.

But I write as if I've lived a lot of things I haven't lived. I've never lived with cancer. I've never been fat. I have different sensibilities. In my critical work I'm an eighteenth-century rationalist of some kind. In my poetry I'm not at all. There's no way of knowing in advance what will get into your work. One collects all the shiny objects that catch one's fancy—a great array of them. Some of them you think are utterly useless. I have a large collection of curios of that kind, and every once in a while I need one of them. They're in my head, but who knows where! It's such a jumble in there. It's hard to find anything.

Is sex easy to write about?

If by "sex" you mean just the sex act—"the earth moved" stuff—well, I don't think I write those scenes much. They can so quickly become comic or pretentious or overly metaphoric. "Her breasts were like apples," that sort of thing. But "sex" is not just which part of whose body was where. It's the relationship between the participants, the furniture in the room, or the leaves on the tree, what gets said before and after, the emotions—act of love, act of lust, act of hate, act of indifference, act of violence, act of despair, act of manipulation, act of hope. Those things have to be part of it.

Striptease has become less interesting since they did away with the costumes. It's become Newtonian. The movement of bodies through space, period. It can get boring.

INTERVIEWER

Has motherhood made you feel differently about yourself?

ATWOOD

There was a period in my early career that was determined by the images of women writers I was exposed to—women writers as genius suicides like Virginia Woolf. Or genius reclusives like Emily Dickinson and Christina Rossetti. Or doomed people of some sort, like the Brontës, who both died young. You could fall back on Harriet Beecher Stowe or Mrs. Gaskell; they both led reasonable lives. But then George Eliot didn't have any children; neither did Jane Austen. Looking back over these women writers, it seemed difficult as a writer and a woman to have children and a domestic relationship. For a while I thought I had to choose between the two things I wanted: children and to be a writer. I took a chance.

INTERVIEWER

In much of your work, love and power seem to be intricately connected—love as a power struggle in *Power Politics*. Do you see any other way between men and women?

Love relationships between men and women do involve power structures because men in this society have different kinds of, and more, power than women do. The problem for a woman in a relationship is how to maintain her integrity, her own personal power while also in a relationship with a man. Being in love with somebody is an experience that breaks down ego barriers. The positive part of that is a feeling of "cosmic consciousness," and the negative pole is a feeling of loss of self. You're losing who you are; you're surrendering—the fortress has fallen. But is it possible to have an equal exchange in a society in which things aren't entirely equal? *Power Politics* is fourteen years old. People tend to put it in the present tense. Each of my books is different—presenting different situations, characters, and involvements. My most domestic novel is *Life Before Man* (1979). In it there's an equilateral triangle. There are two women and one man, and viewed from any one point in the triangle the other two are not behaving properly. But you can go around the triangle and look at it from all sides. To be asked what I think as a person is a different thing. I have a very good relationship with a man and I've had it for some time. The novel is not merely a vehicle for self-expression or for the rendition of one's own personal life. I'm quite conservative in that way. I do see the novel as a vehicle for looking at society—an interface between language and what we choose to call reality, although even that is a very malleable substance. When I create characters in novels, those characters aren't necessarily expressing something that is merely personal. I draw observations from a wide range of things.

How do you work? Can you describe how you write your first draft?

I write in longhand and preferably on paper with margins and thick lines with wide space between the lines. I prefer to write with pens that glide very easily over the paper because my handwriting is fast. Actually, I don't churn out finished copy quickly. Even though I have this fast handwriting, I have to scribble over it and scratch things out. Then I transcribe the manuscript, which is almost illegible, onto the typewriter.

Do you have a time, a day, or a place for writing? Does it matter where you are?

I try to write between ten in the morning and four in the afternoon, when my child comes home from school. Sometimes in the evenings, if I'm really zipping along on a novel.

Do you write a novel from page one through to the end?

No. Scenes present themselves. Sometimes it proceeds in a linear fashion, but sometimes it's all over the place. I wrote two parts of *Surfacing* five years before I wrote the rest of the novel—the scene in which the mother's soul appears as a bird and the first drive to the lake. They are the two anchors for that novel.

INTERVIEWER

What is the most difficult aspect of writing?

ATWOOD

That would be book promotion—that is, doing interviews. The easiest is the writing itself. By "easiest" I don't mean something that is lacking in hard moments or frustration; I suppose I mean "most rewarding." Halfway between book promotion and writing is revision; halfway between book promotion and revision is correcting the galleys. I don't like that much at all.

INTERVIEWER

Do you work closely with editors?

ATWOOD

I used to be an editor, so I do a lot of self-editing. I rewrite a lot before I show things to people. I like to have a manuscript in more or less its final shape before anyone sees it. That doesn't mean I can spell. There's that, and the fiddley things like punctuation—everyone has different ideas about that. So I work with an editor to improve that aspect of the text, of course. Ellen Seligman of McClelland & Stewart was devoted and wonderful when we worked on *Cat's Eye*. Things like: You have *soggy* twice on the same page. Meticulous. And I've had great fun doing some stories by phone with certain magazine editors—Bob Gottlieb of *The New Yorker* and Bill Buford of *Granta*, for instance. These sessions always take place when you're in Switzerland or about to get into the bath, and they have to have it done right away. Bargaining goes on, horse-trading. You can have the dash if I get the semicolon. That sort of thing. But an editor doesn't just edit. She or he sees the book through the whole publishing process. I have close and long-standing relationships with, for instance, Bill Toye of Oxford, Canada; Nan Talese, who's been my U.S. editor since 1976; and Liz Calder of Bloomsbury in the U.K. One of the things you want from an editor is simply the feeling that he or she understands your work. Money is no substitute for that.

INTERVIEWER

I've noticed that money is a very important factor in your thinking. Have you always seen things in such sharp economic terms?

ATWOOD

When you're poor you do. I went through a period of being quite poor, of having to really watch it in order to buy myself time to write, and indeed in order to eat. My poverty wasn't the same as real poverty in that I had some sense of direction. I didn't feel trapped. Actually, because my family lived in the woods, it was rather difficult to tell whether we were rich or poor because none of those things applied. It didn't matter. We had what we needed—we grew a lot of our own vegetables and things. So I grew up outside of that. I wasn't in a social structure in which it mattered at all. Then I was out on my own quite early. I was brought up to believe that I should support myself. I had a bank account quite early on and learned how to use it. I was taught to be financially independent and I always have been. Money is important for women, because you'd be amazed how it alters your thinking to be financially dependent on someone. Indeed, anyone.

Have you ever thought of writing a novel in which a woman had an extremely important job?

Yes, I have thought of doing that. But I've shied away for the same reason that George Eliot never wrote a novel about a successful English nineteenth-century woman writer, although she was one. It's still so atypical as to be a social exception. Besides, I'm not a businessperson. I'm a self-employed person. I don't have to deal in a power structure in the same way. I don't have to claw my way up through the corporate world. There is a successful woman in one of my books. She's the young, female judge that Rennie interviews in *Bodily Harm*. She's just so perfect. She has modern paintings, a wonderful husband, children. She loves her work—remember her? Rennie interviews her and can't stand it. A woman interviewer—of the "lifestyles" variety—once got very peeved with me because she felt I wasn't telling her the real dirt. She wanted the inner guck. I finally said to her, If you had your choice, what would you like me to say to you? She said, Well, that you're leaving Graham, right now, and that I've got the scoop on it, and that I can come home and watch you pack.

INTERVIEWER

Have you always questioned institutions?

ATWOOD

Well, I grew up in the woods outside of any social structures apart from those of my family. So I didn't absorb social structures through my skin the way many children do. If you grow up in a small town you instinctively know who is who and what is what and whom you can safely be contemptuous of.

INTERVIEWER

How do you come by your titles?

ATWOOD

I like "come by," because that's about the way it is. I come by them, much as you come by some unexpected object in a junk store or lying beside the road. Sometimes the title arrives almost at the beginning of the writing of the book—*The Edible Woman* (1969) and *Lady Oracle* are cases in point. Sometimes you've been looking very hard in other directions and the right title will just leap at you from the side. *Bodily Harm* came while I was doing some unrelated reading of a legal nature. Several books have gone through a number of working titles; for *Surfacing* there were two serious previous titles and about twenty possibilities—some of them variations on the final one. *Cat's Eye*—I think that came early on and was very necessary in view of the central physical object in the book. *The Handmaid's Tale* was called "Offred" when I first began it. It changed by page a hundred and ten. I know this because I kept a sort of working diary—not notes, but a running total of pages written—to encourage myself. I've read and continue to read the Bible a lot—partly as a result of being in all those hotel rooms, partly a long-standing habit—so the final title really did come from Genesis 30. I think too that it was one of those words that puzzled me as a child. *Handmaid*. Like *footman*. It's a very odd word.

INTERVIEWER

Is the Bible a literary inspiration to you? I know that you've spoken of having "the gift" in almost religious terms.

ATWOOD

That's not an analogy I'm particularly comfortable with because it is religious. But "the gift" is real. Along with it goes a sense of vocation and dedication. You get the call.

INTERVIEWER

At the end of *Lady Oracle*, Joan says, I'm not going to write Costume Gothics anymore. Maybe I'll write science fiction. Maybe I'll write about the future. In a sense you have done this in *Handmaid's Tale*. There is an evolution in your work toward a larger focus on the world.

ATWOOD

I think the focus has become wider, but surely that happens with every writer. What you do first is learn your craft. That can take years. In order to do that, you have to pick subjects that are small enough for you to handle. You learn how to do a good job with that. Of course, in the larger sense, every novel is—

at the beginning—the same opening of a door onto a completely unknown space. I mean, it's just as terrifying every time. But nevertheless, having made the journey a few times, you have little guideposts, little signposts in the back of your mind. One of the most salutary things is writing a novel that fails, doesn't work, or that you can't finish, because what you learn from these failures is often as important as what you learn from doing something that succeeds. The prospect of having it happen again isn't so terrifying because you know you got through it.

INTERVIEWER

Can you look over your past work with pleasure? Would you change it if you had the chance?

ATWOOD

I don't look over my past work very much. I would not change it any more than I would airbrush a photo of myself. When I do look at my work, I sometimes don't recognize it immediately, or I'm indulgent, as one is toward the work of the young. Or I wonder what I could possibly have been thinking about— and then I remember. I suppose when I'm eighty I'll have a good old pig-out on my past productions, but right now I'm too preoccupied with what's on my plate. What a lot of food metaphors!

INTERVIEWER

Have Canadian critics been hard on you lately?

ATWOOD

My Canadian critics haven't been any harder on me than they usually are. If anything, maybe a bit easier;

I think they're getting used to having me around. Growing a few wrinkles helps. Then they can think you're a sort of eminent fixture. I still get a few young folks who want to make their reputations by shooting me down. Any writer who has been around for a while gets a certain amount of that. I was very intolerant as a youthful person. It's almost necessary, that intolerance; young people need it in order to establish credentials for themselves.

INTERVIEWER
You seem to know a great deal about visual art. Does this come from research or firsthand experience?

ATWOOD
All writers, I suspect—and probably all people— have parallel lives, what they would have been if they hadn't turned into what they are. I have several of these, and one is certainly a life as a painter. When I was ten I thought I would be one; by the time I was twelve I had changed that to dress designer, and then reality took over and I confined myself to doodles in the margins of my textbooks. At university I made pocket money by designing and printing silk-screened posters and by designing theater programs. I continued to draw and paint in a truncated sort of way and still occasionally design—for instance the Canadian covers of my poetry books. It's one of those things I'm keeping in reserve for when I retire. Maybe I can be a sort of awful Sunday painter like Winston Churchill. Several of my friends are painters, so I've witnessed the difficulty of the life. The openings with the bad wine and drying-up cheese, the reviews with the perky headlines that don't quite get it, and so forth.

INTERVIEWER

INTERVIEWER

Is there anything that sticks in your mind as having been your greatest reward as a writer?

ATWOOD

The first poem I ever got published was a real high. Isn't it funny? I mean, all the other things that have happened since then were a thrill, but that was the biggest.

INTERVIEWER

I mean something more personal, though.

ATWOOD

All right, yes. I was in Copenhagen and just walking along, you know, window-shopping in a crowded mall. Denmark has a historical relationship with Greenland, where a lot of Inuit live. Along the street came some Inuit dancers done up in traditional Greenland dress. They had their faces painted and they had furry costumes on, impersonating beasts and monsters, spirits of some kind. They were spirit dancers, growling and making odd noises to the crowd. They had clawed hands and face distorters in their mouths—pieces of wood that made their cheeks stick out in a funny way. One of these furry spirit monsters came over to me, took his face distorter out of his mouth, and said, Are you Margaret Atwood? I said yes. He said, I like your work. And then he put his face distorter back in his mouth and went growling off into the crowd.

(1990)

Grace Paley

THE ART OF FICTION NO. 131

Interviewed by Jonathan Dee, Barbara Jones,
and Larissa MacFarquhar

When Grace Paley visits New York, she stays in her old apartment on West Eleventh Street. Her block has for the most part escaped the gentrification that has transformed the West Village since Paley moved there in the forties. The building where Paley lived for most of her adult life and where she raised her two children by her first husband, the filmmaker Jess Paley, is a rent-controlled brownstone walk-up with linoleum hallways. Mercifully spared midcareer renovations, Paley's apartment retains the disheveled, variegated look of an apartment with children. Paley now lives in Thetford, Vermont, with her second husband, poet and playwright Robert Nichols, but we arranged to speak with her in New York. We met her on the street outside her apartment—she was returning home from a Passover celebration with friends elsewhere in the city. We recognized her from half a block away—a tiny woman with fluffy white hair in a brown overcoat.

People often ask Grace Paley why she has written so little—three story collections and three chapbooks of poetry in seventy years. Paley has a number of answers to this question. Mostly she explains that she is lazy and that this is her major flaw as a writer. Occasionally she will admit that, though it is "not nice" of her to say so, she believes that she can accomplish as much in a few stories as her longer-winded colleagues do in a novel. And she points out that she has had many other important things to do with her time, such as raising children and participating in politics. "Art," she explains, "is too long, and life is too short." Paley is noticeably unaffected by the pressures of mortality which drive most writers to publish. Donald Barthelme scavenged her apartment for the stories that made up her first book, and her agent says she periodically raids Paley's drawers and kitchen cabinets for material. Her first collection of stories, *The Little Disturbances of Man*, did not appear until 1959, when Paley was thirty-seven. Since then she has published just two collections of stories (*Enormous Changes at the Last Minute* in 1974 and *Later the Same Day* in 1985) and three collections of poems—*Leaning Forward* (1985), *New and Collected Poems* (1992), and *Long Walks and Intimate Talks* (1991). Though Paley is better known as a short-story writer than as a poet, her stories are so dense and rigorously pruned that they frequently resemble poetry as much as fiction. Her conversation is as cerebral and distilled as her prose. The oft-noted Paley paradox is the contrast between her grandmotherly appearance and her no-schmaltz personality. Paley says only what is necessary. Ask her a yes-or-no question, and she will answer yes or no. Ask her a foolish question, and she will kindly but clearly convey her impatience. Talking with her, one develops the impression that she listens and speaks in two different, sometimes conflicting capacities. As a person she is tolerant and easygoing, as a user of words, merciless. On politics Paley speaks unreservedly and in earnest, on writing, she is drier, more careful.

Grace Goodside was born in the Bronx in December 1922, seventeen years after her parents immigrated to New York and one year after the invention of the sanitary napkin (as she notes in her poem "Song Stanzas of Private Luck" [1992]). Her father, Isaac, was a doctor who learned English by reading Dickens and was, like her mother, Mary, a committed socialist. The family spoke Russian and Yiddish at home and English to the world with a Bronx twang that remains one of the more noticeable signs of Paley's attitude toward the establishment. Writing has only occasionally been Paley's main occupation. She spent a lot of time in playgrounds when her children were young. She has always been very active in the feminist and peace movements. She has been on the faculty at City College and taught courses at Columbia University and, until recently, Sarah Lawrence College.

INTERVIEWER

What were you doing before you became a published writer?

GRACE PALEY

I was working part-time. I was hanging out a lot. I was kind of lazy. I had my kids when I was about twenty-six, twenty-seven. I took them to the park in the afternoons. Thank God I was lazy enough to spend all that time in Washington Square Park. I say "lazy" but of course it was kind of exhausting running after two babies. Still, looking back I see the pleasure of it. That's when I began to know women very well—as coworkers, really. I had a part-time job as a typist up at Columbia. In fact, when I began to write stories, I typed some up there, and some in the PTA office of P.S. 41 on Eleventh Street. If I hadn't spent that time in the playground, I wouldn't have written a lot of those stories. That's pretty much how I lived. And then we had our normal family life—struggles and hard times. That takes up a lot of time, hard times. Uses up whole days.

INTERVIEWER

Could you tell the story of the publication of your first book?

PALEY

I'd written three stories, and I liked them. I showed them to my former husband, Jess Paley, and he liked them, and he showed them to a couple of friends, and *they* liked them, so I was feeling pretty good about them. The kids were still young at the time, and they played a lot with the neighborhood kids, so I got to know the other mothers in the neighborhood. One of them was Tibby McCormick, who had just gotten unmarried from Ken McCormick, an editor at Doubleday. She knew about these stories, and poor Ken was more or less forced into reading them—you know, The kids are over at her house all the time, you *might* read her stories. So he took them home and read them and he came over to see me and said, Write seven more of them and we'll publish a book. So that's what happened. Luck happened. He also told me that no magazine around would touch them, and he was pretty much right about that too, although two of the stories in that collection were finally taken by *Accent*.

INTERVIEWER
Do you have a particular reader in mind when you write?

PALEY
As far as I know I'm not writing *to* anybody. Writers often write about what they want to read or haven't seen written. Sometimes I write *for* people—I wrote a story called "Debts" (1971) about the mother of a friend of mine. I wanted my friend to like it, although I didn't write it to please her. But that was different from writing *to* someone. I wrote "This Is a Story About My Friend George, the Toy Inventor" (1977) about a guy on Sixth Avenue who later told me I understood him better than his wife. But I wasn't writing it *to* him so much as speaking *for* him. Still, there's always that first storytelling impulse: I want to tell you something...

INTERVIEWER
How do stories begin for you?

PALEY
A lot of them begin with a sentence—they all begin with language. It sounds dopey to say that, but it's true. Very often one sentence is absolutely resonant.

A story can begin with someone speaking. "I was popular in certain circles," for example; an aunt of mine said that, and it hung around in my head for a long time. Eventually I wrote a story, "Goodbye and Good Luck" (1956), that began with that line, though it had nothing to do with my aunt. Another example: "There were two husbands disappointed by eggs," which is the first sentence of "The Used-Boy Raisers" (1959). I was at the house of a friend of mine, thirty-five years ago, and there were her two husbands complaining about the eggs. It was just *right*—so I went home and began the story, though I didn't finish it for months. I'm almost invariably stuck after one page or one paragraph—at which point I have to begin thinking about what the story could possibly be about. I begin by writing paragraphs that don't have an immediate relation to a plot. The sound of the story comes first.

INTERVIEWER

In "A Conversation with My Father" (1971) you make a lot of disparaging remarks about plot.

PALEY

Ever since then, everybody says I have no plot, which gets me really mad. Plot is *nothing*; plot is simply time, a timeline. All our stories have timelines. One thing happens, then another thing happens. What I was really talking about in that story was having a plot settled *in your mind*: This is the way the story's going to go. In the next thirty pages or so, this will happen, this will happen, this will happen. That's what I meant.

So you would never start a story with the ending in mind?

No. When the ending comes to me, that's when I know I'm going to finish the story. Usually it's around the middle. And then I write the end. And then I change it.

How many drafts do you go through in writing a story?

I don't like to count. I never understand what people mean when they say they've done twenty drafts or something. Does that mean they've typed it twenty times, or what? I'm always changing things as I go. It's always substantially different by the time I've finished. I do it till it's done.

Do you take advice from anyone when you write or edit?

I listen to what people tell me, but I don't always act on it. I read a story to my twelve-year-old granddaughter a couple of months ago. She told me what was wrong: there were sentences that were not clear—and she was absolutely right. My husband is a good reader.

How do you know when a story is done?

When I don't have anything else to say. Sometimes I publish the story in a magazine, and I still have something else to say. One story comes to mind: "Faith in the Afternoon" (1960). When it was published in a magazine, it ended with Faith dreaming she was holding this guy's balls. All the guys I knew *loved* it. But when it came time to publish it in a book, I realized that wasn't what it was about; it would have been a cheap way to end it. I went beyond that. Everyone got mad at me—not really angry, just sad.

How did you change it?

I didn't *change* it. I simply realized that Faith was still in the park, and it was probably the late sixties and one of the frequent little theatrical antiwar walks or parades would have to be coming through. Faith was able to have a political imagination as well as an erotic one.

Is the character Faith, who appears in so many of your stories, at all autobiographical?

No. Her life is entirely different from mine. I was never as mad at any husband of mine as she was at her first. On the other hand, I feel very warmly toward my present husband, and she does toward hers too.

But I was never that mad. And I brought my kids up in different circumstances. Faith represents a number of women I have been close to. It's not as though she's *any one* of them—but she *has* become one of them. The whole Faith thing also came about partly by accident. In "The Used-Boy Raisers," I started off by giving Faith those two boys. Then to compensate for it I began giving all the other women daughters, but I was stuck with the major character of my stories having two boys from the beginning. I was also stuck with the name Faith, which I was very sorry for later on. It was too close to my own name, and I didn't really want it to be—but at the time I never thought I would write another story about her.

INTERVIEWER

The character must have some kind of hold on you, though, to keep turning up like that?

PALEY

She's become a very good worker for me.

INTERVIEWER

How do you know a story is working?

PALEY

I read it aloud a lot, and that helps me. It's not so useful for a writer of novels, but for me reading aloud as I work helps me know if it's right.

INTERVIEWER

What about a story like "Lavinia: An Old Story" (1982), written in a black voice—did you read that out loud as you wrote it?

I did read it aloud. I don't know if I could write that story now. I was closer then to a couple of older black women as well as my own grandmother—whose story was exactly the same, which was one of my reasons for writing it. I was able to read the story to them—check it out in some way. There are other stories that may have been risky. These were recently read by some students in James Monroe High School in the Bronx where nearly all the kids were African American. Not being in any political group yet—hopefully they will be—they weren't bothered by my writing "Lavinia: An Old Story" or "The Little Girl" (1974) at all. They argued a few particulars, but were harder on the narrator than I was.

What about people who criticize you for writing in a black voice?

Some have been critical. I know the politics of it, but I know I act out of real feeling and considerable respect for the person. That's why I want to do it—not to show off. It's true that in "The Little Girl" I do have a pretty terrible black character—a rapist, in fact. It's not as though I only deal with sweet situations.

But what's a writer for? The whole point is to put yourself into other lives, other heads—writers have always done that. If you screw up, so someone will tell you, that's all. I think men can write about women and women can write about men. The whole point is to know the facts. Men have so often written about women without knowing the reality of their lives, and worse, without being interested in that daily reality.

INTERVIEWER

Are there any men you think write particularly well about women?

PALEY

I liked Norman Rush's last book, *Mating*. The main character is a very smart woman, very intellectual, very interesting, and very unlike many of the women many *women* write about. I love all the traditional books, but...Well, I feel, like many women, that Anna Karenina shouldn't have killed herself. Still, Kate Chopin in *The Awakening* also has the woman go drown herself for no reason that I can see!

INTERVIEWER

Were you a poet first, before you started writing fiction?

PALEY

I wrote poems all my life. I didn't *really* write stories until I wrote my first book, when I was in my thirties.

INTERVIEWER

You've spoken very specifically about the way a story comes to you. Is it different writing poetry? Is there more of an awareness or an adherence to craft?

PALEY

There's an equal amount of adherence to craft in the use of both forms. I would say that I went to school to study poetry, that's how I learned to write. I got my courage for the way I write stories from first writing poems. My poems of that period were more literary than the stories ever were, or than my poems are now. That was the difference.

INTERVIEWER
What was it like studying with Auden at the New School?

PALEY
He seemed an immortal to me. I had a conversation with him when I was seventeen, and though I only lived twenty blocks away, I never got to talk to him again that year—1939? 1940, probably. I couldn't understand a word he said. He had just come here, he had this lisp, plus his English—his normal way of speaking. He was giving a class on the history of English literature. At one point he said, Are there any poets who would like to speak to me, or who want me to look at their work? There were two hundred and fifty people in the room, and maybe five people put up their hands. I was one of them. Nowadays two hundred and forty would have raised their hands. That I even put my hand up was amazing to me, since I'd just gone through high school without raising it once. And then he said, Meet me in Stewart's Cafeteria. So the next week, I went to meet him at Stewart's Cafeteria and he wasn't there. I immediately called up this boy I had begun to go around with (and later married) and bawled, He wasn't there, he was fooling.

It turned out there were *two* Stewart's Cafeterias on Twenty-Third Street—one east and one west—

he was in the other one. So the next week he said, Where were you, Grace Goodside? Then I did meet him. He read my poems—which were exactly like his.

INTERVIEWER

Exactly?

PALEY

I mean, I really wrote in his style. I was crazy about him. I loved his poems so much that I was using this British language all the time—I was saying *trousers* and *subaltern* and things like that. You understand I was a Bronx kid. We went through a few poems, and he kept asking me, Do you really *talk* like that? And I kept saying, Oh yeah, well, sometimes. That was the great thing I learned from Auden: that you'd better talk your own language. Then I asked him what young writers now ask me—and I always tell them this story—I said to Auden, Well, do you think I should keep writing? He laughed and then became very solemn. If you're a writer, he said, you'll keep writing no matter what. That's not a question a writer should ask. Something like that, not exactly, but close.

INTERVIEWER

Were there other poets that you heard or took a class with?

PALEY

No, but I read poetry all the time. Probably the poets everybody read then. Very catholic taste. I even loved Eliot then, whom I later grew not to love. I knew lots of poems by memory and walked around mumbling them. Yeats, Rilke, Keats, Coleridge. I liked Milton a lot, for some reason. And then there were the Oscar Williams anthologies of 1942 and 1943 with those pictures of the beautiful young poets.

INTERVIEWER

How about fiction writers?

PALEY

Again, you think you're unique in some way but you really never are: you read what people your age are reading. We read a lot of Joyce—*Dubliners* was always very important to me—and Proust. Joyce's stories were the only short stories I really liked. We used to read *Ulysses* aloud when I was eighteen years old. I think that's where I got my habit of reading aloud. Gertrude Stein's *Three Lives* impressed me. The use of the "other voice." Then there were lots of other novels at home that my parents were reading— like *The Forty Days of Musa Dagh*—we worried, we felt for the Armenians. Later I read Chekhov, who meant a lot to me. Then Babel and Turgenev—all the Russians—and Flaubert. I don't think I read more than most good readers, but I read as much.

INTERVIEWER

Did you enjoy the Russian writers because you grew up with Russian at home?

PALEY

Probably. Although it's not just Russian: Russian is very dear to me because it's a family language, but I am Jewish Russian, which is a little different from Russian Russian. My family ran away in 1905 from the

Russian Russians. People say I write like Isaac Babel, but it's not that he has influenced me. I hadn't read him before I wrote. It's our common grandparents who have influenced us both ... in terms of inflection and what one pays attention to. It's not a literary influence so much as a social influence, a linguistic influence, a musical influence. I've just published a new book called *New and Collected Poems* with a blurb on the back from Jean Valentine, a wonderful poet. She says, At last, a Russian writer in English! The publishers felt it was a little weird, but I thought it was great.

INTERVIEWER

Has your writing been influenced by nonliterary media? Art, or music, or painting ... TV?

PALEY

My husband, Robert Nichols, begins his day of writing by looking at paintings—for about an hour every morning. All this year he's been looking at Klee. I'm not like that. I've always listened to a lot of music, but I'm not very visual. Noticeably not. You may be aware that I don't do a lot of description. I've been surrounded by music for most of my life. Always classical. But I think the most powerful sounds are those *voices*, those childhood voices. The tune of those voices. Other languages, Russian and Yiddish, coming up smack against the English. I think you hear that a lot in American literature. TV I don't watch too much. I don't feel snobbish about it, it's just that it can use up too much time. It's terribly seductive.

INTERVIEWER

People have described your writing as wise.

That's because I'm old. When people get old they seem wise, but it's only because they've got a little more experience, that's all. I'm not so wise. Two things happen when you get older. You have more experience, so you either seem wiser, or you get totally foolish. There are only those two options. You choose one, probably the wrong one.

INTERVIEWER

In your choice of subject matter, you and Tillie Olsen have opened the door for a lot of writers.

PALEY

I hope so. Of course that's not up to me or Tillie to say, Yes, there was the door and we opened it—we can't say that. It's not nice. I will say I knew I wanted to write about women and children, but I put it off for a couple of years because I thought, People will think this is trivial, nothing. Then I thought, It's what I *have* to write. It's what I want to read. And I don't see it out there.

Meanwhile, the women's movement had begun to gather force. It needed to become the second wave. It turned out that we were some of the drops in the wave. Tillie was more like a cupful.

INTERVIEWER

Was there anyone on that wave before you who enabled you to write like you did?

PALEY

Well, I didn't know I was on any wave. I knew what I was writing, but I didn't think then that I was part of any movement. I didn't even think I was a feminist! If you had asked me if I was a feminist when I began writing *The Little Disturbances of Man*, I would have said I'm a socialist—or something like that. But by the end of the book I had taught myself a lot and I knew more or less who I was. I opened the door to myself.

INTERVIEWER

Do you still feel supported by the women's movement?

PALEY

I do feel very supported. There's hardly a woman writer who doesn't receive some kind of support from the women's movement. We're very lucky to be living and writing now. I feel supported by lots of men too, but I feel very specifically the attention of women, even in opposition. And they're the ones I get arguments from; they're the ones who say, Why don't you write about this kind of life, or that kind of life? We like the children but why are they all boys? But on the other hand, I was at a conference in California last week, where a young woman kept saying she didn't want to be a woman writer because it trivialized her. The point is that the outside world will trivialize you for almost anything if it wants to. You may as well be who you are.

INTERVIEWER

Why do you suppose she said that?

PALEY

I think she said it because she feels it's true. And there *is* truth to it. A lot of European women feel it very strongly. They are afraid of being anything but totally universal. But we used to have a saying, "I take it from whence it comes," which is a Bronx version of sticks and stones will break my bones, but names will never hurt me. So you take it from whence it comes, that is, if a certain society decides to trivialize you, it will marginalize you.

INTERVIEWER

Do you think American women writers feel that way?

PALEY

I think they fear being marginalized and rightly so. There's an idea that there's this great mainstream, which may be wide but is kind of shallow and slow-moving. It's the tributaries that seem to have the energy.

INTERVIEWER

You've said that when you're writing you are "doing women's politics." Could you say more about that?

PALEY

Did I say that? If I did I probably meant that if the personal is political—as we all say—then writing about women is a political act. Just like black people writing about the lives of blacks. It's very important to people that they have these stories. And the personal is especially political when it spreads fingers out into the world—because sometimes you find that what is most personal is also what connects you most strongly with others.

Has there been a change of climate from when you first started writing to now, in the nineties?

PALEY

In 1959 it was absolutely insane for Ken McCormick to say, yes, he was going to publish a book of short stories. Now everybody in the writing world is reading and writing short stories—that's one thing. Another thing is that a lot more women are writing. A lot of people who wouldn't have written are writing. When a couple of black women speak, the throats of many are opened. Somehow or other they give courage and sound to their sisters.

INTERVIEWER

So you didn't feel that sense of there being a community of women writers in the fifties?

PALEY

I didn't think about it. I just wrote. I didn't say, Oh, there are no women writers, as much as I thought to myself, This subject matter is so trivial. Who in the world would be interested in this stuff?

INTERVIEWER

Did it surprise you when you found that there was a response, the sort of response that Ken McCormick had?

PALEY

I was surprised they published the book, I was surprised they liked the stories. It wasn't even really surprise—I just considered myself lucky.

INTERVIEWER

Do you feel that your subject matter has changed or broadened over the years?

PALEY

As my life has changed, it has, I suppose. I'm still politically very interested in women's lives, so I think about that a lot. But it really isn't up to me to say. Some of these observations other people have to make. I don't see a particular line, I just see that I've written a lot of stories. Yet I know they get different, somewhat, not a lot. I traveled, went to different places. I took an airplane out of the park.

INTERVIEWER

Do you think editors have a responsibility to publish as many women as they do men?

PALEY

Yes. Editors should think about those things. What sometimes starts out seeming artificial, well, it's as though you *have* to be artificial at first. That's what affirmative action is about—it's hard for some people to evolve through artificiality into something natural and decent, a truth you and the world have refused to see. It's like changing your language.

INTERVIEWER

Can you tell when you pick up a manuscript whether it's by a woman writer?

PALEY

You can't always tell. Think of the number of women who sent their manuscripts in with initials so they didn't give themselves away as women. I did that myself when I was young, I mean, with my poems. I'd write G. G. Paley.

INTERVIEWER

You put the initials on the poems because you thought they had a better chance of being accepted?

PALEY

It doesn't happen so much anymore, but that's what used to happen: women hid in order to be seen.

INTERVIEWER

Some writers say writing gets harder.

PALEY

Well, some of it's harder and some of it's easier. The easy part is, you know you're going to finish something. That's the best part. When you first begin to write, you—well, I, at least, used to think, Will I ever get past four paragraphs? But once I finished that first book, I knew I would finish whatever I wanted to. That's the great thing. It's harder because you have already set yourself certain standards, and you're probably trying to do something more demanding—not to change your voice, but trying to understand something different, so far unknown to you.

INTERVIEWER

Your stories are so oriented around dialogue and how people sound. Have you ever written plays?

For a start, plays always seemed to me much more than dialogue. A play that's all dialogue is really pretty uninteresting, unless it's Shaw or Oscar Wilde. So that was one thing. Second of all, I don't like the theater as much as I did when I was really young. And third, when I was writing the early stories, the theater I liked was really the radical theater, street theater. I loved those audiences, and I really didn't like twenty-five-dollar-a-seat audiences, especially when they couldn't afford twelve dollars for a book! So I had a kind of a prejudice against it.

You wrote your father into *Enormous Changes at the Last Minute* and you dedicated it to him. What about your mother?

My mother died when I was young—in my early twenties. I was much closer to my father. My mother was very much like the person in a couple of the stories, in several poems: very serious, always telling my father not to think he's so funny. She was a terrific person, a very kind woman...but it's as though I haven't really wanted to write about her. I have some kind of loyalty to a true portrayal—can I do it? I think about her very factually. With my father I invent and reinvent him. He had many aspects. He could be the working guy in "The Loudest Voice" (1959), very charming, obviously not as principled as his wife; or he could be a man who writes poems or paints—he did most of the paintings in this kitchen. In actual fact he was a doctor, a neighborhood doctor who was much loved. He lived with my mother, my aunt, and my grandmother. The joke was, if he said Pass the salt, three women leaped to their feet—so he was a pain in that respect. My father had different aspects I could use, but my mother was very much one person, the same to everybody. She was wise, she didn't talk a lot. It was easier for me to leap onto the bandwagon of my father's conversation. In other words, I did the easy thing. I've been reprimanded for it by people who knew my mother—they ask me, Where's mama?

INTERVIEWER
Virginia Woolf felt that a writer can't write if she's angry. What do you think about that?

PALEY
You can't write without a lot of pressure. Sometimes the pressure comes from anger, which then changes into a pressure to write. It's not so much a matter of getting distance as simply a translation. I felt a lot of pressure writing some of those stories about women. Writers are lucky because when they're angry, the anger—by habit almost—I wouldn't say transcends but *becomes* an acute pressure to write, to tell. Some guy, he's angry, he wants to take a poke at someone—or he kicks a can, or sets fire to the house, or hits his wife, or the wife smacks the kid. Then again, it's not always violent. Some people go out and run for three hours. Some people go shopping. The pressure from anger is an energy that can be violent or useful or useless. Also the pressure doesn't have to be anger. It could be love. One could be overcome with feelings of lifetime love or justice. Why not?

Other writers, such as Toni Morrison and Flannery O'Connor, use a lot of physical violence in their stories. In yours it's there, but offstage, in the background, in the past. Was this a conscious decision?

I don't *use* violence. Most of the time it's used opportunistically. Still it is a terribly violent country. When I wrote "The Little Girl"—that story about the murder—it took all my strength ... really used me from my toes to my head. It was so hard; it almost took my breath to write that story. I'm not as close to violence as African American mothers who are writers, such as Toni Morrison or June Jordan. Having black sons who are vulnerable to police, to directed race hatred, they must be anxious all the time. Some of my stories are knock-wood stories—like "Samuel" (1968), in which four boys are fooling around on the subway between cars and one falls and is killed. It's a taboo story. I tell it to prevent it from happening, not because it did ... The idea that if you write it into literature it won't happen in life.

But I hate the American expectation of violence. I'm not going to play into any of that. When I must write about violence, I will, but I'll do it straight, not add and add because the level is higher every year. I was just reading Tim O'Brien's *The Things They Carried*, and I felt the American war in Vietnam in my bones. Flannery O'Connor's a terrific writer, but somehow her conception of religion as specializing in death—and also her illness—forced her and her brilliant language in that direction.

You say also that the pressure to write is a pressure of language—how do these two relate?

PALEY

It depends. I wasn't angry when I wrote "Goodbye and Good Luck"—I just felt a certain pressure to use the resonance of the phrase "I was popular in certain circles"—a looking-backness, a storytelling justice for one of my aunts, a reinvention of her life for that purpose—all of which wouldn't leave me alone. The sound of it required me to go on. This is what I mean when I say that art comes from constant mental harassment. You're bugged.

INTERVIEWER

The pressure to write and the pressure to publish are not the same?

PALEY

Not for me. It's not that I don't like being published. I love to see my stuff in print. I really do. But I think I have a peculiar sense of time. I feel like I can always do something. There's time. I never feel like I have to do something fast or it will never appear, or I'll drop dead first. I may—I'm almost seventy. I figure, Well, in a week I'll figure out where to send this to, and then I think, Well, I'm too busy to decide.

INTERVIEWER

Have you ever had a hard time publishing?

I've had a lot of trouble publishing my stories in magazines. People say that I'm a *New Yorker* writer: *The New Yorker* published one of my stories in 1978 and two in 1979 and has never published anything since. I often have stories sent back, though now I have more requests for more stories than I have stories to give, so it balances out. I know I can publish, but I still get things sent back.

INTERVIEWER

Have you ever relied on your writing for income?

PALEY

No. I've always had to teach, or read, or lecture.

INTERVIEWER

What is the relationship between writing and money?

PALEY

It's helpful to have money. I don't think writers have to suffer to starve to death. One of the first things I tell my classes is, If you want to write, keep a low overhead. If you want to live expansively, you're going to be in trouble because then you have to start thinking very hard about whom you're writing to, who your audience is, who the *editor* thinks your audience is, who he *wants* your audience to be.

INTERVIEWER

Did you always want to be a writer?

I always wanted to write. Two different things. I never thought I was going to be a writer, but I was never interested in anything else. I failed at whatever else I undertook—even as an office worker, I was not outstanding.

You've said there are two kinds of people: those with children and those without. Could you say more about that?

It's a different life. Another creature is really dependent on you. I think it's *good* for a writer, though. I know some people say women writers should not have children. Of course, it was worse for them back then. Years ago just to do the kids' wash could take the whole day, so if you were poor it was impossible to write. If you were rich, you could hire a maid; it was possible if you were George Sand. But even now we need help. My kids were in day care from the time they were three years old.

How did you find time to write while raising children, being involved in political activity, teaching?

I wrote at different paces. I wrote my first stories when I was sick and had a few weeks at home. I made a start in a big chunk of time, about three weeks. And after that I just kept going.

Sometimes one or the other part of my life would pull me away from writing—the children, of course and then the civil rights movement and the Vietnam War. Having grown up the way I did, it just seemed natural to become involved. That was what the whole country was about. I was often busy with that from morning until night. I couldn't stand that we were in this war, and I just wrote less. Actually, that isn't quite true. I wrote leaflets, political reports, articles. And poems. As a matter of fact, my reports following my journey through North Vietnam in 1969 were mostly poems.

A lot of other writers were involved too. There were lots of readings. On the East Coast, Denise Levertov and Mitch Goodman had a lot to do with those events. Angry Arts Week—organized by Artists and Writers Protest Against the War—and the Greenwich Village Peace Center are good examples of that energy. Poets rode around the city reading from trucks. Almost any concert that week would begin with a dedication to the war's end. One particular event—"Vietnamese Life"—focused on ordinary Vietnamese life and culture. No egotism allowed, no, Oh how bad I feel about all of this...remember Hortense Calisher reading Vietnamese stories and Susan Sontag reading Lao Tse. Irene Fornés presented a Vietnamese wedding. Wally Zuckerman, who used to build harpsichords, created the wind instruments used in the windy forest of Indochina.

INTERVIEWER

Who were the poets on the trucks?

People who were comfortable on trucks. I wasn't. I worked in the office mostly. I was too shy anyway. Who were they? Well, Sam Abrams, Tuli Kupferberg, Clayton Eshleman, Bob Nichols, Ed Sanders, many more. I've probably got a file somewhere.

INTERVIEWER

How important do you think it is for the writer to rise up at moments like that?

PALEY

It's interesting for the writer. It's normal. Of course, it's hard if you're in the middle of a book. It's a question only Americans ask. Is it good? It certainly isn't antithetical to a passionate interior life—all that noise coming in. You *have* to make music of it somehow.

INTERVIEWER

Do you think political statements belong in literature? Would you write a novel that was a political tract?

PALEY

One man's political tract is another person's presidential statement—in Czechoslovakia, for example. The word *tract* is such a bad word by itself obviously one would have to say, No, nobody should write a tract, nobody should do that. But I think that a love of language, truthfulness, and a sense of form is justification enough.

Anyway characters in fiction can say anything they want. They're often quite willful, you know.

Has anti-Semitism affected your career?

I don't know. It's affected my work. I take being Jewish very seriously. I like it. My first two stories were specifically Jewish. When I took a class at the New School this teacher said to me, You've got to get off that Jewish *dime*, Grace, they're wonderful stories, but ... The idiocy of that remark was that he was telling me this just as Saul Bellow, Philip Roth, and others were getting more generally famous every day. He was Jewish himself, but he wanted me to "broaden" myself.

I don't think anti-Semitism has affected my career much. I'm sure in certain colleges they're not interested in my stories, but you'd be surprised how people don't take it into account. Kids especially, they just want to know how the plot turned out. I always say that racism is like pneumonia and anti-Semitism is like the common cold—everybody has it. I often meet it in this lovely Vermont countryside, sneezing away.

You used to embrace the position of literary outsider, whereas now you are a central figure ...

I wasn't trying to be an outsider. At first I was afraid of hanging out with writers. Otherwise I would surely have seen and tried to talk to Auden again. But I really wasn't interested. When the poets went out on the trucks, I helped organize, but I never read myself. Nor was I in any of those Vietnam anthologies...until about six months ago when a group of nurses put an anthology together of women who had gone to Vietnam during the war. Basically I didn't want to get into that life...I was scared of it.

INTERVIEWER
What were you scared of?

PALEY
I was scared in the way that some people are scared to leave their neighborhoods: you have your people, you have your roots, and you don't want to pull away from them. You're writing about these people and their lives and you don't want suddenly to get into a literary scene. It seemed so logical to me. Besides, I wasn't interested. I was interested in my park friends. I was interested in the meetings I helped organize during those years or in going to the Soviet Union to do certain political tasks, to Sweden to talk to deserters, to Vietnam in 1969.

Though I devoted a good deal of time trying to be completely unliterary, I ended up working with writers on the PEN board and liking them, and it. Also having many beloved literary friends like Kay Boyle and Tillie Olsen, Esther Broner. Don Barthelme lived across the street—he was a beloved family friend. And my second husband is a writer. I was always afraid that if I started to become too literary it would end my street and kitchen life. But it turned out writers were okay. I was surprised. And then my closest friends like Sybil Claiborne, Eva Kollisch, and Vera Williams had always been writing—so there was no escape.

Have you ever found yourself in conflict with the literary establishment?

There are so many different groups of writers. Some liked the first book and didn't like what came after that, but I think it's really *me* they didn't like so much. As I became more feminist some people took a dim view of that. On the other hand other people liked me, not for the stories but for the stuff I did outside. I haven't really seen a lot of criticism of my work; I know it exists and I know it's good and bad, but I don't go out and look for it. The longest review I've ever had was an attack in *Commentary* magazine. Kind of virulent. My publisher doesn't send me terrible things that people have said. I'm not the kind of a writer who gets into literary fights. I prefer political ones. As for my attitude toward other writers, I'm kind of short on disdain or contempt. That is, I don't belong to the school of "I can only live if you die." I tend to be interested in writers whose work is different from mine. Of course I'm saddened and angered equally by work made of contempt, hatred, misogyny, and too many adjectives.

At a recent PEN Congress in which you played a prominent role there was much argument over the proper relationship between the writer and the state. Is it necessarily an adversarial one?

It's not that you *set out* to oppose authority. In the act of writing you simply do. Your job, your reason for writing, is to uncover what the state and the conventions of your town normally hide. That's why you want to write—to tell what hasn't been told. Our PEN Congress was about the conscience of the state and the conscience of the writer. One of its troubles and truths was that George Shultz, intent on making war on Central American people, was the keynote speaker. Another was the fact that out of eleven poets reading, ten were men. This situation has been eased somewhat by the creation of a Women's Committee in the U.S. as well as one in International PEN.

INTERVIEWER

And a final word?

PALEY

The best training is to read and write, no matter what. Don't live with a lover or roommate who doesn't respect your work. Don't lie, buy time, borrow to buy time. Write what will stop your breath if you don't write.

(1992)

Toni Morrison

THE ART OF FICTION NO. 134

Interviewed by Elissa Schappell, with additional
material from Claudia Brodsky Lacour

Toni Morrison detests being called a "poetic writer." She seems to think that the attention that has been paid to the lyricism of her work marginalizes her talent and denies her stories their power and resonance. As one of the few novelists whose work is both popular and critically acclaimed, she can afford the luxury of choosing what praise to accept. But she does not reject all classifications, and, in fact, embraces the title "black woman writer." Her ability to transform individuals into forces and idiosyncrasies into inevitabilities has led some critics to call her the "D. H. Lawrence of the black psyche." She is also a master of the public novel, examining the relationships between the races and sexes and the struggle between civilization and nature, while at the same time combining myth and the fantastic with a deep political sensitivity.

We talked with Morrison one summer Sunday afternoon on the lush campus of Princeton University.

The interview took place in her office, which is decorated with a large Helen Frankenthaler print, pen-and-ink drawings an architect did of all the houses that appear in her work, photographs, a few framed book-jacket covers, and an apology note to her from Hemingway—a forgery meant as a joke. On her desk is a blue glass teacup emblazoned with the likeness of Shirley Temple filled with the number two pencils that she uses to write her first drafts. Jade plants sit in a window and a few more potted plants hang above. A coffeemaker and cups are at the ready. Despite the high ceilings, the big desk, and the high-backed black rocking chairs, the room had the warm feeling of a kitchen, maybe because talking to Morrison about writing is the intimate kind of conversation that often seems to happen in kitchens; or perhaps it was the fact that as our energy started flagging she magically produced mugs of cranberry juice. We felt that she had allowed us to enter into a sanctuary, and that, however subtly, she was completely in control of the situation.

Outside, high canopies of oak leaves filtered the sunlight, dappling her white office with pools of yellowy light. Morrison sat behind her big desk, which despite her apologies for the "disorder" appeared well organized. Stacks of books and piles of paper resided on a painted bench set against the wall. She is smaller than one might imagine, and her hair, gray and silver, is woven into thin steel-colored braids that hang just at shoulder length. Occasionally during the interview Morrison let her sonorous, deep voice break into rumbling laughter and punctuated certain statements with a flat smack of her hand on the desktop. At a moment's notice she can switch from raging about violence in the United States to gleefully skewering the hosts of the trash TV talk shows through which she confesses to channel surfing sometimes late in the afternoon if her work is done.

INTERVIEWER

You have said that you begin to write before dawn. Did this habit begin for practical reasons, or was the early morning an especially fruitful time for you?

TONI MORRISON

Writing before dawn began as a necessity—I had small children when I first began to write and I needed to use the time before they said, Mama—and that was always around five in the morning. Many years later, after I stopped working at Random House, I just stayed at home for a couple of years. I discovered things about myself I had never thought about before. At first I didn't know when I wanted to eat, because I had always eaten when it was lunchtime or dinnertime or breakfast time. Work and the children had driven all of my habits ... I didn't know the weekday sounds of my own house; it all made me feel a little giddy.

I was involved in writing *Beloved* (1987) at that time—this was in 1983—and eventually I realized that I was clearer-headed, more confident, and generally more intelligent in the morning. The habit of getting up early, which I had formed when the children were young, now became my choice. I am not very bright or very witty or very inventive after the sun goes down.

Recently I was talking to a writer who described something she did whenever she moved to her writing table. I don't remember exactly what the gesture was—there is something on her desk that she touches before she hits the computer keyboard—but we began to talk about little rituals that one goes through before beginning to write. I, at first, thought I didn't have a ritual, but then I remembered that I always get up and make a cup of coffee while it is still dark—it must be dark—and then I drink the coffee and watch the light come. And she said, Well, that's a ritual. And I realized that for me this ritual comprises my preparation to enter a space that I can only call nonsecular ... Writers all devise ways to approach that place where they expect to make the contact, where they become the conduit, or where they engage in this mysterious process. For me, light is the signal in the transition. It's not being *in* the light, it's being there *before it arrives*. It enables me, in some sense.

I tell my students one of the most important things they need to know is when they are their best, creatively. They need to ask themselves, What does the ideal room look like? Is there music? Is there silence? Is there chaos outside or is there serenity outside? What do I need in order to release my imagination?

INTERVIEWER
What about your writing routine?

MORRISON
I have an ideal writing routine that I've never experienced, which is to have, say, nine uninterrupted days when I wouldn't have to leave the house or take phone calls. And to have the space—a space where I have huge tables. I end up with this much space [*she indicates a small square spot on her desk*] everywhere I

am, and I can't beat my way out of it. I am reminded of that tiny desk that Emily Dickinson wrote on and I chuckle when I think, Sweet thing, there she was. But that is all any of us have: just this small space and no matter what the filing system or how often you clear it out—life, documents, letters, requests, invitations, invoices just keep going back in. I am not able to write regularly. I have never been able to do that— mostly because I have always had a nine-to-five job. I had to write either in between those hours, hurriedly, or spend a lot of weekend and predawn time.

INTERVIEWER

Could you write after work?

MORRISON

That was difficult. I've tried to overcome not having orderly spaces by substituting compulsion for discipline, so that when something is urgently there, urgently seen or understood, or the metaphor was powerful enough, then I would move everything aside and write for sustained periods of time. I'm talking to you about getting the first draft.

INTERVIEWER

You have to do it straight through?

MORRISON

I do. I don't think it's a law.

INTERVIEWER

Could you write on the bottom of a shoe while riding on a train like Robert Frost? Could you write on an airplane?

MORRISON

Sometimes something that I was having some trouble with falls into place, a word sequence, say, so I've written on scraps of paper, in hotels on hotel stationery, in automobiles. *If* it arrives you *know.* If you know it *really* has come, then you *have* to put it down.

INTERVIEWER

What is the physical act of writing like for you?

MORRISON

I write with a pencil.

INTERVIEWER

Would you ever work on a word processor?

MORRISON

Oh, I do that also, but that is much later, when everything is put together. I type that into a computer and then I begin to revise. But everything I write for the first time is written with a pencil, maybe a ballpoint if I don't have a pencil. I'm not picky, but my preference is for yellow legal pads and a nice number two pencil.

INTERVIEWER

Dixon Ticonderoga number two soft?

MORRISON

Exactly. I remember once trying to use a tape recorder, but it doesn't work.

INTERVIEWER

Did you actually dictate a story into the machine?

Not the whole thing, but just a bit. For instance, when two or three sentences seemed to fall into place, I thought I would carry a tape recorder in the car, particularly when I was working at Random House going back and forth every day. It occurred to me that I could just record it. It was a disaster. I don't trust my writing that is not written, although I work very hard in subsequent revisions to remove the writerly-ness from it, to give it a combination of lyrical, standard, and colloquial language. To pull all these things together into something that I think is much more alive and representative. But I don't trust something that occurs to me and then is spoken and transferred immediately to the page.

INTERVIEWER

Do you ever read your work out loud while you are working on it?

MORRISON

Not until it's published. I don't trust a performance. I could get a response that might make me think it was successful when it wasn't at all. The difficulty for me in writing—*among* the difficulties—is to write language that can work quietly on a page for a reader who doesn't hear anything. Now for that, one has to work very carefully with what is *in between* the words. What is not said. Which is measure, which is rhythm, and so on. So, it is what you don't write that frequently gives what you do write its power.

INTERVIEWER

How many times would you say you have to write a paragraph over to reach this standard?

MORRISON

Well, those that need reworking I do as long as I can. I mean, I've revised six times, seven times, thirteen times. But there's a line between revision and fretting, just working it to death. It is important to know when you are fretting it; when you are fretting it because it is not working, it needs to be scrapped.

INTERVIEWER

Do you ever go back over what has been published and wish you had fretted more over something?

MORRISON

A lot. Everything.

INTERVIEWER

Do you ever rework passages that have already been published before reading them to an audience?

MORRISON

I don't change it for the audience, but I know what it ought to be and isn't. After twenty-some years you can figure it out; I know more about it now than I did then. It is not so much that it would have been different or even better; it is just that, taken into context with what I was trying to effect, or what consequence I wanted it to have on the reader, years later the picture is clearer to me.

How do you think being an editor for twenty years affected you as a writer?

I am not sure. It lessened my awe of the publishing industry. I understood the adversarial relationship that sometimes exists between writers and publishers, but I learned how important, how critical an editor was, which I don't think I would have known before.

Are there editors who are helpful critically?

Oh yes. The good ones make all the difference. It is like a priest or a psychiatrist; if you get the wrong one, then you are better off alone. But there are editors so rare and so important that they are worth searching for, and you always know when you have one.

Who was the most instrumental editor you've ever worked with?

I had a very good editor, superlative for me—Bob Gottlieb. What made him good for me was a number of things—knowing what not to touch; asking all the questions you probably would have asked yourself had there been the time. Good editors are really the third eye. Cool. Dispassionate. They don't love you or your work; for me that is what is valuable—

not compliments. Sometimes it's uncanny; the editor puts his or her finger on exactly the place the writer knows is weak but just couldn't do any better at the time. Or perhaps the writer thought it might fly, but wasn't sure. Good editors identify that place and sometimes make suggestions. Some suggestions are not useful because you can't explain everything to an editor about what you are trying to do. I couldn't possibly explain all of those things to an editor, because what I do has to work on so many levels. But within the relationship if there is some trust, some willingness to listen, remarkable things can happen. I read books all the time that I know would have profited from not a copy editor but somebody just talking through it. And it is important to get a great editor at a certain time, because if you don't have one in the beginning, you almost can't have one later. If you work well without an editor, and your books are well received for five or ten years, and then you write another one—which is successful but not very good—why should you then listen to an editor?

INTERVIEWER

You have told students that they should think of the process of revision as one of the major satisfactions of writing. Do you get more pleasure out of writing the first draft, or in the actual revision of the work?

MORRISON

They are different. I am profoundly excited by thinking up or having the idea in the first place...before I begin to write.

Does it come in a flash?

No, it's a sustained thing I have to play with. I always start out with an idea, even a boring idea, that becomes a question I don't have any answers to. Specifically, since I began the *Beloved* trilogy, the last part of which I'm working on now, I have been wondering why women who are twenty, thirty years younger than I am are no happier than women who are my age and older. What on earth is that about, when there are so many more things that they can do, so many more choices? *All right*, so this is an embarrassment of riches, but so what. Why is everybody so miserable?

Do you write to figure out exactly how you feel about a subject?

No, I know how I *feel*. My feelings are the result of prejudices and convictions like everybody else's. But I am interested in the complexity, the vulnerability of an idea. It is not, This is what I believe, because that would not be a book, just a tract. A book is, This may be what I believe, but suppose I am wrong... what could it be? Or, I don't know what it is, but I am interested in finding out what it might mean to me, as well as to other people.

Did you know as a child you wanted to be a writer?

No. I wanted to be a reader. I thought everything that needed to be written had already been written or would be. I only wrote the first book because I thought it wasn't there, and I wanted to read it when I got through. I am a pretty good reader. I love it. It is what I do, really. So, if I can read it, that is the highest compliment I can think of. People say, I write for myself, and it sounds so awful and so narcissistic, but in a sense if you know how to read your own work—that is, with the necessary critical distance—it makes you a better writer and editor. When I teach creative writing, I always speak about how you have to learn how to read your work; I don't mean enjoy it because you wrote it. I mean, go away from it, and read it as though it is the first time you've ever seen it. Critique it that way. Don't get all involved in your thrilling sentences and all that...

Do you have your audience in mind when you sit down to write?

Only me. If I come to a place where I am unsure, I have the characters to go to for reassurance. By that time they are friendly enough to tell me if the rendition of their lives is authentic or not. But there are so many things only I can tell. After all, this is my work. I have to take full responsibility for doing it right as well as doing it wrong. Doing it wrong isn't bad, but doing it wrong and thinking you've done it right is. I remember spending a whole summer writing something I was very impressed with, but couldn't get back to until winter. I went back confident that those fifty pages were really first-rate, but when I read them each page of the fifty was terrible. It was really ill-conceived. I knew that I could do it over, but I just couldn't get over the fact that I thought it was so good at the time. And that is scary because then you think it means you don't know.

INTERVIEWER

What about it was so bad?

MORRISON

It was pompous. Pompous and unappetizing.

INTERVIEWER

I read that you started writing after your divorce as a way of beating back the loneliness. Was that true, and do you write for different reasons now?

MORRISON

Sort of. Sounds simpler than it was. I don't know if I was writing for that reason or some other reason— or one that I don't even suspect. I do know that I don't like it here if I don't have something to write.

INTERVIEWER

Here, meaning where?

MORRISON

Meaning out in the world. It is not possible for me to be unaware of the incredible violence, the willful ignorance, the hunger for other people's pain. I'm always conscious of that though I am less aware of it under certain circumstances—good friends at

dinner, other books. Teaching makes a big difference, but that is not enough. Teaching could make
me into someone who is complacent, unaware, rather
than part of the solution. So what makes me feel as
though I belong here out in this world is not the
teacher, not the mother, not the lover, but what goes
on in my mind when I am writing. Then I belong
here and then all of the things that are disparate and
irreconcilable can be useful. I can do the traditional
things that writers always say they do, which is to
make order out of chaos. Even if you are reproducing
the disorder, you are sovereign at that point. Strug-
gling through the work is extremely important—
more important to me than publishing it.

INTERVIEWER

If you didn't do this, then the chaos would—

MORRISON

Then I would be part of the chaos.

INTERVIEWER

Wouldn't the answer to that be either to lecture about
the chaos or to be in politics?

MORRISON

If I had a gift for it. All I can do is read books and
write books and edit books and critique books. I
don't think that I could show up on a regular basis
as a politician. I would lose interest. I don't have
the resources for it, the gift. There are people who
can organize other people and I cannot. I'd just get
bored.

When did it become clear to you that your gift was to be a writer?

It was very late. I always thought I was probably adept, because people used to say so, but their criteria might not have been mine. So, I wasn't interested in what they said. It meant nothing. It was by the time I was writing *Song of Solomon* (1977), the third book, that I began to think that this was the central part of my life. Not to say that other women haven't said it all along, but for a woman to say, I am a writer, is difficult.

Why?

Well, it isn't so difficult *anymore*, but it certainly was for me and for women of my generation or my class or my race. I don't know that all those things are folded into it, but the point is you're moving yourself out of the gender role. You are not saying, I am a mother, I am a wife. Or if you're in the labor market, I am a teacher, I am an editor. But when you move to *writer*, what is that supposed to mean? Is that a job? Is this the way you make your living? It's an intervention into terrain that you are not familiar with—where you have no provenance. At the time I certainly didn't personally know any other women writers who were successful; it looked very much like a male preserve. So you sort of hope you're going to be a little minor person around the edges. It's almost as if you needed permission to write. When I read women's biographies and autobiographies, even accounts of how they got started writing, almost every one of them had a little anecdote that told about the moment someone gave them permission to do it. A mother, a husband, a teacher—somebody—said, Okay, go ahead—you can do it. Which is not to say that men have never needed that; frequently when they are very young, a mentor says, You're good, and they take off. The entitlement was something they could take for granted. I couldn't. It was all very strange. So, even though I knew that writing was central to my life, that it was where my mind was, where I was most delighted and most challenged, I couldn't say it. If someone asked me, What do you do? I wouldn't say, Oh I'm a writer. I'd say, I'm an editor, or, A teacher. Because when you meet people and go to lunch, if they say, What do you do? and you say, I'm a writer, they have to think about that, and then they ask, What have you written? Then they have to either like it or not like it. People feel obliged to like or not like and say so. It is perfectly all right to hate my work. It really is. I have close friends whose work I loathe.

INTERVIEWER

Did you feel you had to write in private?

MORRISON

Oh yes, I wanted to make it a private thing. I wanted to own it myself. Because once you say it, then other people become involved. As a matter of fact, while I was at Random House I never said I was a writer.

INTERVIEWER

Why not?

Oh, it would have been awful. First of all they didn't hire me to do that. They didn't hire me to be one of *them*. Secondly, I think they would have fired me.

INTERVIEWER

Really?

MORRISON

Sure. There were no in-house editors who wrote fiction. Ed Doctorow quit. There was nobody else— no real buying, negotiating editor in trade who was also publishing her own novels.

INTERVIEWER

Did the fact that you were a woman have anything to do with it?

MORRISON

That I didn't think about too much. I was so busy. I only know that I will never again trust my life, my future, to the whims of men, in companies or out. Never again will their judgment have anything to do with what I think I can do. That was the wonderful liberation of being divorced and having children. I did not mind failure, ever, but I minded thinking that someone male knew better. Before that, all the men I knew *did* know better, they really did. My father and teachers were smart people who knew better. Then I came across a smart person who was very important to me who *didn't* know better.

INTERVIEWER

Was this your husband?

Yes. He knew better about his life, but not about mine. I had to stop and say, Let me start again and see what it is like to be a grown-up. I decided to leave home, to take my children with me, to go into publishing and see what I could do. I was prepared for that not to work either, but I wanted to see what it was like to be a grown-up.

INTERVIEWER

Can you talk about that moment at Random House when they suddenly realized that they had a writer in their midst?

MORRISON

I published a book called *The Bluest Eye* (1970). I didn't tell them about it. They didn't know until they read the review in the *New York Times*. It was published by Holt. Somebody had told this young guy there that I was writing something and he had said in a very offhand way, If you ever complete something send it to me. So I did. A lot of black men were writing in 1968, 1969, and he bought it, thinking that there was a growing interest in what black people were writing and that this book of mine would also sell. He was wrong. What was selling was: Let me tell you how powerful I am and how horrible you are, or some version of that. For whatever reasons, he took a small risk. He didn't pay me much, so it didn't matter if the book sold or not. It got a really horrible review in the *New York Times Book Review* on Sunday and then got a very good daily review.

You mentioned getting permission to write. Who gave it to you?

No one. What I needed permission to do was to succeed at it. I never signed a contract until the book was finished because I didn't want it to be homework. A contract meant somebody was waiting for it, that I *had* to do it, and they could ask me about it. They could get up in my face and I don't like that. By not signing a contract, I do it, and if I want you to see it, I'll let you see it. It has to do with self-esteem. I am sure for years you have heard writers constructing illusions of freedom, anything in order to have the illusion that it is all mine and only I can do it. I remember introducing Eudora Welty and saying that nobody could have written those stories but her, meaning that I have a feeling about most books that at some point somebody would have written them *anyway*. But then there are some writers without whom certain stories would never have been written. I don't mean the subject matter or the narrative but just the way in which they did it—their slant on it is truly unique.

Who are some of them?

Hemingway is in that category, Flannery O'Connor. Faulkner, Fitzgerald ...

Haven't you been critical of the way these authors depicted blacks?

No! Me, critical? I have been revealing how white writers imagine black people, and some of them are brilliant at it. Faulkner was brilliant at it. Hemingway did it poorly in places and brilliantly elsewhere.

How so?

In not using black characters, but using the aesthetic of blacks as anarchy, as sexual license, as deviance. In his last book, *The Garden of Eden*, Hemingway's heroine is getting blacker and blacker. The woman who is going mad tells her husband, I want to be your little African queen. The novel gets its charge that way: her white, white hair and her black, black skin... almost like a Man Ray photograph. Mark Twain talked about racial ideology in the most powerful, eloquent, and instructive way I have ever read. Edgar Allan Poe did not. He loved white supremacy and the planter class, and he wanted to be a gentleman, and he endorsed all of that. He didn't contest it or critique it. What is exciting about American literature is that business of how writers say things under, beneath, and around their stories. Think of *Pudd'nhead Wilson* and all these inversions of what race is, how sometimes nobody can tell, or the thrill of discovery. Faulkner in *Absalom, Absalom!* spends the entire book tracing race and you can't find it. No one can see it, even the character who *is* black can't see it. I did this lecture for my students that took me forever, which was tracking all the moments of withheld, partial, or disinformation, when a racial fact or clue *sort* of comes out but doesn't quite arrive. I just wanted to chart it. I listed its appearance, disguise, and disappearance on every page—I mean every phrase! Everything, and I delivered this thing to my class. They all fell asleep! But I was so fascinated, technically. Do you know how hard it is to withhold that kind of information but hinting, pointing all of the time? And then to reveal it in order to say that it is *not* the point anyway? It is technically just astonishing. As a reader you have been forced to hunt for a drop of black blood that means everything and nothing. The insanity of racism. So the structure is the argument. Not what this one says or that one says ... it is the *structure* of the book, and you are there hunting this black thing that is nowhere to be found and yet makes all the difference. No one has done anything quite like that ever. So, when I critique, what I am saying is, I don't care if Faulkner is a racist or not; I don't personally care but I am fascinated by what it means to write like this.

INTERVIEWER

What about black writers ... how do they write in a world dominated by and informed by their relationship to a white culture?

MORRISON

By trying to alter language, simply to free it up, not to repress it or confine it, but to open it up. Tease it. Blast its racist straitjacket. I wrote a story entitled

"Recitatif" (1983), in which there are two little girls in an orphanage, one white and one black. But the reader doesn't know which is white and which is black. I use class codes, but no racial codes.

INTERVIEWER

Is this meant to confuse the reader?

MORRISON

Well, yes. But to provoke and enlighten. I did that as a lark. What was exciting was to be forced as a writer not to be lazy and rely on obvious codes. Soon as I say, Black woman... I can rest on or provoke predictable responses, but if I leave it out then I have to talk about her in a complicated way—as a person.

INTERVIEWER

Why wouldn't you want to say, The black woman came out of the store?

MORRISON

Well, you can, but it has to be important that she is black.

INTERVIEWER

What about *The Confessions of Nat Turner*?

MORRISON

Well, here we have a very self-conscious character who says things like, I looked at my black hand. Or, I woke up and I felt black. It is very much on Bill Styron's mind. He feels charged in Nat Turner's skin... in this place that feels exotic to him. So it reads exotically to us, that's all.

There was a tremendous outcry at that time from people who felt that Styron didn't have a right to write about Nat Turner.

He has a right to write about whatever he wants. To suggest otherwise is outrageous. What they should have criticized, and some of them did, was Styron's suggestion that Nat Turner hated black people. In the book Turner expresses his revulsion over and over again...he's so distant from blacks, so superior. So the fundamental question is, Why would anybody follow him? What kind of leader is this who has a fundamentally racist contempt that seems unreal to any black person reading it? Any white leader would have some interest and identification with the people he was asking to die. That was what these critics meant when they said Nat Turner speaks like a white man. That racial distance is strong and clear in that book.

You must have read a lot of slave narratives for *Beloved*.

I wouldn't read them for information because I knew that they had to be authenticated by white patrons, that they couldn't say everything they wanted to say because they couldn't alienate their audience; they had to be quiet about certain things. They were going to be as good as they could be under the circumstances and as revelatory, but they never say how terrible it was. They would just say, Well, you know, it was really awful, but let's abolish slavery so life can go on. Their narratives had to be very understated. So while I looked at the documents and felt *familiar* with slavery and overwhelmed by it, I wanted it to be truly *felt*. I wanted to translate the historical into the personal. I spent a long time trying to figure out what it was about slavery that made it so repugnant, so personal, so indifferent, so intimate, and yet so public.

In reading some of the documents I noticed frequent references to something that was never properly described—*the bit*. This thing was put into the mouth of slaves to punish them and shut them up without preventing them from working. I spent a long time trying to find out what it looked like. I kept reading statements like, I put the bit on Jenny, or, as Equiano says, "I went into a kitchen" and I saw a woman standing at the stove, and she had a brake (*b-r-a-k-e*, he spells it) "in her mouth," and I said, What is that? and somebody told me what it was, and then I said, I never saw anything so awful in all my life. But I really couldn't image the thing—did it look like a horse's bit or what?

Eventually I did find some sketches in one book in this country, which was the record of a man's torture of his wife. In South America, Brazil, places like that, they kept such mementos. But while I was searching, something else occurred to me—namely, that this bit, this item, this personalized type of torture, was a direct descendant of the inquisition. And I realized that of course you can't buy this stuff. You can't send away for a mail-order bit for your slave. Sears doesn't carry them. So you have to make it. You have to go out in the backyard and put some stuff together and construct it and then affix it to a person. So the whole process had a very personal quality for the person who made it, as well as for the person who wore it. Then I realized that describing it would never be helpful; that the reader didn't need to *see* it so much as *feel* what it was like. I realized that it was important to imagine the bit as an active instrument, rather than simply as a curio or an historical fact. And in the same way I wanted to show the reader what slavery *felt* like, rather than how it looked.

There's a passage in which Paul D. says to Sethe, I've never told anybody about it, I've sung about it sometimes. He tries to tell her what wearing the bit was like, but he ends up talking about a rooster that he swears smiled at him when he wore it—he felt cheapened and lessened and that he would never be worth as much as a rooster sitting on a tub in the sunlight. I make other references to the desire to spit, to sucking iron, and so on; but it seemed to me that describing what it *looked* like would distract the reader from what I wanted him or her to experience, which was what it *felt* like. The kind of information you can find between the lines of history. It sort of falls off the page, or it's a glance and a reference. It's right there in the intersection where an institution becomes personal, where the historical becomes people with names.

INTERVIEWER

When you create a character is it completely created out of your own imagination?

MORRISON

I never use anyone I know. In *The Bluest Eye* I think I used some gestures and dialogue of my mother in certain places, and a little geography. I've never done that since. I really am very conscientious about that. It's never based on anyone. I don't do what many writers do.

Why is that?

There is this feeling that artists have—photographers, more than other people, and writers—that they are acting like a succubus...this process of taking from something that's alive and using it for one's own purposes. You can do it with trees, butterflies, or human beings. Making a little life for oneself by scavenging other people's lives is a big question, and it does have moral and ethical implications.

In fiction, I feel the most intelligent, and the most free, and the most excited, when my characters are fully invented people. That's part of the excitement. If they're based on somebody else, in a funny way it's an infringement of a copyright. That person *owns* his life, has a patent on it. It shouldn't be available for fiction.

Do you ever feel like your characters are getting away from you, out of your control?

I take control of them. They are very carefully imagined. I feel as though I know all there is to know about them, even things I don't write—like how they part their hair. They are like ghosts. They have nothing on their minds but themselves and aren't interested in anything but themselves. So you can't let them write your book for you. I have read books in which I know that has happened—when a novelist has been totally taken over by a character. I want to say, You can't do that. If those people could write books they would, but they can't. *You* can. So, you have to say, Shut up. Leave me alone. I am doing this.

INTERVIEWER
Have you ever had to tell any of your characters to shut up?

MORRISON
Pilate, I did. Therefore she doesn't speak very much. She has this long conversation with the two boys and every now and then she'll say something, but she doesn't have the dialogue the other people have. I had to do that, otherwise she was going to over-whelm everybody. She got terribly interesting; char-acters can do that for a little bit. I had to take it back. It's *my* book; it's not called "Pilate."

INTERVIEWER
Pilate is such a strong character. It seems to me that the women in your books are almost always stronger and braver than the men. Why is that?

MORRISON
That isn't true, but I hear that a lot. I think that our expectations of women are very low. If women just stand up straight for thirty days, everybody goes, Oh! How brave! As a matter of fact, somebody wrote about Sethe, and said she was this powerful,

statuesque woman who wasn't even human. But at the end of the book, she can barely turn her head. She has been zonked; she can't even feed herself. Is that tough?

Maybe people read it that way because they thought Sethe made such a hard choice slashing Beloved's throat. Maybe they think that's being strong. Some would say that's just bad manners.

Well, Beloved surely didn't think it was all that tough. She thought it was lunacy. Or, more importantly, How do you know death is better for me? You've never died. How could you know? But I think Paul D., Son, Stamp Paid, even Guitar make equally difficult choices; they are principled. I do think we are too accustomed to women who don't talk back or who use the weapons of the weak.

What are the weapons of the weak?

Nagging. Poison. Gossip. Sneaking around instead of confrontation.

There have been so few novels about women who have intense friendships with other women. Why do you think that is?

It has been a discredited relationship. When I was writing *Sula* (1973), I was under the impression that for a large part of the female population a woman friend was considered a secondary relationship. A man and a woman's relationship was primary. Women, your own friends, were always secondary relationships when the man was not there. Because of this, there's that whole cadre of women who don't like women and prefer men. We had to be taught to like one another. *Ms.* magazine was founded on the premise that we really have to stop complaining about one another, hating, fighting one another, and joining men in their condemnation of ourselves—a typical example of what dominated people do. That is a big education. When much of the literature was like that—when you read about women together (not lesbians or those who have formed long relationships that are covertly lesbian, like in Virginia Woolf's work), it is an overtly male view of females together. They are usually male dominated—like some of Henry James's characters—or the women are talking about men, like Jane Austen's girlfriends…talking about who got married, and how to get married, and are you going to lose him, and I think she wants him and so on. To have heterosexual women who are friends, who are talking only about themselves to each other, seemed to me a very radical thing when *Sula* was published in 1973…but it is hardly radical now.

INTERVIEWER

It is becoming acceptable.

Yes, and it's going to get boring. It will be overdone and as usual it will all run amok.

Why do writers have such a hard time writing about sex?

Sex is difficult to write about because it's just not sexy enough. The only way to write about it is not to write much. Let the reader bring his own sexuality into the text. A writer I usually admire has written about sex in the most off-putting way. There is just too much information. If you start saying "the curve of..." you soon sound like a gynecologist. Only Joyce could get away with that. He said all those forbidden words. He said *cunt*, and that was shocking. The forbidden word can be provocative. But after a while it becomes monotonous rather than arousing. Less is always better. Some writers think that if they use dirty words they've done it. It can work for a short period and for a very young imagination, but after a while it doesn't deliver. When Sethe and Paul D. first see each other, in about half a page they get the sex out of the way, which isn't any good anyway—it's fast and they're embarrassed about it—and then they're lying there trying to pretend they're not in that bed, that they haven't met, and then they begin to think different thoughts, which begin to merge so you can't tell who's thinking what. That merging to me is more tactically sensual than if I had tried to describe body parts.

What about plot? Do you always know where you're going? Would you write the end before you got there?

When I really know what it is about, then I can write that end scene. I wrote the end of *Beloved* about a quarter of the way in. I wrote the end of *Jazz* (1992) very early and the end of *Song of Solomon* very early on. What I really want is for the plot to be *how* it happened. It is like a detective story in a sense. You know who is dead and you want to find out who did it. So, you put the salient elements up front and the reader is hooked into wanting to know, How did that happen? Who did that and why? You are forced into having a certain kind of language that will keep the reader asking those questions. In *Jazz*, just as I did before with *The Bluest Eye*, I put the whole plot on the first page. In fact, in the first edition the plot was on the cover, so that a person in a bookstore could read the cover and know right away what the book was about, and could, if they wished, dismiss it and buy another book. This seemed a suitable technique for *Jazz* because I thought of the plot in that novel, the threesome, as the melody of the piece, and it is fine to follow a melody—to feel the satisfaction of recognizing a melody whenever the narrator returns to it. That was the real art of the enterprise for me— bumping up against that melody time and again, seeing it from another point of view, seeing it afresh each time, playing it back and forth.

When Keith Jarrett plays "Ol' Man River," the delight and satisfaction is not so much in the melody itself but in recognizing it when it surfaces and when it is hidden, and when it goes away completely, what is put in its place. Not so much in the original line as in all the echoes and shades and turns and pivots Jarrett plays around it. I was trying to do something similar with the plot in *Jazz*. I wanted the story to be the vehicle that moved us from page one to the end, but I wanted the delight to be found in moving away from the story and coming back to it, looking around it, and through it, as though it was a prism, constantly turning.

This playful aspect of *Jazz* may well cause a great deal of dissatisfaction in readers who just want the melody, who want to know what happened, who did it, and why. But the jazzlike structure wasn't a secondary thing for me—it was the raison d'être of the book. The process of trial and error by which the narrator revealed the plot was as important and exciting to me as telling the story.

INTERVIEWER

You also divulge the plot early on in *Beloved*.

MORRISON

It seemed important to me that the action in *Beloved*—the fact of infanticide—be immediately known, but deferred, unseen. I wanted to give the reader all the information and the consequences sur- rounding the act, while avoiding engorging myself or the reader with the violence itself. I remember writing the sentence where Sethe cuts the throat of the child very, very late in the process of writing the book. I remember getting up from the table and walking outside for a long time—walking around the yard and coming back and revising it a little bit and going back out and in and rewriting the sentence over and over again ... Each time I fixed that sentence so that it was exactly right, or so I thought, but then I would be unable to sit there and would have to go away and come back. I thought that the act itself had to be not only buried but also understated, because if the language was going to compete with the violence itself it would be obscene or pornographic.

INTERVIEWER

Style is obviously very important to you. Can you talk about this in relation to *Jazz*?

MORRISON

With *Jazz*, I wanted to convey the sense that a musician conveys—that he has more but he's not gonna give it to you. It's an exercise in restraint, a holding back—not because it's not there, or because one had exhausted it, but because of the riches, and because it can be done again. That sense of knowing when to stop is a learned thing and I didn't always have it. It was probably not until after I wrote *Song of Solomon* that I got to feeling secure enough to experience what it meant to be thrifty with images and language and so on. I was very conscious in writing *Jazz* of trying to blend that which is contrived and artificial with improvisation. I thought of myself as like the jazz musician—someone who practices and practices and practices in order to be able to invent and to make his art look effortless and graceful. I was always conscious of the constructed aspect of the writing process, and that art appears natural and elegant only as a result of constant practice and awareness of its formal structures. You must practice thrift in order to achieve that luxurious quality of wastefulness—that sense that you have enough to waste, that you are holding back—without actually wasting anything. You shouldn't overgratify, you should never satiate. I've always felt that that peculiar sense of hunger at the end of a piece of art—a yearning for more—is really very, very powerful. But there is at the same time a kind of contentment, knowing that at some other time there will indeed be more because the artist is endlessly inventive.

INTERVIEWER
Were there other ... ingredients, structural entities?

MORRISON
Well, it seems to me that migration was a major event in the cultural history of this country. Now, I'm being very speculative about all of this—I guess that's why I write novels—but it seems to me something modern and new happened after the Civil War. Of course, a number of things changed, but the era was most clearly marked by the disowning and dispossession of ex-slaves. These ex-slaves were sometimes taken into their local labor markets, but they often tried to escape their problems by migrating to the city. I was fascinated by the thought of what the city must have meant to them, these second- and third-generation ex-slaves, to rural people living there in their own number. The city must have seemed so exciting and wonderful, so much the place to be.

I was interested in how the city worked. How classes and groups and nationalities had the security of numbers within their own turfs and territories, but also felt the thrill of knowing that there were other turfs and other territories, and felt the real glamour and excitement of being in this throng. I was interested in how music changed in this country. Spirituals and gospel and blues represented one kind of response to slavery—they gave voice to the yearning for escape, in code, literally, on the Underground Railroad.

I was also concerned with personal life. How did people love one another? What did they think was free? At that time, when the ex-slaves were moving into the city, running away from something that was constricting and killing them and dispossessing them over and over and over again, they were in a very limiting environment. But when you listen to their music—the beginnings of jazz—you realize that they are talking about something else. They are talking about love, about loss. But there is such grandeur, such satisfaction in those lyrics... they're never happy—somebody's always leaving—but they're not whining. It's as though the whole tragedy of choosing somebody, risking love, risking emotion, risking sensuality, and then losing it all didn't matter, since it was their choice. Exercising choice in who you love was a major, major thing. And the music reinforced the idea of love as a space where one could negotiate freedom.

Obviously, jazz was considered—as all new music is—to be devil music; too sensual and provocative, and so on. But for some black people jazz meant claiming their own bodies. You can imagine what that must have meant for people whose bodies had been owned, who had been slaves as children, or who remembered their parents' being slaves.

Blues and jazz represented ownership of one's own emotions. So of course it is excessive and overdone: tragedy in jazz is relished, almost as though a happy ending would take away some of its glamour, its flair. Now advertisers use jazz on television to communicate authenticity and modernity; to say "trust me," and to say "hip."

These days the city still retains the quality of excitement it had in the jazz age—only now we associate that excitement with a different kind of danger. We chant and scream and act alarmed about the homeless; we say we want our streets back, but it is from our awareness of homelessness and our employment of strategies to deal with it that we get our sense of the urban. Feeling as though we have the armor, the shields, the moxie, the strength, the toughness, and the smarts to be engaged and survive encounters with the unpredictable, the alien, the strange, and the violent is an intrinsic part of what it means to live in the city. When people "complain" about homelessness they are actually bragging about it: New York has more homeless than San Francisco. No, no, no, San Francisco has more homeless. No, you haven't been to Detroit. We are almost competitive about our endurance, which I think is one of the reasons why we accept homelessness so easily.

INTERVIEWER

So the city freed the ex-slaves from their history?

MORRISON

In part, yes. The city was seductive to them because it promised forgetfulness. It offered the possibility of freedom—freedom, as you put it, from history. But although history should not become a straitjacket, which overwhelms and binds, neither should it be forgotten. One must critique it, test it, confront it, and understand it in order to achieve a freedom that is more than license, to achieve true, adult agency. If you penetrate the seduction of the city, then it becomes possible to confront your own history—to forget what ought to be forgotten and use what is useful—such true agency is made possible.

How do visual images influence your work?

I was having some difficulty describing a scene in *Song of Solomon* ... of a man running away from some obligations and himself. I used an Edvard Munch painting almost literally. He is walking and there is nobody on his side of the street. Everybody is on the other side.

Song of Solomon is such a painted book in comparison with some of your others like *Beloved*, which is sepia toned.

Part of that has to do with the visual images that I got being aware that in historical terms women, black people in general, were very attracted to very bright-colored clothing. Most people are frightened by color anyway.

Why?

They just are. In this culture quiet colors are considered elegant. Civilized Western people wouldn't buy bloodred sheets or dishes. There may be something more to it than what I am suggesting. But the slave population had no access even to what color there was, because they wore slave clothes, hand-me-downs, work clothes made out of burlap and sacking. For them a colored dress would be luxurious; it wouldn't matter whether it was rich or poor cloth...just to have a red or a yellow dress. I stripped *Beloved* of color so that there are only the small moments when Sethe runs amok buying ribbons and bows, enjoying herself the way children enjoy that kind of color. The whole business of color was why slavery was able to last such a long time. It wasn't as though you had a class of convicts who could dress themselves up and pass themselves off. No, these were people marked because of their skin color, as well as other features. So color is a signifying mark. Baby Suggs dreams of color and says, Bring me a little lavender. It is a kind of luxury. We are so inundated with color and visuals. I just wanted to pull it back so that one could feel that hunger and that delight. I couldn't do that if I had made it the painterly book *Song of Solomon* was.

INTERVIEWER

Is that what you are referring to when you speak about needing to find a controlling image?

MORRISON

Sometimes, yes. There are three or four in *Song of Solomon*—I knew that I wanted it to be painterly, and I wanted the opening to be red, white, and blue. I also knew that in some sense he would have to "fly." In *Song of Solomon* it was the first time that I had written about a man who was the central, the driving engine of the narrative; I was a little unsure about my ability to feel comfortable inside him. I could always look at him and write from the outside, but those would have been just perceptions. I had to be able not only to look at him but to feel how it really must have felt. So in trying to think about this, the image in my mind was a train. All the previous books have been women centered, and they have been pretty much in the neighborhood and in the yard; this was going to move out. So, I had this feeling about a train … sort of revving up, then moving out as he does, and then it sort of highballs at the end; it speeds up, but it doesn't brake, it just highballs and leaves you sort of suspended. So that image controlled the structure for me, although that is not something I articulate or even make reference to; it only matters that it works for me. Other books look like spirals, like *Sula*.

INTERVIEWER

How would you describe the controlling image of *Jazz*?

MORRISON

Jazz was very complicated because I wanted to re-represent two contradictory things—artifice and improvisation—where you have an artwork planned, thought through, but at the same time appears invented, like jazz. I thought of the image being a book. Physically a book, but at the same time it is writing itself. Imagining itself. Talking. Aware of what it is doing. It watches itself think and imagine. That seemed to me to be a combination of artifice and improvisation—where you practice and plan in order to invent. Also the willingness to fail, to be wrong, because jazz is performance. In a performance you make mistakes, and you don't have the luxury of revision that a writer has; you have to make something out of a mistake, and if you do it well enough it will take you to another place where you never would have gone had you not made that error. So, you have to be able to risk making that error in performance. Dancers do it all the time, as well as jazz musicians. *Jazz* predicts its own story. Sometimes it is wrong because of faulty vision. It simply did not imagine those characters well enough, admits it was wrong, and the characters talk back the way jazz musicians do. It has to listen to the characters it has invented and then learn something from them. It was the most intricate thing I had done, though I wanted to tell a very simple story about people who do not know that they are living in the jazz age and to never use the word *jazz*.

INTERVIEWER

One way to achieve this structurally is to have several voices speaking throughout each book. Why do you do this?

MORRISON

It's important not to have a totalizing view. In American literature we have been so totalized—as though there is only one version. We are not one indistinguishable block of people who always behave the same way.

Is that what you mean by "totalized"?

Yes. A definitive or an authoritarian view from somebody else or someone speaking for us. No singularity and no diversity. I try to give some credibility to all sorts of voices, each of which is profoundly different. Because what strikes me about African American culture *is* its variety. In so much of contemporary music everybody sounds alike. But when you think about black music, you think about the difference between Duke Ellington and Sidney Bechet or Satchmo or Miles Davis. They don't sound anything alike, but you know that they are all black performers, because of whatever that quality is that makes you realize, Oh yes, this is part of something called the African American music tradition. There is no black woman popular singer, jazz singer, blues singer who sounds like any other. Billie Holiday does not sound like Aretha, doesn't sound like Nina, doesn't sound like Sarah, doesn't sound like any of them. They are really powerfully different. And they will tell you that they couldn't possibly have made it as singers if they sounded like somebody else. If someone comes along sounding like Ella Fitzgerald, they will say, Oh we have one of those ... It's interesting to me how those women have this very distinct, unmistakable image. I would like to write like that. I would like to write novels that were unmistakably mine, but nevertheless fit first into African American traditions and second of all, into this whole thing called literature.

First African American?

Yes.

... rather than the whole of literature?

Oh yes.

Why?

It's richer. It has more complex sources. It pulls from something that's closer to the edge, it's much more modern. It has a human future.

Wouldn't you rather be known as a great exponent of literature rather than as an African American writer?

It's very important to me that my work be African American; if it assimilates into a different or larger pool, so much the better. But I shouldn't be *asked* to do that. Joyce is not asked to do that. Tolstoy is not. I mean, they can all be Russian, French, Irish, or Catholic, they write out of where they come from, and I do too. It just so happens that that space for me is African American; it could be Catholic, it could be Midwestern. I'm those things too, and they are all important.

Why do you think people ask, Why don't you write something that we can understand? Do you threaten them by not writing in the typical Western, linear, chronological way?

MORRISON

I don't think that they mean that. I think they mean, Are you ever going to write a book about white people? For them perhaps that's a kind of a compliment. They're saying, You write well enough, I would even let you write about me. They couldn't say that to anybody else. I mean, could I have gone up to André Gide and said, Yes, but when are you going to get serious and start writing about black people? I don't think he would know how to answer that question. Just as I don't. He would say, What? I will if I want to, or, Who are you? What is behind that question is, there's the center, which is white, and then there are these regional blacks or Asians, or any sort of marginal people. That question can only be asked from the center. Bill Moyers asked me that when-are-you-going-to-write-about question on television. I just said, Well, maybe one day ... but I couldn't say to him, you know, you can only ask that question from the center. The center of the world! I mean, he's a white male. He's asking a marginal person when are you going to get to the center, when are you going to write about white people. I can't say, Bill, why are you asking me that question? Or, As long as that question seems reasonable is as long as I won't, can't. The point is that he's patronizing; he's saying, You write well enough; you could come on into the center if you wanted to. You don't have to stay out there on the margins. And I'm saying, Yeah, well, I'm gonna stay out here on the margin, and let the center look for me.

Maybe it's a false claim, but not fully. I'm sure it was true for the ones we think of as giants now. Joyce is a good example. He moved here and there, but he wrote about Ireland wherever he was, didn't care where he was. I am sure people said to him, Why...? Maybe the French asked, When you gonna write about Paris?

INTERVIEWER

What do you appreciate most in Joyce?

MORRISON

It is amazing how certain kinds of irony and humor travel. Sometimes Joyce is hilarious. I read *Finnegans Wake* after graduate school and I had the great good fortune of reading it without any help. I don't know if I read it right, but it was hilarious! I laughed constantly! I didn't know what was going on for whole blocks but it didn't matter because I wasn't going to be graded on it. I think the reason why everyone still has so much fun with Shakespeare is because he didn't have any literary critic. He was just doing it; and there were no reviews except for people throwing stuff on stage. He could just do it.

INTERVIEWER

Do you think if he had been reviewed he would have worked less?

MORRISON

Oh, if he'd cared about it, he'd have been very self-conscious. That's a hard attitude to maintain, to pretend you don't care, pretend you don't read.

INTERVIEWER

Do you read your reviews?

MORRISON

I read everything.

INTERVIEWER

Really? You look deadly serious.

MORRISON

I read everything written about me that I see.

INTERVIEWER

Why is that?

MORRISON

I have to know what's going on!

INTERVIEWER

You want to see how you're coming across?

MORRISON

No, no. It's not about me or my work, it's about what is going on. I have to get a sense, particularly of what's going on with women's work or African American work, contemporary work. I teach a literature course. So I read any information that's going to help me teach.

Are you ever really surprised when they compare you to the magic realists, such as Gabriel García Márquez?

Yes, I used to be. It doesn't mean anything to me. Schools are only important to me when I'm teaching literature. It doesn't mean anything to me when I'm sitting here with a big pile of blank yellow paper ... what do I say? I'm a magic realist? Each subject matter demands its own form, you know.

Why do you teach undergraduates?

Here at Princeton, they really do value undergraduates, which is nice because a lot of universities value only the graduate school or the professional research schools. I like Princeton's notion. I would have loved that for my own children. I don't like freshman and sophomores being treated as the staging ground or the playground or the canvas on which graduate students learn how to teach. They need the best instruction. I've always thought the public schools needed to study the best literature. I always taught *Oedipus Rex* to all kinds of what they used to call remedial or development classes. The reason those kids are in those classes is that they're bored to death; so you can't give them boring things. You have to give them the best there is to engage them.

INTERVIEWER

One of your sons is a musician. Were you ever musical, did you ever play the piano?

MORRISON

No, but I come from a family of highly skilled musicians. Highly skilled, meaning most of them couldn't read music but they could play everything that they heard ... instantly. They sent us, my sister and me, to music lessons. They were sending me off to learn how to do something that they could do naturally. I thought I was deficient, retarded. They didn't explain that perhaps it's more important that you learn how to *read* music ... that it's a good thing, not a bad thing. I thought we were sort of lame people going off to learn how to walk, while, you know, they all just stood up and did it naturally.

INTERVIEWER

Do you think there is an education for becoming a writer? Reading perhaps?

MORRISON

That has only limited value.

INTERVIEWER

Travel the world? Take courses in sociology, history?

MORRISON

Or stay home ... I don't think they have to go anywhere.

INTERVIEWER

Some people say, Oh, I can't write a book until I've lived my life, until I've had experiences.

That may be—maybe they can't. But look at the people who never went anywhere and just thought it up. Thomas Mann. I guess he took a few little trips...I think you either have or you acquire this sort of imagination. Sometimes you do need a stimulus. But I myself don't ever go anywhere for stimulation. I don't want to go anywhere. If I could just sit in one spot I would be happy. I don't trust the ones who say I have to go do something before I can write. You see, I don't write autobiographically. First of all, I'm not interested in real-life people as subjects for fiction—including myself. If I write about somebody who's a historical figure like Margaret Garner, I really don't know anything about her. What I knew came from reading two interviews with her. They said, Isn't this extraordinary. Here's a woman who escaped into Cincinnati from the horrors of slavery and was not crazy. Though she'd killed her child, she was not foaming at the mouth. She was very calm; she said, I'd do it again. That was more than enough to fire my imagination.

INTERVIEWER

She was sort of a cause célèbre?

MORRISON

She was. Her real life was much more awful than it's rendered in the novel, but if I had known all there was to know about her I never would have written it. It would have been finished; there would have been no place in there for me. It would be like a recipe already cooked. There you are. You're already this person. Why should I get to steal from you? I don't like that. What I really love is the process of invention. To have characters move from the curl all the way to a full-fledged person, that's interesting.

INTERVIEWER

Do you ever write out of anger or any other emotion?

MORRISON

No. Anger is a very intense but tiny emotion, you know. It doesn't last. It doesn't produce anything. It's not creative ... at least not for me. I mean, these books take at least three years!

INTERVIEWER

That is a long time to be angry.

MORRISON

Yes. I don't trust that stuff anyway. I don't like those little quick emotions, like, I'm lonely, *ohhh*, God ... I don't like those emotions as fuel. I mean, I have them, but—

INTERVIEWER

—they're not a good muse?

MORRISON

No, and if it's not your brain thinking cold, cold thoughts, which you can dress in any kind of mood, then it's nothing. It has to be a cold, cold thought. I mean cold, or cool at least. Your brain. That's all there is.

(1993)

Jan Morris

THE ART OF THE ESSAY NO. 2

Interviewed by Leo Lerman

J an Morris was born James Humphrey Morris on October 2, 1926, in Somerset, England. As she recalled in her memoir, *Conundrum* (1974), "I was three or perhaps four years old when I realized that I had been born into the wrong body, and should really be a girl." First intimations. But he would live as a man for the next thirty-six years, mentioning his sexual confusion only to his wife, Elizabeth, whom he married at twenty-two in Cairo, where he was working for the local Arab News Agency.

Morris left boarding school at the age of seventeen and served for the next five years in the 9th Queen's Royal Lancers, one of Britain's best cavalry regiments. He then moved to Cairo, but soon returned to Britain, attending Oxford for two years before reentering journalism as a reporter for the *Times*, which assigned him, because no one else was available, to cover the Hillary and Tenzing expedition to Mount Everest. At twenty-six, having never before climbed a mountain, he scaled three-quarters (twenty-two thousand feet) of Everest to report the first conquest of the mountain. It was a world scoop, and won him international renown. He went on to a distinguished career as a foreign correspondent, for both the *Times* and the *Guardian*.

In 1956, he was awarded a Commonwealth Fellowship, which allowed him to travel through America for a year and resulted in his first book: *As I Saw the U.S.A.* (1956). A similar book was published to great acclaim in 1960, *The World of Venice*, the product of a year's sabbatical in that city with his family. Morris ended his career as a full-time journalist in 1961, in part because of a newspaper policy that prevented him from expanding his journalistic assignments into books. He went on to publish numerous books, including *The Road to Huddersfield: A Journey to Five Continents* (1963), *The Presence of Spain* (1965), and the Pax Britannica trilogy (1968–78).

In 1964, there was another change, personal rather than professional: Morris started taking hormone pills to begin his transformation into a female. The process was completed in 1972, when he traveled to Casablanca for the definitive operation. Her first book as Jan Morris, *Conundrum*, chronicles the passing from male to female. But when asked to discuss the sex change further, she demurs, preferring to let that account speak for itself and referring to the whole matter simply as "the conundrum thing." Since then she has published thirteen books, including *Travels* (1976), *Manhattan '45* (1987), *Hong Kong* (1988), and two novels, *Last Letters from Hav* (1985), and *Fisher's Face* (1995).

Divorce necessarily followed the sex change (it is required by British law), although Morris still lives with her former wife, currently in a house in North Wales called Trefan Morys. Morris describes the house in her book *Pleasures of a Tangled Life* (1989): "I love it above all inanimate objects, and above a good many animate ones too ... It consists in essence simply of two living-rooms, one above the other, each about forty feet long. Both are full of books, and there is a little suite of functional chambers on two floors at one end, linked by a spiral staircase." They have four children.

At seventy-one, she looks remarkably youthful, perhaps a result of the hormone pills. And she still travels, this summer to Hong Kong to cover the transfer of power from Britain to China. The interview was begun in 1989 under the auspices of the 92nd Street Y, at Hunter College in New York City, and continued through telephone calls and letters.

INTERVIEWER

You resist being called a travel writer.

JAN MORRIS

Yes. At least I resist the idea that travel writing has got to be factual. I believe in its imaginative qualities and its potential as art and literature. I must say that my campaign, which I've been waging for ages now, has borne some fruit because intelligent bookshops nowadays do have a stack called something like travel *literature*. But what word does one use?

Writing about place?

Yes, that's what I do. Although I think of myself more as a *belletrist*, an old-fashioned word. *Essayist* would do; people understand that more or less. But the thing is, my subject has been mostly concerned with place. It needn't be. I believe my best books to be far more historical than topographical. But like most writers, I think far too much about myself anyway, and in my heart of hearts don't think I am worth talking about in this way.

Basically, what you are then is a historian.

Well, my best books have been histories. That's all.

So let's start with your Pax Britannica trilogy. Did you have Gibbon's *Decline and Fall of the Roman Empire* in mind when you began?

No, not at all. When I began the trilogy I didn't know I was going to write it. I ought to tell you how I got into writing it. I'm old enough to remember the empire when it still was the empire. I was brought up in a world whose map was painted very largely red, and I went out into the world when I was young in a spirit of imperial arrogance. I felt, like most British people my age, that I was born to a birthright of supremacy; out I went to exert that supremacy. But gradually in the course of my later adolescence and youth my views about this changed.

Did they change at a particular moment?

Yes. I was living in what was then Palestine, and I had occasion to call upon the district commissioner of Gaza. He was an Englishman. It was a British mandate in those days, and he was the British official in charge of that part of Palestine. I knocked on his door and out he came. Something about this guy's hat made me think twice about him. It was kind of a bohemian hat. Rather a floppy, slightly rakish or raffish hat; a very, very civilian hat—a sort of fawn color, but because it was bleached by imperial suns and made limp by tropical rainstorms all of the empire was in that hat. He seemed to be rather a nice man. I admired him. He had none of my foolish, cocky arrogance at all. He was a gentleman in the old sense of the word. And through him, and through meeting some of his colleagues, I began to see that my imperial cockiness was nonsense and that the empire, in its last years at least, wasn't a bit arrogant, it wasn't a bit cocky. People like that were simply trying to withdraw from an immense historical process and hand it over honorably to its successors. Because of this, my view of the empire changed.

I went on and wrote a book about an imperial adventure, which was a crossing of southeast Arabia, with the sultan of Oman, but under the auspices of the raj, really. One of the reviewers of the book said,

Why does this author fiddle around along the edges, along the perimeters of this imperial subject? Why not get down to the heart of it? For once a writer did take notice of what a reviewer suggested: because of what he said, I decided I'd write a large, celebratory volume at the center of the imperial story, 1897, which was the time of the queen's Diamond Jubilee and the climax of the whole imperial affair. I wrote that book, and I loved doing it. Then I thought, Well, I'll add one on each side of it and make a triptych. I'll have a volume showing how Queen Victoria came to the throne and the empire splurged into this great moment of climax. Then we'll have the climactic piece. Finally, we'll have an elegiac threnody, letting the thing die down until the end, which I took to be the death of Winston Churchill. Nothing at all to do with Gibbon.

INTERVIEWER

In what's now the Queen Victoria volume you demonstrated something you do frequently. You began with the particular, with Emily Eden, and then spread out over the British Empire. The reader sort of grows up with Queen Victoria. In the preface of the first volume you state that you are "chiefly attracted by the aesthetic of empire." Did this dictate a different approach?

MORRIS

Yes, it did. Because I did not set out to exhibit a moral stance about the empire. I treated it as an immense exhibition. By and large, I accepted the moral views of those who were doing it at the time. Things that would seem wicked to us now didn't always seem wicked to people in the Victorian age. I accepted that. Since this is an escapist point of view, really, I decided that I would not in any way make it an analysis of empire but rather an evocation. The looks and smells and sensations of it. What I later tried to imagine was this: supposing in the last years of the Roman Empire one young centurion, old enough to remember the imperial impulses and the imperial splendor but recognizing that it was passing, sat down and wrote a large book about his sensations at that moment. Wouldn't that be interesting? Said I, But somebody *could* do it about this still greater empire, the British Empire. Who is that? I asked myself. Me!

INTERVIEWER

As empire began its decline, more frightening than the loss of territory, you say, was the possibility that the British might have lost the will to rule. In what ways was empire's decline an expression of British character at the time?

MORRIS

In several ways it was. In the more honorable way, I think it was in the way that I was trying to express my responses to the district commissioner of Gaza. There were a great many very decent men who were devoting their lives to the empire. Perhaps, when they began their careers, they did it in a paternalistic way, which is in itself a form of arrogance; by the time I got into it, very few of them were arrogant. They were only anxious to hand it over honorably and at a reasonable speed. I think they did it very well on the whole. Compared with the record of the French leaving their empire, the British did it in a successful, kindly way. But at the same time, of course, the British had been absolutely shattered by two world wars. The first one left the empire physically larger than ever before. The second one was an obvious death knell for it. The British came out of the Second World War an extremely tired and disillusioned nation, exemplified by the fact that they immediately gave the boot to their great hero, Winston Churchill. All they were interested in then was getting back to their island and trying to make it a more decent place to live. In that respect, the will to empire had most certainly gone. And the sense of enterprise and of adventure and of push and of just a touch of arrogance too—of swagger, at least—that had been essential to the extension of the empire. All that had been kicked out of the British. Perhaps a very good thing too.

INTERVIEWER

There was such a show of panache, such a show of grandeur, such pageantry.

MORRIS

You mean the ending of it or the running of it?

INTERVIEWER

The running of it.

MORRIS

The ending of it too was done with a certain panache, a lot of grand pullings down of flags and trumpet calls and royalty going out to kiss prime ministers lately released from jail.

You begin the trilogy as James Morris. The second volume was written during the ten years of sexual ambiguity when you were taking female hormones but had not yet changed your gender. And the third was written as Jan Morris. To what extent is the character of the trilogy seasoned by this change?

MORRIS

I truly don't think at all, really. I've reread the books myself with this in mind. I don't think there is a great deal of difference. It was a purely intellectual or aesthetic, artistic approach to a fairly remote subject. It wasn't anything, I don't think, that could be affected much by my own personal affairs... less than other things I've written.

INTERVIEWER

The very heart of this question is: Do you feel your sensibilities at all changed?

MORRIS

That is a different question. The trilogy: I started it and finished it in the same frame of mind. But I suppose it is true that most of my work has been a protracted potter, looking at the world and allowing the world to look at me. And I suppose there can be no doubt that both the world's view of me and my view of the world have changed. Of course they have. The point of the book *Pleasures of a Tangled Life* is to try to present, or even to present to myself, what kind of sensibility has resulted from this experience. I'm sick to death of talking about the experience itself, as you can imagine, after twenty years. But I've come to recognize that what I am is the result of the experience itself. The tangle that was there is something that has gone subliminally through all my work. The one book I think isn't affected is the Pax Britannica trilogy.

INTERVIEWER
At the end of the trilogy you say that you've come to view empire less in historical than in redemptory terms. What do you mean?

MORRIS
I was thinking of Teilhard de Chardin's concept of "infurling," in which he thought that history, by a process of turning in upon itself, was very gradually bringing humanity and nature into a unity. When I was in Canada I came across an old newspaper article about a lecture on imperialism given in about 1902. Nearly all imperialist talk of that time was about the majesty of the British economic power or the strength of the navy. But this one wasn't at all; this lecturer viewed empire as an agent of love. He thought that among all these mixed emotions there was a common thread of love—of people being fond of each other and trying to do the best for each other. And I've come to think that the good is simply more resilient than the bad. If you have a great historical process like the British Empire, the bad is dross; it is thrown away. The good is what stays on. There was some good in imperialism. It did enable people to get to know each other better than they had before. It allowed people to break away from shackling old traditions and heritages. It introduced the world to fresh ideas and new opportunities. These are the

contributions that matter for the redemption and the unity of us all. Although I am at heart against empires, I do think that the British did leave behind them a great number of friends.

At the end of the trilogy you ask, "Is that the truth? Is that how it was? It is *my* truth... Its emotions are coloured by mine, its scenes are heightened or diminished by my vision... If it is not invariably true in the fact, it is certainly true in the imagination." In what way is this statement true of any history?

Oh, I think it can be untrue of some histories... There are people who write history as a deliberate distortion because they want to deliver a message or shove over a creed. Mine wasn't false in that sense. I tried to present both sides of the story. I didn't try to distort anything to fit another purpose.

I was thinking of that extra inch or half inch that Lytton Strachey added onto the archbishop. Such is the temptation when one is writing history—to add that extra inch.

Of course, there is one small distortion in my kind of history in that it aims to entertain. So it does in effect ignore little matters like economics. But I have a story too. In *Pleasures*, I have a piece about first enjoying food and drink. Until I was in my midtwenties, I didn't take much interest in them. But when I lunched in Australia at the famous cartoon-ist George Molnar's house on the lawn overlooking Sydney Harbor, the meal was something quite simple but delicious: pâté, crusty rolls, a bottle of wine, an apple, this sort of thing. There was something about the way this man presented and served the food. He crunched the bread in sort of a lascivious way. He spread the pâté kind of unguently. He almost slurped the wine. I thought it was so marvelous. When I came to describe it, I could see it all again so clearly: the dancing sea, the clear Australian sky, the green lawn; above us were the wings of the Sydney Opera House, like a benediction over this experience. It was only when I finished the chapter that I remembered that the Sydney Opera House hadn't been built yet!

INTERVIEWER

I would like to ask you about *The World of Venice*. Judging from the book and from the entire trilogy, you seem supremely interested in declines and falls. Are you trying to tell us about the decline and fall of the whole world, of reality in our time? And if so, is there any new beginning?

MORRIS

I certainly don't think that I'm trying to describe the decline and fall of the world. Rather, it seems more vigorous as every year goes by. Perhaps it is because I am aware of the excitement of the present age—the explosive beauty of the new technologies that are overcoming us, the vivacity of the world—that I am attracted to decline, to the melancholy spectacle of things that get old and die. But another reason I tend to write about decline is because I don't believe in pretending it doesn't exist. I believe in age; I believe in recognizing age. I'm sure that I shall always love Venice, but in a way I do wish it wasn't being touched up. I think it's trying to deny its age, pretending that it isn't antiquated and decrepit, which it is, really. One part of me is very attracted to that decline, and another part of me is fascinated by the fact that Venice denies that decline so adamantly. Such a scenario is not part of my view of the world in the 1990s. Rather, I take the opposite stance. I see the world today as in a very vigorous, virile, and interesting state.

INTERVIEWER

You first published *The World of Venice* in 1960 as James Morris. In the preface to the 1974 reprinted edition, you, as Jan Morris, see the book as a period piece: "Venice seen through a particular pair of eyes at a particular moment," which "cannot be modernized, as I supposed, with a few deft strokes of the felt-tipped pen." Would Jan have written a different book than James?

MORRIS

It's extremely hard to say. As a reprint it was no longer a contemporary portrait of the city because a lot had changed in the meantime. I resigned myself to the fact that the Venice I had described was my Venice, really. As to whether Jan Morris would write the book differently...I used to think that as Jan I tend to concentrate more on the smaller things, the details, rather than on the grand sweep of things. But as I've got older, I've come to think that the grand sweep and the details are exactly the same; the macrocosm and the microcosm are identical.

255

You speak of the book on Venice as "a highly subjective, romantic, impressionistic picture, less of a city
than of an experience." Is that true of any city you
portray? Is it more true in some cases than in others?

MORRIS

It's true of them all, certainly. I'm not the sort of
writer who tries to tell other people what they are
going to get out of the city. I don't consider my
books travel books. I don't like travel books, as I said
before. I don't believe in them as a genre of literature.
Every city I describe is really only a description of
me looking at the city or responding to it. Of course,
some cities have a more brilliant image. In this case
the city overtakes me so that I find I am not, after all,
describing what I feel about the city but describing
something very, very powerful about the city itself.
For example, Beijing: I went to that city in my usual
frame of mind, in which I follow two precepts. The
first I draw from E. M. Forster's advice that in order
to see the city of Alexandria best one ought to wander
around aimlessly. The other I take from the Psalms;
you might remember the line "grin like a dog and
run about the city."

INTERVIEWER

And scare the hell out of the populace!

MORRIS

Yes. Well, I went into Beijing wandering aimlessly
and grinning like a dog and running about in the
usual way, but it didn't work! Beijing was too big for
me. Its size imposed upon what I wrote about the city.

In the introduction to your collection of writings about cities you say that you've accomplished at last what you set out to do.

MORRIS

I drew an imaginary, figurative line between two cities, Budapest and Bucharest. All cities above that line qualify as what seem to me "great cities," and all below that line could be very interesting but not in the same class. So I resolved that before I died I would visit and write about all the cities above the Bucharest line. I could do some below if I wanted to, but I would try to do all the ones above. In the end I did. Beijing was the last one.

INTERVIEWER

Is there any place you haven't written about that you would like to?

MORRIS

I think I'm tired of writing about places qua places— if I ever did that. But I've never been into Tibet proper (only on the frontier) and I would like to go there, also Vladivostok—both places where the situation would be as interesting to write about as the locality.

INTERVIEWER

Is there any place you have been unable to capture?

MORRIS

I always think London has defeated me; probably heaps of other places too—who am I to judge?

You say that by 1980 you had fallen out of love with Venice. What happened?

I fall in and out of love with Venice very frequently as a matter of fact. I've known Venice since the end of the Second World War. For most of that time Venice has been trying to find a role for itself, to be a creative, living city, or to be a kind of museum city that we all go and look at. At one time it was intended to be a dormitory town for the big industrial complex around the lagoon and Mestre. That fell through because of pollution, so Venice was out on a limb again. The attempt to bring it into the modern world had failed. Then one day I saw that the golden horses of Saint Mark's were no longer on the facade of the basilica. They'd taken the statues down and put them inside. Outside they'd placed some dummies... good replicas, but without the sheen and the scratches, the age and the magic of the old ones. I thought, This is the moment when Venice has decided. It won't be a great diplomatic, mercantile, or political city, nor will it be a great seaport of the East. Instead it will be a museum that we can all visit. Maybe that's the right thing for it, anyway. Age has crept up on it. It can't do it anymore. Perhaps that's the answer. For a time I went along with that, but in the last five or ten years mass tourism has taken such a turn, especially in Europe and particularly in Venice. It seems to me that the poor old place is too swamped with tourism to survive as even a viable museum unless it takes really drastic steps to keep people out.

Still, there are strange, haunted squares in Venice that one can find, away from tourists.

MORRIS

There are haunted squares where one can sit in Indianapolis!

INTERVIEWER

Those dummy horses are very significant to me too, but to me they meant something slightly different. They seemed to be symbols of the decline and fall of reality in my time.

MORRIS

If it is true about the decline and fall of reality, then its chief agency is tourism. Tourism encourages unreality. It's easier in the tourist context to be unreal than real. It's the easiest thing in the world to buy a funny old Welsh hat and pop it on and sit outside selling rock in some bogus tavern. It's much easier than being real, contemporary. Tourism encourages and abets this sham-ness wherever it touches. I detest it.

INTERVIEWER

For those who don't know what "rock" is, it's a very sweet candy.

MORRIS

And it can have the name of the place written all the way through it. However much you chew it, it still says *Wales*. Wales, Wales, Wales.

In your book *Conundrum* you answer almost every conceivable question about your decision to change your gender and the process involved. Your life seems made up of journeys, both in terms of travel and of personal exploration. To what extent was travel a relief or escape from feeling trapped in a man's body?

MORRIS

You mean just ordinary travel, don't you, not travel in a metaphysical sense?

INTERVIEWER

We can come to metaphysical travel later.

MORRIS

Well, I used to think it hadn't anything to do with escape because I've always enjoyed traveling; it's one of my great pleasures. My original travels were not quite voluntary. I went abroad with the British army, and there wasn't much sense of escape in that. But later I did begin to believe that maybe there was some sort of allegorical meaning to my traveling. I thought that the restlessness I was possessed by was, perhaps, some yearning, not so much for the sake of escape as for the sake of quest: a quest for unity, a search for wholeness. I certainly didn't think of it that way in the beginning, but I've come to think it might be so.

INTERVIEWER

From what I know of you, both personally and through your writing, I think it must be so.

I've become obsessed with the idea of reconciliation, particularly reconciliation with nature but with people too, of course. I think that travel has been a kind of search for that, a pursuit for unity and even an attempt to contribute to a sense of unity.

INTERVIEWER

Your description of climbing Mount Everest is such an extraordinary symbolic venture.

MORRIS

Well, it's nice to have it thought of as symbolism, but I really don't think of it that way. It was just an assignment, and I did it.

INTERVIEWER

So you have nothing to say about metaphysical travel then?

MORRIS

No, because it seems to me such an inner, indeed inmost matter that, old pro as I am, I can't put it into words.

INTERVIEWER

Is there a book you've written as Jan that James would not have written?

MORRIS

Pleasures of a Tangled Life. The whole point of this book of essays is to try to present the sensibility that has been created or has evolved out of "the conundrum experience," as we say in our evasive, euphemistic way. People who come to interview me at home often ask, Do you mind if we talk about the conundrum thing? The book tries to present, to readers as well as myself, what kind of a sensibility has resulted from this sort of thing. I think the conundrum aspect runs subliminally through the whole book. I recognize that the pleasures, nearly all of them, are ones that I enjoy in a particular way because of "the conundrum thing."

INTERVIEWER

Let's talk about *Sydney* (1992). How do you prepare yourself for a particular book?

MORRIS

First of all I decide why I want to write the book. The reason I wanted to write *Sydney* gets me back to the good old empire once again. It seems to me that when the tide of empire withdrew it left behind on the sands of the world a whole lot of objects, some of them unpleasant, some of them dull, but one of them particularly glittering. Not the nicest object, rather a sharp, hard object, but a brilliant one. And that seemed to me the city of Sydney, New South Wales, a city that is not only a remnant of that old empire but also, in a way, the New City. It is creating new people in the same way that America created new people in the 1780s. So I decided that would be a good book to do. I wanted to conclude my commitment, my obsession with the empire. And I thought Sydney was a good place to end with. Somebody reviewing *Sydney* said that most of the books I'd written were cousins to empire in some way; they're related.

At what point during the progress of the book do you feel that you've captured your subject, that the place is yours?

MORRIS

It varies. I usually write the first draft in a sort of stream-of-consciousness way, without thinking very hard about it. I let it all go through. Then when I go back to the second draft, very often I find that what I've already got is much better than what I've planned. Sometimes the unconscious bit is very much better than the conscious bit. I'm a weak person, and so I do, in fact, always replace the unconscious with the conscious bit, but I'm often wrong in doing so. Sometimes I go back and see that the early draft is better and more natural. Incidentally, talking of stream of consciousness, after forty years of trying I've finished Joyce's *Ulysses*. I must say I still think life is too short for *Finnegans Wake*.

INTERVIEWER

Do you feel you got to the *bottom* of Sydney in this book?

MORRIS

No, I don't think so. I got to the bottom, as I say, of my own feelings about it. Sydney is not a city that at first sight is going to incite one's sensibilities. It wants to be frank, macho, fun, you know. But the more I felt the city, the more I thought about the city, the more I realized that sort of *wistful* quality in it, which perhaps is behind all such macho places, really.

A wistful quality?

MORRIS

Yes. It's a kind of yearning. Often what I feel about
the Australians themselves is that they resist it a bit
because they don't feel they ought to feel these sort of
feelings. But they probably do, really, I think. It has
something to do with the landscape. D. H. Lawrence
got it all those years ago.

INTERVIEWER

But when you have a city, such as Sydney, that's a
little bit elusive in terms of its wistful quality, how
does that reveal itself to you? Is the realization an
active process on your part, or is it something that
just flowers as you spend time there?

MORRIS

I think that it is purely passive. All I do, really, is
to go to the place and just think about nothing else
whatever except that place. I have to say in the case
of Sydney that if its transcendental quality hadn't
emerged the book might have been a little bit boring.
I didn't know it was going to show itself. I felt it more
and more the longer I stayed there.

INTERVIEWER

So it wasn't an immediate transcendence?

MORRIS

No. A lot of people see *Sydney* as if it were a "road to
Damascus" experience. It wasn't.

You use anecdotes and stories in certain places to punctuate the narrative. Do you consciously use the techniques of fiction to move a narrative along?

MORRIS

I do believe in the techniques of fiction, so I'm very gratified you should ask this. I really don't see that there's much difference between writing a book of this kind and writing a novel. The situations that arise are the sort of situations you'd often make up—the background you would devise for a novel, the characters you would produce for a novel. And you have an added attraction, of course: the fact that the overwhelming character of the whole book is the city itself, which is an advantage you have over the novelist. Paul Theroux said to me once that he liked writing travel books because they gave him a plot; he didn't have to think one up. It works the other way around too. I edited the travel writings of Virginia Woolf. *To the Lighthouse* is in many ways a travel book: the descriptions of the journey across the bay, the views that she provides, are exactly what she would do if she were writing a work of literary travel.

INTERVIEWER

What aspect did the sensibility and change of sensibility based on "the conundrum experience," which you discussed in *Pleasures of a Tangled Life*, play in writing *Sydney*?

MORRIS

Well, of course, *Pleasures of a Tangled Life* was a very much more varied book. It dealt specifically with personal aspects of life, personal views: what happened to me at home, how I feel about different aspects of life and of living and of art and of religion... So, naturally, that presents a sensibility far more directly, doesn't it, more immediately, than a book like *Sydney*. On the other hand, I think if you compare with a compassionate eye, a sympathetic eye, a book like *Sydney* with a book like *Oxford*, which I wrote in 1965, I think you would think, if you were intelligent enough, that there was a different person writing. You might not think the style had changed enormously, but I think you'd find the mind behind it or the feeling behind it, the sensibility behind it, had changed. Yes, I think I would think that about *Sydney*. It's a gentler book, of course.

INTERVIEWER

When you're researching a book, do you travel alone?

MORRIS

I generally travel alone, but sometimes with my partner, with whom I've lived for forty years. But dearly though I love her, if I'm going to be working I find I'm better on my own. Love is rather inhibiting in my view. We are always thinking about what each other wants to do. Whereas to be writing about a place you've got to be utterly selfish. You've only got to think about the place that you're writing. Your antenna must be out all the time picking up vibrations and details. If you've got somebody with you, especially somebody you're fond of, it doesn't work so well. So, although I never have the heart to tell her this, I would really rather not have her come along.

If you're going to be any kind of writer you've got to be utterly selfish.

And lonely, I suppose.

How long do you stay in a place?

That depends entirely on the nature of the thing that I'm writing. If I'm commissioned by a magazine to write an essay, what I do is go to the place for a week and think about nothing but that place. And then, the last few days, in a kind of frenzy of ecstasy or despair, I write three drafts of the essay, one draft each day. I write continuously—it doesn't matter how many hours—until the thing is done. I love the feeling of wrapping the whole thing up, popping it off in the post and going somewhere else. It is very satisfying. I do think that the impact of it, the suddenness and abruptness of it, makes it go better.

The best book about a place I've ever written is the one about Spain. I hardly knew Spain, but I was commissioned to go there for six months to write a book about it. So I bought a Volkswagen camper bus, and off I set to this country that I knew nothing about. The impact was tremendous; I thought about nothing but Spain for the entire six months. When it was finished I remember watching an airplane going overhead and thinking, There goes my lovely manuscript, on its way to New York. That book, because it was done in a mood of high ecstasy and excitement, was the best of the lot.

How does your mood affect your impression of a place? What you write about it?

I am nothing if not a professional, and I long ago learned to aim off for mood, weather, or chance encounters: but of course if I spent a week somewhere with a permanent headache, in perpetual drizzle, encountering only grumpy citizens, I can see that my essay might not be as exuberant as it might be.

You mentioned being lonely...

Yes. Well, I'm not lonely when I travel, but like every writer, I'm a bit lonely when I have to sit down and write the thing, because you can only do that by yourself. I do it rather laboriously, three times over. It's a long process. During that time I'm pretty reclusive and shuttered. But traveling, no, less so than it used to be, really, because, you know, I've been doing it an awfully long time. Wherever I go now I know people. So there's no need for me to be lonely if I don't want to be lonely. The lonely part of it is the technicality of being a writer, which is naturally a lonely one anyway. You can't talk to people while you're writing. You can't work while the television is on.

You could have music.

Lately I bought a little electronic keyboard so that every now and then I break off and play something.

What do you play?

Sometimes if I've got the score, I play the solo part of concertos. I'm very good on the Mendelssohn violin concertos.

How important are languages? How many languages do you speak and to what extent is that critical in investigating a place?

Well, it has been crucial in a way in my choice of subjects. Because so much of my time has been spent with the British Empire and its cousinships, English was the lingua franca so that was no problem. But because I am a poor linguist I've done very few—no books, really, except *Venice*—about cities where the foreign language is essential. I speak sort of pidgin French and Italian. I learned some Arabic years ago, but that wouldn't, for example, qualify me to write a book about Moscow or Berlin, would it? And unlike some of my colleagues, I'm not sure I've got the dedication to learn an entirely new language in order to write a book about that country. Colin Thubron, for example, to write a book about traveling through China actually sat down and learned Mandarin.

So what did you do, say, when you were investigating Venice? Did you use translators?

Well, I'm not too bad on Italian. Do you know that story? Hemingway said what an easy language Italian was, and his Italian friend said, In that case, Mr. Hemingway, why not undertake the use of grammar? When I went to Spain, commissioned to do a short, sixty-thousand-word book, I bought a recorded language course. And the book's been in print ever since.

Has technology, notably the advent of the word processor, changed your technique or style in any way?

I do use a word processor, but it hasn't changed my writing in any way whatever. The belief that style and mental capacity depend upon the instrument one uses is a superstition. I will write with anything at any time. I've used them all—the fountain pen, manual typewriter, electric typewriter—and none has made the slightest difference. But with a word processor I won't type the first few drafts on disk because there is the temptation simply to fiddle with the text, to juggle with it. The word processor is useful to me only for the final draft of the thing. I do think that the word processor for a writer's last draft is a wonderful thing because you can go on and on polishing the thing.

INTERVIEWER

Do you feel that having been a man at one time in your life gives you more courage to make excursions on your own?

MORRIS

Yes. There's a hangover from the confidence I had as a man. When I started, the feminist movement hadn't really happened, so, of course, there was more of a gulf between a male and female traveler. Now things are very, very different. Many women are unnecessarily timid about travel. I don't believe it is so different for a woman or a man nowadays. Of course, there are actual physical dangers of a different kind. But the general run of hazard is exactly the same for men as for women, and the treatment that a woman gets when traveling is, by and large, better. People are less frightened of you. They tend to trust you more. The relationship between women, between one woman and another, is a much closer one than the relationship between men. Wherever a woman travels in the world she's got a few million friends waiting to help her.

INTERVIEWER

You say that you read about and study a place you've never been to before going there to write about it. Do you find that the place turns out to be largely what you expect it to be or exactly what you did not expect it to be?

It's a long time since I've had to write about a place I didn't know. Nowadays, I generally write about places I know about already. But I think some of the great travel books have not prepared me for the place I'm going to. One of them is one of my favorite books, Doughty's *Arabia Deserta*; it's a marvelous book and a great work of art, but the image it presents of the desert and its life isn't the image I felt. I'm not grumbling at all. He wasn't trying to tell me what *I* was going to see in the desert. He was just telling me what the desert was like to him. But that's one book that doesn't seem to match up to my own conceptions of the desert. Sterne, for example, too. I can't say that France seems very much like *A Sentimental Journey* to me. There are some other people too, like Kingslake, who wrote deliberately in an entertaining mode, consciously painting an arresting picture of life. It isn't much like it when you get there.

INTERVIEWER

Back to the dissolution of empires. We've watched the waning and extinction of another great empire, the Soviet Union.

MORRIS

The tragedy of the Soviet Union was that it marked the decline of an ideological empire. The British Empire really had no ideology, except one that had evolved by a kind of rule of thumb, changing as it went along. There was a general rule of fair play about it. But the moral purpose behind the Soviet Empire seems to have been a different thing altogether. I've always been very attracted to the idea of communism. If I'd been alive in those days I probably would have been a communist. The tragedy of it was, it seems to me, that it was so soon perverted. The revolution was betrayed. It sank into the horrors of Stalinism, sliding slowly into the awful mires of inefficiency, disillusion, unhappiness, and despair that we see now. The failure of it seems to be that although it set out ideologically to provide welfare for a people, it utterly lacked the idea of giving its people happiness. If political ideology doesn't take into account the human desire for happiness, it seems to me bound to fail. Perhaps this is why your system is so successful, because it actually does talk about the pursuit of happiness, doesn't it? That's a different matter altogether.

INTERVIEWER

I once met someone who had visited London and had refused to go back so as not to obliterate the memory she had of it twenty-eight years earlier. Have you ever felt that way about any place?

MORRIS

Yes, I think I have. I've often had doubts about going back, but I find that often they are ill founded. Chicago is one of them. I first went to Chicago in 1953, and I've been commissioned several times since then to go back. Each time I thought, This is a mistake. It's not going to be what you thought it was; you'll be disappointed. But it wasn't so. Recently I wrote a very long essay about it, and it came off just as well as it had in previous times. Although in principle I agree with your friend, in practice it doesn't seem to be true.

Why do you think Chicago works so well for you? Has it changed?

Yes, of course, it has changed enormously since I first went there, but it's not the change that excites me; it's the sameness—the fact that it still feels like most of us foreigners really want America to feel. There's a touch of an immensely urbane, sophisticated Norman Rockwell to Chicago that we innocents like.

You've called Chicago the perfect city. Is that still true?

I don't think I said "perfect." What I do mean is that, among twentieth-century cities, Chicago comes nearest to the ideal of a perfect city ... an aesthetically perfect city. The shape of it seems to me fine and logical, and the buildings are magnificent. It is the most underrated of all the metropolises of the world in my opinion. I don't think many people say, I must go and look at that Chicago! Dickens did, though. As he drove in by train the conductor came through and said, Mr. Dickens, you're entering the boss city of the universe.

You've written thirty-two books to date, by our count eighteen as James, fourteen as Jan. You've accomplished everything you set out to do?

By no means. There's one particular thing I've failed to do. This experience of mine that every now and then crops up ... I think I've failed to use it artistically in the way I might have used it. A sex change is a very extraordinary thing for someone to have gone through and particularly extraordinary for a writer, I think. But although, as I say and you recognize, the effects of it appear kind of subliminally through everything I've written, I don't believe I've created a work of art around it.

I think *Fisher's Face* was, as some percipient critics saw, a kind of artistic product of this predicament—it is my favorite among my books—but I still haven't devised any more explicit way of using it. Perhaps I've left it too late?

(1997)

Joan Didion

THE ART OF NONFICTION NO. I

Interviewed by Hilton Als

The last time this magazine spoke with Joan Didion, in August of 1977, she was living in California and had just published her third novel, *A Book of Common Prayer*. Didion was forty-two years old and well-known not only for her fiction but also for her work in magazines—reviews, reportage, and essays—some of which had been collected in *Slouching Towards Bethlehem* (1968). In addition, Didion and her husband, John Gregory Dunne (who was himself the subject of a *Paris Review* interview in 1996), had written a number of screenplays together, including *The Panic in Needle Park* (1971); a 1972 adaptation of her second novel, *Play It As It Lays* (1970); and *A Star Is Born* (1976). When Didion's first interview appeared in these pages in 1978, she was intent on exploring her gift for fiction and nonfiction. Since then, her breadth and craft as a writer have only grown deeper with each project.

Joan Didion was born in Sacramento, and both her parents, too, were native Californians. She studied English at Berkeley, and in 1956, after graduating, she won an essay contest sponsored by *Vogue* and moved to New York City to join the magazine's editorial staff. While at *Vogue*, she wrote fashion copy, as well as book and movie reviews. She also became a frequent contributor to *National Review*, among other publications. In 1963, Didion published her first novel, *Run River*. The next year she married Dunne, and soon afterward, they moved to Los Angeles. There, in 1965, they adopted their only child, Quintana Roo.

In 1973, Didion began writing for *The New York Review of Books*, where she has remained a regular contributor. While she has continued to write novels in recent decades—*Democracy* (1984) and *The Last Thing He Wanted* (1996)—she has increasingly explored different forms of nonfiction: critical essay, political reportage, memoir. In 1979, she published a second collection of her magazine work, *The White Album*, which was followed by *Salvador* (1983), *Miami* (1987), *After Henry* (1992), *Political Fictions* (2001), and *Where I Was From* (2003). In the spring of 2005, Didion was awarded a Gold Medal from the American Academy of Arts and Letters.

In December of 2003, shortly before their fortieth anniversary, Didion's husband died. Last fall, she published *The Year of Magical Thinking*, a book-length meditation on grief and memory. It became a best seller, and won the National Book Award for nonfiction; Didion is now adapting the book for the stage as a monologue. Two months before the book's publication, Didion's thirty-nine-year-old daughter died after a long illness.

Our conversation took place over the course of two afternoons in the Manhattan apartment Didion shared with her husband. On the walls of the spacious flat, one could see many photographs of Didion, Dunne, and their daughter. Daylight flooded the book-filled parlor. "When we got the place, we assumed the sun went all through the apartment. It doesn't," Didion said, laughing. Her laughter was the additional punctuation to her precise speech.

INTERVIEWER

By now you've written at least as much nonfiction as you have fiction. How would you describe the difference between writing the one or the other?

JOAN DIDION

Writing fiction is for me a fraught business, an occasion of daily dread for at least the first half of the novel, and sometimes all the way through. The work process is totally different from writing nonfiction. You have to sit down every day and make it up. You have no notes—or sometimes you do, I made extensive notes for *A Book of Common Prayer*—but the notes give you only the background, not the novel itself. In nonfiction the notes give you the piece. Writing nonfiction is more like sculpture, a matter of shaping the research into the finished thing. Novels are like paintings, specifically watercolors. Every stroke you put down you have to go with. Of course you can rewrite, but the original strokes are still there in the texture of the thing.

Do you do a lot of rewriting?

When I'm working on a book, I constantly retype my own sentences. Every day I go back to page one and just retype what I have. It gets me into a rhythm. Once I get over maybe a hundred pages, I won't go back to page one, but I might go back to page fifty-five, or twenty, even. But then every once in a while I feel the need to go to page one again and start rewriting. At the end of the day, I mark up the pages I've done—pages or *page*—all the way back to page one. I mark them up so that I can retype them in the morning. It gets me past that blank terror.

Did you do that sort of retyping for *The Year of Magical Thinking*?

I did. It was especially important with this book because so much of it depended on echo. I wrote it in three months, but I marked it up every night.

The book moves quickly. Did you think about how your readers would read it?

Of course, you always think about how it will be read. I always aim for a reading in one sitting.

At what point did you know that the notes you were writing in response to John's death would be a book for publication?

John died December 30, 2003. Except for a few lines written a day or so after he died, I didn't begin making the notes that became the book until the following October. After a few days of making notes, I realized that I was thinking about how to structure a book, which was the point at which I realized that I was writing one. This realization in no way changed what I was writing.

Was it difficult to finish the book? Or were you happy to have your life back—to live with a lower level of self-scrutiny?

Yes. It was difficult to finish the book. I didn't want to let John go. I don't really have my life back yet, since Quintana died only on August 26.

Since you write about yourself, interviewers tend to ask about your personal life; I want to ask you about writing and books. In the past you've written pieces on V. S. Naipaul, Graham Greene, Norman Mailer, and Ernest Hemingway—titanic, controversial iconoclasts whom you tend to defend. Were these the writers you grew up with and wanted to emulate?

Hemingway was really early. I probably started reading him when I was just eleven or twelve. There was just something magnetic to me in the arrangement of those sentences. Because they were so simple— or rather they appeared to be so simple, but they weren't.

Something I was looking up the other day, that's been in the back of my mind, is a study done several years ago about young women's writing skills and the incidence of Alzheimer's. As it happens, the subjects were all nuns, because all of these women had been trained in a certain convent. They found that those who wrote simple sentences as young women later had a higher incidence of Alzheimer's, while those who wrote complicated sentences with several clauses had a lower incidence of Alzheimer's. The assumption—which I thought was probably erroneous—was that those who tended to write simple sentences as young women did not have strong memory skills.

Though you wouldn't classify Hemingway's sentences as simple.

No, they're deceptively simple because he always brings a change in.

Did you think you could write that kind of sentence? Did you want to try?

I didn't think that I could do them, but I thought that I could learn—because they felt so natural. I could see how they worked once I started typing them out. That was when I was about fifteen. I would just type those stories. It's a great way to get rhythms into your head.

INTERVIEWER

Did you read anyone else before Hemingway?

DIDION

No one who attracted me in that way. I had been reading a lot of plays. I had a misguided idea that I wanted to act. The form this took was not acting, however, but reading plays. Sacramento was not a place where you saw a lot of plays. I think the first play I ever saw was the Lunts in the touring company of *O Mistress Mine*. I don't think that that's what inspired me. The Theatre Guild used to do plays on the radio, and I remember being very excited about listening to them. I remember memorizing speeches from *Death of a Salesman* and *Member of the Wedding* in the period right after the war.

INTERVIEWER

Which playwrights did you read?

DIDION

I remember at one point going through everything of Eugene O'Neill's. I was struck by the sheer theatricality of his plays. You could see how they worked. I read them all one summer. I had nosebleeds, and for some reason it took all summer to get the appointment to get my nose cauterized. So I just lay still on the porch all day and read Eugene O'Neill. That was all I did. And dab at my face with an ice cube.

INTERVIEWER
What you really seem to have responded to in these early influences was style—voice and form.

DIDION
Yes, but another writer I read in high school who just knocked me out was Theodore Dreiser. I read *An American Tragedy* all in one weekend and couldn't put it down—I locked myself in my room. Now that was antithetical to every other book I was reading at the time because Dreiser really had no style, but it was powerful.

And one book I totally missed when I first read it was *Moby-Dick*. I reread it when Quintana was assigned it in high school. It was clear that she wasn't going to get through it unless we did little talks about it at dinner. I had not gotten it at all when I read it at her age. I had missed that wild control of language. What I had thought discursive were really these great leaps. The book had just seemed a jumble; I didn't get the control in it.

INTERVIEWER
After high school you wanted to go to Stanford. Why?

DIDION
It's pretty straightforward—all my friends were going to Stanford.

INTERVIEWER

But you went to Berkeley and majored in literature. What were you reading there?

DIDION

The people I did the most work on were Henry James and D. H. Lawrence, who I was not high on. He irritated me on almost every level.

INTERVIEWER

He didn't know anything about women at all.

DIDION

No, nothing. And the writing was so clotted and sentimental. It didn't work for me on any level.

INTERVIEWER

Was he writing too quickly, do you think?

DIDION

I don't know, I think he just had a clotted and sentimental mind.

INTERVIEWER

You mentioned reading *Moby-Dick*. Do you do much rereading?

DIDION

I often reread *Victory*, which is maybe my favorite book in the world.

INTERVIEWER

Conrad? Really? Why?

The story is told thirdhand. It's not a story the narrator even heard from someone who experienced it. The narrator seems to have heard it from people he runs into around the Strait of Malacca. So there's this fantastic distancing of the narrative, except that when you're in the middle of it, it remains very immediate. It's incredibly skillful. I have never started a novel—I mean except the first, when I was starting a novel just to start a novel—I've never written one without rereading *Victory*. It opens up the possibilities of a novel. It makes it seem worth doing. In the same way, John and I always prepared for writing a movie by watching *The Third Man*. It's perfectly told.

Conrad was also a huge inspiration for Naipaul, whose work you admire. What drew you to Naipaul?

I read the nonfiction first. But the novel that really attracted me—and I still read the beginning of it now and then—is *Guerrillas*. It has that bauxite factory in the opening pages, which just gives you the whole feel of that part of the world. That was a thrilling book to me. The nonfiction had the same effect on me as reading Elizabeth Hardwick—you get the sense that it's possible simply to go through life noticing things and writing them down and that this is okay, it's worth doing. That the seemingly insignificant things that most of us spend our days noticing are really significant, have meaning, and tell us something. Naipaul is a great person to read before you have to do a piece. And Edmund Wilson, his essays for *The American Earthquake*. They have that everyday-traveler-in-the-world aspect, which is the opposite of an authoritative tone.

Was it as a student at Berkeley that you began to feel that you were a writer?

No, it began to feel almost impossible at Berkeley because we were constantly being impressed with the fact that everybody else had done it already and better. It was very daunting to me. I didn't think I could write. It took me a couple of years after I got out of Berkeley before I dared to start writing. That academic mind-set—which was kind of shallow in my case anyway—had begun to fade. Then I did write a novel over a long period of time, *Run River*. And after that it seemed feasible that maybe I could write another one.

You had come to New York by then and were working at *Vogue*, while writing at night. Did you see writing that novel as a way of being back in California?

Yes, it was a way of not being homesick. But I had a really hard time getting the next book going. I couldn't get past a few notes. It was *Play It As It Lays*, but it wasn't called that—I mean it didn't have a name and it wasn't what it is. For one, it was set in New York. Then, in June of 1964, John and I went to California and I started doing pieces for *The Saturday*

Evening Post. We needed the money because neither one of us was working. And during the course of doing these pieces I was out in the world enough that an actual story for this so-called second novel presented itself, and then I started writing it.

INTERVIEWER
What had you been missing about California? What were you not getting in New York?

DIDION
Rivers. I was living on the East Side, and on the weekend I'd walk over to the Hudson and then I'd walk back to the East River. I kept thinking, All right, they are rivers, but they aren't California rivers. I really missed California rivers. Also the sun going down in the West. That's one of the big advantages to Columbia-Presbyterian hospital—you can see the sunset. There's always something missing about late afternoon to me on the East Coast. Late afternoon on the West Coast ends with the sky doing all its brilliant stuff. Here it just gets dark.

The other thing I missed was horizons. I missed that on the West Coast, too, if we weren't living at the beach, but I noticed at some point that practically every painting or lithograph I bought had a horizon in it. Because it's very soothing.

INTERVIEWER
Why did you decide to come back east in 1988?

DIDION
Part of it was that Quintana was in college here, at Barnard, and part of it was that John was between

books and having a hard time getting started on a new one. He felt that it was making him stale to be in one place for a long time. We had been living in Brentwood for ten years, which was longer than we had ever lived in any one place. And I think he just thought it was time to move. I didn't particularly, but we left. Even before moving, we had a little apartment in New York. To justify having it, John felt that we had to spend some periods of time there, which was extremely inconvenient for me. The apartment in New York was not very comfortable, and on arrival you would always have to arrange to get the windows washed and get food in... It was cheaper when we stayed at the Carlyle.

INTERVIEWER

But when you finally moved to New York, was it a bad move?

DIDION

No, it was fine. It just took me about a year, maybe two years all told. The time spent looking for an apartment, selling the house in California, the actual move, having work done, remembering where I put things when I unpacked—it probably took two years out of my effective working life. Though I feel that it's been the right place to be after John died. I would not have wanted to be in a house in Brentwood Park after he died.

INTERVIEWER

Why not?

For entirely logistical reasons. In New York I didn't
need to drive to dinner. There wasn't likely to be a
brush fire. I wasn't going to see a snake in the pool.

You said that you started writing for *The Saturday
Evening Post* because you and John were broke. Is
that where the idea of working for movies came
from—the need for cash?

Yes it was. One of the things that had made us go to
Los Angeles was we had a nutty idea that we could
write for television. We had a bunch of meetings
with television executives, and they would explain to
us, for example, the principle of *Bonanza*. The principle of *Bonanza* was: break a leg at the Ponderosa. I
looked blankly at the executive and he said, Somebody rides into town, and to make the story work,
he's got to break a leg so he's around for two weeks.
So we never wrote for *Bonanza*. We did, however,
have one story idea picked up by *Chrysler Theatre*.
We were paid a thousand dollars for it.

That was also why we started to write for the
movies. We thought of it as a way to buy time. But
nobody was asking us to write movies. John and his
brother Nick and I took an option on *The Panic in
Needle Park* and put it together ourselves. I had read
the book by James Mills and it just immediately said
movie to me. I think that the three of us each put in a
thousand dollars, which was enormous at the time.

How did you make it work as a collaboration? What were the mechanics?

On that one, my memory is that I wrote the treatment, which was just voices. Though whenever I say I did something, or vice versa, the other person would go over it, run it through the typewriter. It was always a back-and-forth thing.

Did you learn anything about writing from the movie work?

Yes. I learned a lot of fictional technique. Before I'd written movies, I never could do big set-piece scenes with a lot of different speakers—when you've got twelve people around a dinner table talking at cross purposes. I had always been impressed by other people's ability to do that. Anthony Powell comes to mind. I think the first book I did those big scenes in was *A Book of Common Prayer*.

But screenwriting is very different from prose narrative.

It's *not* writing. You're making notes for the director—for the director more than the actors. Sydney Pollack once told us that every screenwriter should go to the Actors Studio because there was no better way to learn what an actor needed. I'm guilty of not thinking enough about what actors need. I think instead about what the director needs.

John wrote that Robert De Niro asked you to write a scene in *True Confessions* without a single word of dialogue—the opposite of your treatment for *The Panic in Needle Park*.

Yeah, which is great. It's something that every writer understands, but if you turn in a scene like that to a producer, he's going to want to know where the words are.

At the other end of the writing spectrum, there's *The New York Review of Books* and your editor there, Robert Silvers. In the seventies you wrote for him about Hollywood, Woody Allen, Naipaul, and Patty Hearst. All of those essays were, broadly speaking, book reviews. How did you make the shift to pure reporting for the *Review*?

In 1982, John and I were going to San Salvador, and Bob expressed interest in having one or both of us write something about it. After we'd been there a few days, it became clear that I was going to do it rather than John, because John was working on a novel. Then when I started writing it, it got very long. I gave it to Bob, in its full length, and my idea was that he would figure out something to take from it. I didn't hear from him for a long time. So I wasn't expecting much, but then he called and said he was going to run the whole thing, in three parts.

INTERVIEWER
So he was able to find the through-line of the piece?

DIDION
The through-line in *Salvador* was always pretty clear: I went somewhere, this is what I saw. Very simple, like a travel piece. How Bob edited *Salvador* was by constantly nudging me toward updates on the situation and by pointing out weaker material. When I gave him the text, for example, it had a very weak ending, which was about meeting an American evangelical student on the flight home. In other words it was the travel piece carried to its logical and not very interesting conclusion. The way Bob led me away from this was to suggest not that I cut it (it's still there), but that I follow it—and so ground it— with a return to the political situation.

INTERVIEWER
How did you decide to write about Miami in 1987?

DIDION
Ever since the Kennedy assassination, I had wanted to do something that took place in that part of the world. I thought it was really interesting that so much of the news in America, especially if you read through the assassination hearings, was coming out of our political relations with the Caribbean and Central and South America. So when we got the little apartment in New York, I thought, Well, that's

something useful I can do out of New York: I can fly to Miami.

INTERVIEWER
Had you spent time down south before that?

DIDION
Yes, in 1970. I had been writing a column for *Life*, but neither *Life* nor I was happy with it. We weren't on the same page. I had a contract, so if I turned something in, they had to pay me. But it was soul searing to turn things in that didn't run. So after about seven columns, I quit. It was agreed that I would do longer pieces. And I said that I was interested in driving around the Gulf Coast, and somehow that got translated into "The Mind of the White South." I had a theory that if I could understand the South, I would understand something about California, because a lot of the California settlers came from the Border South. So I wanted to look into that. It turned out that what I was actually interested in was the South as a gateway to the Caribbean. I should have known that at the time because my original plan had been to drive all over the Gulf Coast.

We began that trip in New Orleans and spent a week there. New Orleans was fantastic. Then we drove around the Mississippi Coast, and that was fantastic too, but in New Orleans, you get a strong sense of the Caribbean. I used a lot of that week in New Orleans in *Common Prayer*. It was the most interesting place I had been in a long time. It was a week in which everything everybody said was astonishing to me.

Three years later you started writing for *The New York Review of Books*. Was that daunting? In your essay "Why I Write" (1976) you express trepidation about intellectual, or ostensibly intellectual, matters. What freed you up enough to do that work for Bob?

DIDION

His trust. Nothing else. I couldn't even have imagined it if he hadn't responded. He recognized that it was a learning experience for me. Domestic politics, for example, was something I simply knew nothing about. And I had no interest. But Bob kept pushing me in that direction. He is really good at ascertaining what might interest you at any given moment and then just throwing a bunch of stuff at you that might or might not be related, and letting you go with it.

When I went to the political conventions in 1988—it was the first time I'd ever been to a convention—he would fax down to the hotel the front pages of the *New York Times* and the *Washington Post*. Well, you know, if there's anything you can get at a convention it's a newspaper. But he just wanted to make sure.

And then he's meticulous once you turn in a piece, in terms of making you plug in all relevant information so that everything gets covered and defended before the letters come. He spent a lot of time, for example, making sure that I acknowledged all the issues in the Terri Schiavo piece, which had the potential for eliciting strong reactions. He's the person I trust more than anybody.

INTERVIEWER

Why do you think he pushed you to write about politics?

DIDION

I think he had a sense that I would be outside it enough.

INTERVIEWER

No insider reporting—you didn't know anyone.

DIDION

I didn't even know their names!

INTERVIEWER

But now your political writing has a very strong point of view—you take sides. Is that something that usually happens during the reporting process, or during the writing?

DIDION

If I am sufficiently interested in a political situation to write a piece about it, I generally have a point of view, although I don't usually recognize it. Something about a situation will bother me, so I will write a piece to find out what it is that bothers me.

INTERVIEWER

When you moved into writing about politics, you moved away from the more personal writing you'd been doing. Was that a deliberate departure?

DIDION

Yes, I was bored. For one thing, that kind of writing is limiting. Another reason was that I was getting a very strong response from readers, which was depressing because there was no way for me to reach out and help them back. I didn't want to become Miss Lonelyhearts.

And the pieces on El Salvador were the first in which politics really drive the narrative.

Actually it was a novel, *Common Prayer.* We had gone to a film festival in Cartagena and I got sick there, some kind of salmonella. We left Cartagena and went to Bogotá, and then we came back to Los Angeles and I was sick for about four months. I started doing a lot of reading about South America, where I'd never been. There's a passage by Christopher Isherwood in a book of his called *The Condor and the Cows*, in which he describes arriving in Venezuela and being astonished to think that it had been down there every day of his life. That was the way that I felt about South America. Then later I started reading a lot about Central America because it was becoming clear to me that my novel had to take place in a rather small country. So that was when I started thinking more politically.

But it still didn't push you into an interest in domestic politics.

I didn't get the connection. I don't know why I didn't get the connection, since I wasn't interested in the politics of these countries per se, but rather in how American foreign policy affected them. And the extent to which we are involved abroad is entirely driven by our own domestic politics. So I don't know why I didn't get that.

I started to get this in *Salvador*, but not fully until *Miami*. Our policy with Cuba and with exiles has been totally driven by domestic politics. It still is. But it was very hard for me to understand the process of domestic politics. I could get the overall picture, but the actual words people said were almost unintelligible to me.

INTERVIEWER

How did it become clearer?

DIDION

I realized that the words didn't have any actual meaning, that they described a negotiation more than they described an idea. But then you begin to see that the lack of specificity is specific in itself, that it is an obscuring device.

INTERVIEWER

Did it help you when you were working on *Salvador* and *Miami* to talk to the political figures you were writing about?

DIDION

In those cases it did. Though I didn't talk to a lot of American politicians. I remember talking to the then president of El Salvador, who was astounding. We were talking about a new land reform law and I explained that I couldn't quite understand what was being said about it. We were discussing a provision—Provision 207—that seemed to me to say that landowners could arrange their affairs so as to be unaffected by the reform.

He said, 207 always applied only to 1979. That is what no one understands. I asked did he mean that 207 applied only to 1979 because no landowner would work against his interests by allowing tenants on his land after 207 took effect? He said, Exactly, no one would rent out land under 207. They would have to be crazy to do that.

Well, that was forthright. There are very few politicians who would say exactly.

INTERVIEWER

Was it helpful to talk with John about your experiences there?

DIDION

It was useful to talk to him about politics because he viscerally understood politics. He grew up in an Irish Catholic family in Hartford, a town where politics was part of what you ate for breakfast. I mean, it didn't take *him* a long time to understand that nobody was saying anything.

INTERVIEWER

After *Salvador*, you wrote your next novel, *Democracy*. It seems informed by the reporting you were doing about America's relationship to the world.

DIDION

The fall of Saigon, though it takes place offstage, was the main thing on my mind. Saigon fell while I was teaching at Berkeley in 1975. I couldn't get those images out of my head, and that was the strongest impulse behind *Democracy*. When the book came out, some people wondered why it began with the bomb tests in the Pacific, but I think those bomb tests formed a straight line to pushing the helicopters off the aircraft carriers when we were abandoning Saigon. It was a very clear progression in my mind. Mainly, I wanted to show that you could write a romance and still have the fall of Saigon, or the Iran-Contra Affair. It would be hard for me to stay with a novel if I didn't see a very strong personal story at the center of it.

Democracy is really a much more complete version of *Common Prayer*, with basically the same structure. There is a narrator who tries to understand the character who's being talked about and reconstruct the story. I had a very clear picture in my mind of both those women, but I couldn't tell the story without standing way far away. Charlotte, in *Common Prayer*, was somebody who had a very expensive dress with a seam that was coming out. There was a kind of fevered carelessness to her. *Democracy* started out as a comedy, a comic novel. And I think that there is a more even view of life in it. I had a terrible time with it. I don't know why, but it never got easy.

In Brentwood we had a big safe-deposit box to put manuscripts in if we left town during fire season. It was such a big box that we never bothered to clean it out. When we were moving, in 1988, and I had to go through the box, I found I don't know how many different versions of the first ninety pages of *Democracy*, with different dates on them, written over several years. I would write ninety pages and not be able to go any further. I couldn't make the switch. I don't know how that was solved. Many of those drafts began with Billy Dillon coming to Amagansett to tell Inez that her father had shot her sister. It was very hard to get from there to any place. It didn't work. It was too conventional a narrative. I never hit the spot where I could sail through. I never got to that point, even at the very end.

INTERVIEWER
Was that a first for you?

DIDION
It was a first for a novel. I really did not think I was going to finish it two nights before I finished it. And when I did finish it, I had a sense that I was just abandoning it, that I was just calling it. It was sort of like Vietnam itself—why don't we say just we've won and leave? I didn't have a real sense of completion about it.

INTERVIEWER
Your novels are greatly informed by the travel and reporting you do for your nonfiction. Do you ever do research specifically for the fiction?

DIDION
Common Prayer was researched. We had someone working for us, Tina Moore, who was a fantastic researcher. She would go to the UCLA library, and I would say, Bring me back anything on plantation life in Central America. And she would come back and say, This is really what you're looking for— you'll love this. And it would not be plantation life in

Central America. It would be Ceylon, but it would be fantastic. She had an instinct for what was the same story, and what I was looking for. What I was looking for were rules for living in the tropics. I didn't know that, but that's what I found. In *Democracy* I was more familiar with all the places.

INTERVIEWER

The last novel you wrote was *The Last Thing He Wanted*. That came out in 1996. Had you been working on it for a long time?

DIDION

No. I started it in the early fall or late summer of 1995, and I finished it at Christmas. It was a novel I had been thinking about writing for a while. I wanted to write a novel about the Iran-Contra Affair, and get in all that stuff that was being lost. Basically it's a novel about Miami. I wanted it to be very densely plotted. I noticed that conspiracy was central to understanding that part of the world; everybody was always being set up in some way. The plot was going to be so complicated that I was going to have to write it fast or I wouldn't be able to keep it all in my head. If I forgot one little detail it wouldn't work, and half the readers didn't understand what happened in the end. Many people thought that Elena tried to kill Treat Morrison. Why did she want to kill him? they would ask me. But she didn't. Someone else did, and set her up. Apparently I didn't make that clear.

I had begun to lose patience with the conventions of writing. Descriptions went first; in both fiction and nonfiction, I just got impatient with those long paragraphs of description. By which I do not mean—obviously—the single detail that gives you the scene. I'm talking about description as a substitute for thinking. I think you can see me losing my patience as early as *Democracy*. That was why that book was so hard to write.

INTERVIEWER

After *Democracy* and *Miami*, and before *The Last Thing He Wanted*, there was the nonfiction collection *After Henry*, which strikes me as a way of coming back to New York and trying to understand what the city was.

DIDION

It has that long piece "Sentimental Journeys" (1991), about the Central Park jogger, which began with that impulse. We had been in New York a year or two, and I realized that I was living here without engaging the city at all. I might as well have been living in another city, because I didn't understand it, I didn't get it. So I realized that I needed to do some reporting on it. Bob and I decided I would do a series of short reporting pieces on New York, and the first one would be about the jogger. But it wasn't really reporting. It was coming at a situation from a lot of angles. I got so involved in it that, by the time I finished the piece, it was too long. I turned it in and Bob had some comments—many, many comments, which caused it to be even longer because he thought it needed so much additional material, which he was right about. By the time I'd plugged it all in, I'd added another six to eight thousand words. When I finally had finished it, I thought, That's all I have to do about New York.

Although it is about the city, "Sentimental Journeys" is really about race and class and money.

It seemed to me that the case was treated with a lot of contempt by the people who were handling it.

How so?

The prosecution thought they had the press and popular sentiment on their side. The case became a way of expressing the city's rage at being broke and being in another recession and not having a general comfort level, the sense that there were people sleeping on the streets—which there were. We moved here six months after the '87 stock market crash. Over the next couple of years, its effect on Madison Avenue was staggering. You could not walk down Madison Avenue at eight in the evening without having to avoid stepping on people sleeping in every doorway. There was a German television crew here doing a piece on the jogger, and they wanted to shoot in Harlem, but it was late in the day and they were losing the light. They kept asking me what the closest place was where they could shoot and see poverty. I said, Try Seventy-Second and Madison. You know where Polo is now? That building was empty and the padlocks were broken and you could see rats scuttling around inside. The landlord had emptied it—I presume because he wanted to get higher rents—and then everything had crashed. There was nothing there. That entire block was a mess.

So from California you had turned your attention to the third world, and now you were able to recognize New York because of the work you had done in the third world.

A lot of what I had seen as New York's sentimentality is derived from the stories the city tells itself to rationalize its class contradictions. I didn't realize that until I started doing the jogger piece. Everything started falling into place on that piece. Bob would send me clips about the trial, but on this one I was on my own, because only I knew where it was going.

In some of your early essays on California, your subject matter was as distinctively your own as your writing style. In recent decades, though, it's not so much the story but your take on the story that makes your work distinctive.

The shift came about as I became more confident that my own take was worth doing. In the beginning, I didn't want to do any stories that anyone else was doing. As time went by, I got more comfortable with that. For example, on the Central Park jogger piece I could not get into the courtroom because I didn't have a police pass. This forced me into another approach, which turned out to be a more interesting one. At least to me.

Wasn't it around the same time that you were also doing the "Letter from Los Angeles" for Robert Gottlieb at *The New Yorker*?

DIDION

Yes. Though I wasn't doing more than two of those a year. I think they only ran six to eight thousand words, but the idea was to do several things in each letter. I had never done that before, where you just really discuss what people are talking about that week. It was easy to do. It was a totally different tone from the *Review*. I went over those *New Yorker* pieces when I collected them. I probably took out some of *The New Yorker*'s editing, which is just their way of making everything sound a certain way.

INTERVIEWER

Can you characterize your methods as a reporter?

DIDION

I can't ask anything. Once in a while if I'm forced into it I will conduct an interview, but it's usually pro forma, just to establish my credentials as somebody who's allowed to hang around for a while. It doesn't matter to me what people say to me in the interview because I don't trust it. Sometimes you do interviews where you get a lot. But you don't get them from public figures.

When I was conducting interviews for the piece on Lakewood, it was essential to do interviews because that was the whole point. But these were not public figures. On the one hand, we were discussing what I was ostensibly there doing a piece about, which was the Spur Posse, a group of local high school boys who had been arrested for various infractions. But on the other hand, we were talking, because it was the first thing on everyone's mind, about the defense industry going downhill, which was what the town was about. That was a case in which I did interviewing and listened.

INTERVIEWER

Did the book about California, *Where I Was From*, grow out of that piece, or had you already been thinking about a book?

DIDION

I had actually started a book about California in the seventies. I had written some of that first part, which is about my family, but I could never go anywhere with it for two reasons. One was that I still hadn't figured out California. The other was that I didn't want to figure out California because whatever I figured out would be different from the California my mother and father had told me about. I didn't want to engage that.

INTERVIEWER

You felt like you were still their child?

DIDION

I just didn't see any point in engaging it. By the time I did the book they were dead.

You said earlier that after *The White Album* you were tired of personal writing and didn't want to become Miss Lonelyhearts. You must be getting a larger personal response from readers than ever with *The Year of Magical Thinking*. Is that difficult?

DIDION

I have been getting a very strong emotional response to *Magical Thinking*. But it's not a crazy response; it's not demanding. It's people trying to make sense of a fairly universal experience that most people don't talk about. So this is a case in which I have found myself able to deal with the response directly.

INTERVIEWER

Do you ever think you might go back to the idea of doing little pieces about New York?

DIDION

I don't know. It is still a possibility, but my basic question about New York was answered for me: it's criminal.

INTERVIEWER

That was your question?

DIDION

Yes, it's criminal.

INTERVIEWER

Do you find it stimulating in some way to live here?

I find it really comfortable. During the time we lived in California, which lasted twenty-four years, I didn't miss New York after the first year. And after the second year I started to think of New York as sentimental. There were periods when I didn't even come to New York at all. One time I realized that I had been to Hong Kong twice since I had last been to New York. Then we started spending more time in New York. Both John and I were really happy to have been here on 9/11. I can't think of any place else I would have rather been on 9/11, and in the immediate aftermath.

INTERVIEWER

You could have stayed in Sacramento forever as a novelist, but you started to move out into the worlds of Hollywood and politics.

DIDION

I was never a big fan of people who don't leave home. I don't know why. It just seems part of your duty in life.

INTERVIEWER

I'm reminded of Charlotte in *A Book of Common Prayer*. She has no conception of the outside world but she wants to be in it.

DIDION

Although a novel takes place in the larger world, there's always some drive in it that is entirely personal—even if you don't know it while you're doing it. I realized some years after *A Book of Common Prayer* was finished that it was about my anticipating

Quintana's growing up. I wrote it around 1975, so she would have been nine, but I was already anticipating separation and actually working through that ahead of time. So novels are also about things you're afraid you can't deal with.

INTERVIEWER

Are you working on one now?

DIDION

No. I haven't felt that I wanted to bury myself for that intense a period.

INTERVIEWER

You want to be in the world a bit.

DIDION

Yeah. A little bit.

(2006)

Hilary Mantel

THE ART OF FICTION NO. 226

Interviewed by Mona Simpson

Hilary Mantel was born Hilary Thompson in Hadfield, Derbyshire, a mill town fifteen miles east of Manchester. Her memoir, *Giving Up the Ghost* (2003), chronicles a grim childhood in a working-class Irish Catholic family: "From about the age of four I had begun to believe I had done something wrong." When she was seven, her mother's lover, Jack Mantel, moved in with the Thompsons. "The children at school question me about our living arrangements, who sleeps in what bed. I don't understand why they want to know but I don't tell them anything. I hate going to school. Often I am ill." Four years later, Jack Mantel and Hilary's mother moved the family to Cheshire, after which Hilary never saw her father again. To quote once more from *Giving Up the Ghost*: "The story of my own childhood is a complicated sentence that I am always trying to finish, to finish and put behind me."

Mantel graduated from the University of Sheffield, with a B.A. in jurisprudence. During her university years, she was a socialist. She worked in a geriatric hospital and in a department store. In 1972, she married Gerald McEwen, a geologist, and soon after, the couple moved to Botswana for five years, where Mantel wrote the book that became *A Place of Greater Safety* (1992). The couple divorced in 1980, but in 1982 they married again, in front of a registrar, who wished them better luck this time.

All her life, Mantel has suffered from a painful, debilitating illness, which was first misdiagnosed and treated with antipsychotic drugs. In Botswana, through reading medical textbooks, she identified and diagnosed her own disease, a severe form of endometriosis. Since then, Mantel has written a great deal about the female body, her own and others'. An essay that begins with a consideration of Kate Middleton's wardrobe and moves on to a discussion of the royal body generated so much controversy that (as she told the *New Statesman*) "if the pressmen saw any fat woman of a certain age walking along the street, they ran after her shouting, 'Are you Hilary?'"

Mantel's early novels—*Wolf Hall* (2009) was her tenth novel, her twelfth book—reflect the grimness she describes from her childhood and share a bleak, dark humor. The two completed books of the projected Cromwell trilogy, *Wolf Hall* and *Bring Up the Bodies* (2012), are not without darkness, but considering their subject—the bloody rise and fall of Henry VIII's chief minister—they are remarkably vivid on the pleasures of work, home, and ordinary happiness. Both were awarded the Man Booker Prize, making Mantel the first woman to win the prize twice. This

winter, a stage adaptation, *Wolf Hall, Parts One &
Two*, enjoyed a sell-out run in London; a *Wolf Hall*
miniseries aired at the same time on the BBC. In
February, Mantel was made a dame.

Over the three days we spent together, she was
working like an impassioned college student, until
three or four A.M., and even after a day in the theater
seeing both plays back to back, followed by a late
supper, she was ready to meet and talk in the morning at nine.

INTERVIEWER

You started with historical fiction and then you
returned to it. How did that happen?

HILARY MANTEL

I only became a novelist because I thought I had
missed my chance to become a historian. So it began
as second best. I had to tell myself a story about the
French Revolution—the story of the revolution by
some of the people who made it, rather than by the
revolution's enemies.

INTERVIEWER

Why that story?

MANTEL

I'd read all the history books and novels I could
lay my hands on, and I wasn't satisfied with what I
found. All the novels were about the aristocracy and
their sufferings. And I thought those writers were
missing a far more interesting group—the idealistic
revolutionaries, whose stories are amazing. There

was no novel about them. I set about writing it—at least, a story about some of them—so I could read it. And of course, for a long time it seemed as if I were the only person who ever would. My idea was to write a sort of documentary fiction, guided entirely by the facts. Then, not many months in, I came to a point where the facts about a certain episode ran out, and I spent a whole day making things up. At the end of it, I thought, I quite liked that. It sounds naive, not knowing that I would have to make things up, but I had a great belief that all the material was out there, somewhere, and if I couldn't find it, that would be my fault.

INTERVIEWER

But the majority of human history is lost, isn't it?

MANTEL

Yes, and when you realize that, then you can say, I don't know exactly how this episode occurred, but, for example, I do know where and when it took place.

INTERVIEWER

Would you ever change a fact to heighten the drama?

MANTEL

I would never do that. I aim to make the fiction flexible so that it bends itself around the facts as we have them. Otherwise I don't see the point. Nobody seems to understand that. Nobody seems to share my approach to historical fiction. I suppose if I have a maxim, it is that there isn't any necessary conflict between good history and good drama. I know that history is not shapely, and I know the truth is often inconvenient and incoherent. It contains all sorts of superfluities. You could cut a much better shape if you were God, but as it is, I think the whole fascination and the skill is in working *with* those incoherencies.

INTERVIEWER
In containing the contradictions?

MANTEL
Exactly. The contradictions and the awkwardness—that's what gives historical fiction its value. Finding a shape, rather than imposing a shape. And allowing the reader to live with the ambiguities. Thomas Cromwell is the character with whom that's most essential. He's almost a case study in ambiguity. There's the Cromwell in popular history and the one in academic history, and they don't make any contact really. What I have managed to do is bring the two camps together, so now there's a new crop of Cromwell biographies, and they will range from the popular to the very authoritative and academic. So we will have a coherent Cromwell—perhaps.

INTERVIEWER
When Raymond Carver wrote a story about Chekhov's death, he invented details and a character. Janet Malcolm traced how subsequent biographies now include the character from his fiction. History grabbed him up.

MANTEL
Yes, and once you know that you are working with historians in that way, then you have to raise your game. You have a responsibility to make

your research good. Of course, you don't mean for these things to happen. In *A Place of Greater Safety*, Camille Desmoulins wonders why he was always running into Antoine Saint-Just. We must be some sort of cousins because I used to see him at christenings, he says. It's now become a "fact" that they were cousins. Things get passed around so easily on the Internet. And fact becomes fiction and fiction becomes fact, without anyone stepping in to arbitrate and say, What are your sources?

INTERVIEWER

You worked on *A Place of Greater Safety*, your first novel about the French Revolution, decades before it was published.

MANTEL

I started it when I was twenty-two, a year after university. That would be 1974. I wrote it in the evenings and on weekends. I did more of the research up front than I would have done at a later stage—luckily for me, because in spring of '77, we went to live in Botswana, where there were no sources to speak of, as you can imagine. I had an intense few weeks before we went, when I said to myself, Get everything you haven't got, because this is your only chance.

It was a strange life. I was living partly in Botswana and partly in the 1790s. I was intensely engaged with my French Revolution book. But I became a teacher by accident. I was roped in by local ladies to work on a volunteer project doing a few hours a week at a little informal school set up for teenage girls. From there, I went to teach at the local secondary school. I was twenty-five and my oldest pupils were older than I was. Their ages ranged from twelve to twenty-six. We tended to have twelve-year-old girls and eighteen-year-old boys in the same classroom, which is an explosive mixture. The institution was a highly unpleasant place. Frantz Fanon would have loved it—the extent of cultural alienation, the horrific forms that colonialism takes that one doesn't detect at the time, the tensions. We had a number of teachers from Zimbabwe, who divided themselves by language—so the teachers who were Ndebele people simply didn't talk to the Shona people. There was a teacher from West Africa who was treated like a leper by all the teachers from southern Africa. The only way they made common cause was by hating the Nigerian. The Indian staff didn't bother with the African staff, and the African staff gave the Indians as hard a time as possible. Botswana is the size of France, so it was a boarding school with day pupils, but many of the children came from hundreds of miles away. And to them our little bush town was New York. There was the culture shock the children lived with, the distance from their families. And then there was the horrible, sexually predatory behavior, which, to my shame, I didn't entirely see at the time. I only dimly perceived it. Both masters and boys preying on the girls. This was Botswana just pre-AIDS. I had only very limited means of detecting what was going on, and, if I did detect it, what on earth was I going to do about it? You know, those layers of corruption permeated every aspect of life. Yet one went along day to day, teaching George Eliot.

INTERVIEWER

Did you a have a prescribed curriculum?

Yes, these children were sitting exams set, moderated, and marked in England. It's very hard to teach Eliot when you have some pupils in your class whose vocabulary is around six hundred words, basic English. On the other hand, there were some children who were from a background where their English was more fluent, who were very capable of appreciating it on the linguistic level, though not on the cultural level. Imagine trying to explain, This is George Eliot, she's writing in the nineteenth century. She's writing about the eighteenth century and she's not doing it very well. Try to explain fox hunting to a child who has never seen a fox, never seen a horse, never seen a hedge, never seen a green field, never seen snow. Yet in some ways they responded to the fierce morality. They cast it in terms of their own morality. We didn't have television, and obviously we didn't have theater. So you were teaching literature to people who had none of the familiar means of forming a picture of the outside world. Teaching Shakespeare in Botswana was difficult, you'd think, but again they loved it. I never told them it was supposed to be difficult. I got good results, I have to say. I suppose I threw myself into it—you know, I didn't have the world weariness of the other teachers. Then some unpleasant incidents drove me out of the school.

INTERVIEWER

What happened?

MANTEL

I was on evening duty, and somebody jumped on me. It wasn't a sexual thing. There were a group of pupils, with one person hitting me. Compared to what could have happened, it was trivial. It was dark, they were not my pupils, I couldn't identify them, the school wasn't interested in finding out. It was a shambles. I felt unsupported by the headmaster, and so I left, but I didn't want to go, because I liked my pupils.

After I left the school, I just wrote.

INTERVIEWER
Had you always wanted to be a writer?

MANTEL
Never. I didn't think in terms of becoming a writer until I actually picked up my pen to become one. And that was born out of a feeling that my health was causing me problems. By the time I was nineteen, I knew there was something wrong but I didn't have a diagnosis, I didn't have any help, and I realized that doors were closing. I wasn't going to be some of the things I thought I might be. The best thing I could do was to get a trade that was under my control. But then, when I looked back, I realized that even though I hadn't said to myself as a child, I want to be a writer, I'd actually instituted a training course. I always wonder if other people's lives have been like that, when they turn into writers. From the age of about eight, I was hyperconscious about what I read, and my reading was always analytical. I was never simply absorbing stories but always asking myself, How is this done? When I walked to school every morning, from the age of eleven to eighteen, I "did" the weather and I didn't stop until I had one perfect paragraph. So I had a huge mental file of weather. When I wrote *Every Day Is Mother's Day* (1985), I picked a sentence from

my mental file and dropped it into the book—it gave me great pleasure to do so. I didn't worry about the ten thousand sentences that didn't get used because they were all a means to an end. The point of the exercise was not to stop until I'd pinned it down precisely and had exactly the right word. It was all about style, not story. By the time I got into my teens, I had nothing to say, but I had a very good style in which to say it. When I studied law, it completely broke my style, because you have to write in a very prescribed and tight way. When I started writing my novel, I had to rebuild my style. As for my subject, the French Revolution was beyond anything I had to say about my own life. It was so much bigger than me. Bigger than anybody. But there wasn't the possibility of writing any other book because I had none.

By December of '79, I had finished *A Place of Greater Safety*, but I couldn't sell it, I couldn't get anywhere with it at all. I had twelve weeks' leave in England before I was due to return to Botswana. I'd made initial contact with a publisher, who seemed interested, so that was my first port of call. And they turned the book down. Then I found myself in hospital. I was very ill, I had major surgery. As I emerged, something in me said, I don't think you will sell this book. It wasn't that I had lost faith in the book— because I never did—I just knew the impossibility of maneuvering from where I was. It was not a good time for historical fiction, and I knew from writing to agents and the dusty answers I got that even getting the book read was going to be impossible.

So I formed a cunning plan. I thought, I'll write another novel. I'll write a contemporary novel. That was *Every Day Is Mother's Day*. I started it in Africa.

I finished it in Saudi Arabia. At times I had very little sense of where I was going with it or whether there would be any profit or success at the end of it. It was written in the teeth of everything. It was an act of defiance—I thought, I'm not going to be beaten. I got an agent, I got a publisher, then I wrote the sequel. It wasn't planned as two books. It was, for me, a way of getting a foot in the door. But once I had secured a contract, I just rolled up my sleeves and I set about *Vacant Possession* (1986) in a way that I've never worked before. I would write through the morning, Gerald would come home midafternoon, would have his siesta, and when he woke up, I would read him what I had written in the morning. I've never written like that since.

INTERVIEWER

Gerald's a geologist—did you train him to be a literary reader?

MANTEL

That wasn't what I needed. It sounds horrible, but I needed a listening ear. I needed someone to write for, someone who wanted to know what would happen next.

INTERVIEWER

Did you prefer historical fiction, even then? Or were they equal but different enterprises?

MANTEL

I have to be frank. Writing a contemporary novel was just a way to get a publisher. My heart lay with historical fiction, and I think it still does.

Though you went on to write quite a few contemporary novels.

Well, things changed. I realized that writing a contemporary novel wasn't just a way in, it was a trade in itself. We returned to England from Saudi Arabia just as *Vacant Possession* was published. By then I had my mass of material from Saudi Arabia, which I knew I must use, because I had a unique opportunity. So again, that book, *Eight Months on Ghazzah Street* (1988), demanded to be written. And by then I had the idea for *Fludd* (1989), which had long been simmering in my mind.

During all that time you didn't give your publisher *A Place of Greater Safety*. Why not?

Because I was absorbed in what I was doing. I thought, Just push on while the going's good. *Fludd* was one of those books that came in an instant. You know, you've got the first sentence, you've got the last sentence. A thing like that can go off the boil. So again, I had a sense of urgency.

A lot of your subsequent themes emerged in those first two books—anorexia, diets, a drowned baby, an obsession with "the royals."

The epigraph to *Every Day Is Mother's Day* is Pascal—"Two errors; one, to take everything literally; two, to take everything spiritually." And it's the epigraph for the lot, isn't it?

How did you go about writing *Eight Months on Ghazzah Street*?

I kept diaries all the time, and I kept my notes. But there are a lot of problems with that novel. I think it's too fuzzy. I don't think I really crunched down on it. That was inexperience, and the distressing business of having to make things up. I always see that book through a dust haze, but I do remember the moment when, if it were another book, I'd say it crystallized, but being *Eight Months on Ghazzah Street*, it didn't crystallize at all. We lived in the city center and one day I went up onto the roof of our apartment block, which was the only outside space available. I craned my neck and saw a crate on the neighbor's balcony. I thought, My novel's in that box. There was something incredibly sinister about it. And yet, what was it? It was a box. In my experience, those are the moments that set a novel. You just have to wait. Supposing I hadn't gone up to the roof, what would the novel have been? I have no idea.

The odd thing about *Ghazzah Street* was that a lot of what I said proved to be pretty accurate when terrorist activity was exposed in Saudi Arabia. People were doing just what I said—they were stockpiling arms in little flats around the city.

I wrote *Ghazzah Street*, then I wrote *Fludd*, not very quickly actually, over a couple of years. By this stage, you see, I'd earned two thousand pounds from my first novel, and four thousand pounds from my second novel. For *Ghazzah Street* and *Fludd*, I got a two-book contract for £17,500—not enough to live on. It was at that point that I became a film critic. Then I became a book reviewer as well. I did one film review a week, several books reviews a month. I was an industry.

INTERVIEWER

How could you do it? Did you become a fast reader?

MANTEL

Long hours. I don't think I changed my reading speed. I take lots of notes. I might not have been the world's most insightful reviewer, but I was an extremely conscientious one. Once I got the film column, I was highly visible, and I had more work coming in than I could handle. But I was making a living. I was solvent. And I felt I was building something. There's something very seductive about opening a newspaper if your name is almost always in it. Every weekend, two papers, three papers. If you're an un-networked person from nowhere, which is exactly what I was, then you realize that you're drilling away into the heart of the cultural establishment.

INTERVIEWER

Did the book reviewing make you see your own work within a context? Did you feel your novels were related to other schools of fiction?

No, to be honest, I never have. I think I've had a curve of development that was just mine. This is why, for so long, I made no money. Though I had a good reputation critically, I had very few readers because I wouldn't find a formula and stick to it. Until the Cromwell novels, I had no identity in the mind of the reading public. It's very hard for a publisher to market an author who doesn't display any consistency in what she's interested in or how she writes.

INTERVIEWER

Ian McEwan jumps all over the map, doesn't he?

MANTEL

I think he is more consistent in his preoccupations. You and I will know that my books are intimately connected, that there is coherence, but from a commercial point of view, they've not been an attractive package. And then there is the divide between contemporary fiction and historical fiction. When I began work on the French Revolution, it seemed to me the most interesting thing that had ever happened in the history of the world, and it still does in many ways. I had no idea how little the British public knew or cared or wished to know about the French Revolution. And that's still the case. They want to know about Henry VIII.

INTERVIEWER

So you feel readers' interests are predominantly subject based.

Yes, the imagination is parochial. I couldn't have picked anything less promising, from a commercial point of view, than the French Revolution.

How did *A Place of Greater Safety* get published, in the end?

It was because of a newspaper article. This was in 1992. I had four books out. I had my reviewing career. I wasn't making a lot of money, but I was getting somewhere. And there was this monster book on the shelf. I hadn't looked into it for years. I thought, What if it's no good? Because if it is no good, then that's my twenties written off. And it also means that I commenced my career with a gigantic mistake. But inside me there was still a belief that it would be published one day. And a friend of mine, the Irish writer Clare Boylan, rang me up and said she was doing an article for the *Guardian* about people's unpublished first novels, and had I got one? I could have lied, but it was as if the devil jumped out of my mouth, and I said, Yes, I have! And of course she rang around a number of authors, and they were saying things like, Yes, I wrote my first novel at the age of eight, and I've still got it in a shoe box. I was the only person who actually wanted to see her first novel published. On my way to deliver it to my agent, I had lunch with another novelist. The manuscript was a huge parcel under my chair—unwelcome, like a surprise guest.

We should have given it a chair to itself. He said, Don't do it.

You were twenty-seven when you'd written it and now you were forty.

Something like that. A lot of things had happened in French Revolution scholarship since then. The bicentenary had come and gone, and there had been a revolution in feminist history. When I read my draft, I saw that the women were wallpaper. There had been no material. Today you would think, Well, I must invent some, then. At the time I hadn't seen the need—I hadn't thought the women were interesting. My life was more like the life of an eighteenth-century man than like the life of an eighteenth-century woman. And I suppose I didn't really ask myself the questions. Now I thought, I've got to work this harder.

How long did you take to revise?

I did it in the course of one summer. The publication process was horrendous. Basically, the novel was written in the present tense. Someone in the publishing house didn't want that, so changed it, and I changed it back, and so on, through proofs. The result was that, if you look at the book now, there are paragraphs where two tenses are employed. One day

I'm going to straighten it out. But the work I had to do in those weeks was brutal, because I had to revise on a schedule. I worked immensely long hours. Something in me was never quite the same after that. It would be romantic to say that summer was the making of me, but it actually wasn't like that. It brutalized me. I'm not sure if I can really express it, but it was after that, I shut down. I shut down such a lot of my life in order to do it, and never opened up again.

INTERVIEWER

Do you mean you entered a level of isolation for the work, or restriction? A deeper commitment?

MANTEL

Restriction, yes. I think it's good for me as a writer. I don't think it's very good for me as a human being. A sort of grimness entered into me, I think, which is still there. I suppose that book always was more important to me than anything else.

INTERVIEWER

It was *the* book, until the Cromwell books.

MANTEL

Yes. It was me doing what I do. And I think, for better or worse, it's me doing what only I could do. Nobody else works by this method, with my ideal of fidelity to history. Regardless of whether that's a good thing, or gets good results, it is a thing I do.

INTERVIEWER

You said you withdrew from life. What did you eliminate?

Friends. Personal relationships. Fun. Everything just went. I don't think I had many close friends before, but it seems to me that after that summer I never relaxed again. And the only people who could be my friends were people who were enormously tolerant of my really not being there for months at a time. Because of my health, my energy has always had to be harvested, preserved, and directed at work. And then if there was any left over, fine, but usually there wasn't. I never lived in London, so I didn't hang out with literary people in my off-duty hours. I was not isolated, though, from other writers. Instead of going to literary parties, I went to committees. I sat on the Council of the Royal Society of Literature, on the management committee of the Society of Authors. For six years I sat on the Advisory Committee for Public Lending Right, which advised the government on giving authors an income from books borrowed from libraries. That was my involvement in the literary world. It was technical, if you like. It was useful work, but most people would have regarded it as extremely dull.

INTERVIEWER

Did you have friends who were helpful with the work itself?

MANTEL

I'm going to say no, on the whole. Gerald is my first reader, but I don't expect literary criticism from him. He's not going to say, Oh, that reminds me of something in Muriel Spark. He's going to react as a human being to it. And isn't that what we want?

I have other people I hold in mind as I write, to whom I might show something at an early stage. A fan who became a friend, Jan Rogers—she was a BBC producer, and it was she who got me writing for radio. She is knowledgeable about revolutionary history, she got me more deeply into Irish history, and she woke me up to literary theory. I have a friend called Jane Haynes, a psychotherapist—that's another strand of interest.

I don't really talk about writing very much to other writers. There's one writer—Adam Thorpe. Adam lives in France and I never see him, but if he were to walk in, we'd have a proper conversation. It would be about writing. And I think he's the only person I have that kind of relationship with, and I haven't heard from him for months.

I keep a big correspondence going with Mary Robertson, whom my Cromwell books are dedicated to. I write to Mary almost every week, sometimes far more often.

INTERVIEWER

How did you become friends?

MANTEL

Some years ago, probably fifteen years ago, I was invited to the Huntington Library, to a conference along with Martin Amis, Ian McEwan, Christopher Hitchens—the lads, you know. I casually mentioned to a woman there that I was thinking of writing something down the line about Thomas Cromwell. And she said, When you do, we have a woman here you need to meet. I thought no more of it until the time came, then I said, You have a woman, I believe.

And therein we fell into correspondence—very tentatively at first. Mary had long ago written a Ph.D. thesis on Thomas Cromwell's ministerial household. She'd also written a couple of papers on his property holdings. But she had not really asked herself what this man was like, because that was not her job.

What was your correspondence like?

Luminous. I didn't really ask her questions. I'd bounce suggestions off her. I'd say, I've come across this and my thought about it is that. What if I were to speculate? Would you see anything against it? Is this really a gap in the record? Or is it just something that I personally don't know? Her interest and knowledge were there, ready to be revived.

Did you find other people who specialized in More and Wolsey?

No, no. I didn't know any historians. I do now, but when I began I only knew Mary. She's a fountain of information. But she was also a muse, and I needed a muse. I needed someone to write for. I needed someone to say, I'm holding up a torch for you, even when it's so dark you can't see your way to the next paragraph. I needed someone to say, Do it, I care, it's important. Someone who was enthralled—just like Gerald was when I used to read him *Vacant Possession*. The wonderful thing was that Mary became so engaged.

I didn't feed the text to her bit by bit, but I would tell her how it was shaping, what I was thinking, what I was contemplating. It was a wonderful thing.

I remember, for instance, one particular Saturday morning, when I was writing. There's an episode when there's a tournament, Gregory Cromwell is in it, and someone rushes in to tell Cromwell that the king has fallen from his horse and is dead. But when he comes in, Cromwell's first thought is, My son is dead. He stands up, and then he grasps the situation. He dries the ink on the document he is writing, then he picks up an ornamental dagger from his desk and goes out to face what is to come. Now, when I came to the point where he dries the document, I couldn't see what he did, and I needed to see. Until I could see, I could not continue. So I e-mailed Mary and said, Documents, ink, methods of drying. She dropped everything. We spent a whole weekend e-mailing— to discuss how you might dry ink. That's not really an archivist's concern. But it was the action of a very good friend. We've met about three times now. She came over to Stratford for the plays. It was magic. Because I never imagined them turning into plays. Or Mary sitting beside me, in the audience.

INTERVIEWER

How long were you thinking of the Cromwell novels before you started?

MANTEL

Thirty years. But I didn't start work until 2005. I don't do a block of research and then write. It's a fluid movement between one thing and another. I have masses and masses of material for the third

Cromwell novel. I'm generating it all the time, every day. At the moment, it arrives in a completely random order. There has to be a stage where I stay at home, sit down at my desk, and begin stitching it together, and I hardly have stayed at home for a year.

Why not?

I've been working on the plays. First with Mike Poulton, the adaptor, on the scripts. Then with the actors in rehearsal. I became a professional audience member. That's how I have learned—tracing the process and how it pays off. Working with Ben Miles, the actor who's playing Thomas Cromwell, is a creative process different from anything I have tried before. He asked me, for example, if I could provide him with some memories of Cromwell's daughters as children. This is not, obviously, something you can find in the book. These little girls barely exist in history. They're names. So we're moving into territory that is difficult for me because I like to have facts to steer by, but I found once I began that I could unspool thousands of words. It's exhilarating, and it's unnerving at times. What has happened is that the projects have begun to play off each other—the two books that are adapted into plays and the third book still in process. An insight will produce a new bit of script, which will generate some prose, which I then write into the third book as a flashback. Or perhaps Ben will describe something that comes to him in performance, a crosscurrent of emotion, let's say—you're saying one thing but the picture in your mind is something else. I can use that.

Or he will give me an image. Literally, sometimes—a photograph. And I can use that, too.

Had you ever thought of working in the theater before?

Long ago I seriously thought about applying to drama school instead of university. But I already knew my health wouldn't hold up. I could act, to a degree, it's what I do as a writer, it's how I build characters—I act them from the inside.

Has your health improved?

I couldn't have sustained this collaboration even a year ago. I couldn't have worked on other people's schedules. I always had to work on my own, so that I was in control. But now I've been able to attend rehearsals and be at the shows at night and then come home and go to bed at three o'clock and then get up the next day and do it over again. I'm not sure that it's wise. But what has wisdom got to do with it? I've had to live in such a cautious way, in such a constrained way for many years. In the last six months I've started to enjoy myself, and it's given me a lot of optimism. I hope *The Mirror and the Light* will be a play, once the novel is done. The other possibility is that I simply go off and write an original play, which I think is quite likely to happen.

I'm sixty-two next month. About four months ago, I noticed that I'm no longer in pain every day.

I find myself feeling better than I have since I was twenty, and therefore, I think I can do things. There are a lot of novels I want to write, but there are also plays I want to write. It's a bit unusual to start at this age, but why not?

INTERVIEWER

Is Gerald your first reader as you work on *The Mirror and the Light*?

MANTEL

I can talk to him or not. He never says, Tell me what you're writing. He gives me space. And he's completely accepting that, at a certain point, my writing might be going out to another person, and my emotional energy with it. He doesn't say, Where's my share? He'll listen to me if I need to be listened to, and I hope that nowadays I don't try his patience too much. I think I used to, particularly when we were in Botswana, where I was so intensely engaged with my material and there was nobody I could talk to about writing. It was me, my secret revolution, and Gerald. Oh, I think it must have been very boring at times. The writer is going round and round, and they insist they've got a problem, but you can't see what it is. Now our relationship's changed a lot because we're business partners.

INTERVIEWER

What kind of business partners?

MANTEL

From two years or so ago, three years now, Gerald doesn't work on his own account, he just works with me. He hasn't been a geologist for many years.

When we came back to England in the mideighties, he went into IT—he worked for IBM for nine years and traveled a great deal. We both traveled a great deal. And we existed in fairly separate spheres. Then we had sort of overlapping crises. Gerald had a serious illness in 2008, just as I was in the closing stages of *Wolf Hall*, and it made a disjunction in our lives. By the time he recovered, life had changed for me because I'd won my first Booker. And it was at that point that I began to need serious help with, you know, office support, just somebody to run my life. Then I had this real horror year. I had complicated surgery, and the aftermath went badly. My lifelong problem was endometriosis, and it has now burnt itself out, but it left a lot of damage internally. I was very ill, housebound for six months. I lost 2010. This was between the two novels. When I did get back to work, I completed *Bring Up the Bodies* very quickly. We went through a year where it wasn't certain what we would do, and whether Gerald would actually pick up and resume his career.

So then we decided he would come and work with me and we would move to Devon and just change everything. And now here we are.

It means a great deal of unselfishness on Gerald's part. I worry about that. Somebody said to him last week, Isn't it like being Mrs. Thatcher's husband? Which I thought was unflattering to us both. The other thing I worry about is if he's lonely, because I'm preoccupied with my work and I don't expect to have people around me, whereas Gerald had colleagues all those years. However, with these theater productions, we're plunged into a world of sociability. And he's become part of the group.

INTERVIEWER

You've described your work for the plays as paying attention to the audience. This is unusual for novelists, who write a long time and receive a response only much later.

MANTEL

A live audience is such an intricate and fascinating thing. It needs permission to relax and to laugh. Also, it needs a reason to listen. We're asking people to listen very closely to these plays. We also want them to be amused. You can feel the mood of an audience change second by second, and it's fascinating to watch experienced actors—their instincts alive—shape and respond to an audience, control it. Writing would be a very different game if that kind of feedback were available to you. Instead, your reader feels very distant. With historical fiction, the big thing is the constant check you keep on information. What have I told my readers? Of what I've told them, how much do I think they hang on to, at first reading? Have I told them too much, have I spoon-fed them? Or have I told them too little, mystified them? It's not just historical fiction, of course, all fiction is like that. And if it's a choice between spoon-feeding and mystification, I think I choose mystification, because you always have to assume that your reader is at least as intelligent as you are, if not more so.

INTERVIEWER

You want to survive rereading, of course.

That's a big and ambitious thing to say to yourself as a young writer—I want to write books that can be reread. At first you get a little exasperated with yourself when you can't convey everything in one go, but then you realize that there are things in your fiction that you didn't get until later, so you begin to see that not as a failure but as an intrinsic part of the process. Not everything will be available at first reading.

What gave you that confidence?

When I began writing, I launched into *A Place of Greater Safety*, a vast novel involving mountains of research, for which there was no discernible public demand. And knowing that it would take me years, without any contacts, not knowing any historians, not knowing any writers or publishers, so when I look back, it seems like a very strange decision. I suppose that, because I was twenty-two, I knew I had time on my side. Still, it's lucky that I couldn't see just exactly how long it would take.

When I began writing I had a perfect belief that, although I might not know how to do many things, I did know how to write a novel. Other people might have disputed that, looking at my efforts, and no one was in a hurry to endorse my confidence, but I did know within myself that I could write a novel. The reason was I'd read so many that the pattern was internalized. I've always been an intensely ambitious individual and whatever I was going to do, I was not going to let go until I got where I thought I ought to be. It's a question of, What will you sacrifice? What other things will you let go, to clear the space for your book? What develops later is something rather different, as you proceed from book to book, every book throwing up different demands, needing different techniques.

INTERVIEWER

You're always a beginner.

MANTEL

You absolutely are—every day. You have no right to assume that you'll be able to write because you could write yesterday. On the other hand, when there are dark times, you can say, I've faced this before. You learn that you will always have to mark time, that you shouldn't rush, that if you wait, the book will come to you. But you only build up this knowledge through long experience. Your daily work is very much about the line, the paragraph. It's not about the grand design of your career.

INTERVIEWER

Have other contemporary writers been important to your development? Sebald? Munro? McEwan?

MANTEL

I was set very early. There was Shakespeare, there was Robert Louis Stevenson, and then there was reading *Jane Eyre*—specifically *Jane Eyre*, none of the other Brontë books. I was nine or ten. That was my first experience of realizing that there was another head in the world that felt like mine—the passage right at the beginning, when Jane's relatives accuse her of being unchildlike. For a young reader that's an important moment, when you recognize that your self exists in the world and that your self exists in literature. I totally identified with Jane as an unchildlike child. I never was very much interested in her love story.

Kidnapped I read probably every couple of years at least. It never loses its magic for me.

INTERVIEWER
Do you reread *Jane Eyre*, too?

MANTEL
When I reread *Jane Eyre*, I just think, Jesus, why don't you leave that bit out, and that bit out, and that bit out. I start working on it, as if I could fix it, but *Kidnapped* is perfect. There's nothing in it that shouldn't be there, nor is it lacking anything. I know Stevenson modestly said it was just a story for boys, but it's actually a perfect novel.

I always find it difficult to talk about this business of influences because I've never consciously said, I want to be like that author, or looked at someone's book and thought, That's a good trick, I'll try it. I've never tried to imitate a style. I don't think that's really what influence is about. Still, when I read Stevenson, I thought, This is how a story should be. And when I read *Jane Eyre*, I found that I existed in fiction. *Kidnapped* came first and remains the book to which I'm most attached, perhaps precisely because it's about a boy, it's about male friendship and the construction of masculinity, and it's about the boy who leaves home and can't go back because there's nothing to go back to. That's a story I've been telling all my life. It has evolved with various novels, but it's a basic narrative to me. Last summer, Gerald planned a week in Scotland for us. He chose a beautiful hotel two miles down the road from where the central incident in *Kidnapped* takes place, which is a real-life incident. I did what Stevenson says you should do—Get yourself a map, you'll understand what follows much better. For the first time, I traced the route of the flight in the heather, went to see the site of the murder, went over all the territory and then started avidly reading, fitting together the picture. There was not a night during our holiday when I went to sleep before four A.M. And by the end of the six days, I understood a whole swathe of Scottish history. Well, it was a very happy thing, but it wasn't great for Gerald, because all we'd both wanted to do was drive around and look at scenery, but the itinerary was steered by my obsession.

It's interesting to think what would have been the outcome if I'd read *Jane Eyre* first.

INTERVIEWER

Did you read *Middlemarch*?

MANTEL

Not until I was grown up. I'm not fond of Eliot. And I've never made my way through a Virginia Woolf book. I can't. I can read her essays, and I can read about her, and I can read all around her. I can't read her novels. You know, it sounds terribly disrespectful to Virginia, but I like books in which things happen. I think it's Faulkner who says, Write down what they say and write down what they do. To a large extent I do that, more than people imagine. I don't have pages and pages in which I say, Cromwell thought. I tell you what he says, I tell you what he does, and you read between the lines. I would prefer to read case histories than to read a novelist's take on the psychology of an imagined person. My favorite person, my hero, is Oliver Sacks. I've exchanged letters with him, and there's one that I haven't stuck in my file for the Huntington archive. I've kept it in my own files. It's really precious.

INTERVIEWER

Do you have other favorites?

MANTEL

Ivy Compton-Burnett is the love of my life. If I can't write—and it happens, your spring gets broken—all I need is a couple of hours with Ivy, and I'm back. There's a sort of click there. It's not that you imitate her, it's an almost mechanical restoration of rhythm and sensibility. I'm reset. It's almost all dialogue, you know, and there is very little by way of "he said" and "she said," so you have to count back, and the characters have only quite a small register, so they say what they have to say almost in formulaic terms, but then you think, Did she really say that? The harshness, the ruthlessness of the narratives and the appalling things that happen between the lines, almost incidentally—well, she's just like nobody else. For me she's magic. We are a very small fan club. Twenty years or more I've been hammering away, trying to get people to read her.

But what I was starting to say earlier, about influences, is that, in my case at least, they are not especially "literary." Your worldview is acquired not just from novels, but from all sorts of books. The big event in my life was getting an adult library card when I was fourteen, because that meant I was free. But while I was reading my way earnestly, with great dedication, through the French and the Russians, I was also reading Marx. That was just as important, probably more important. Among writers themselves, the question is not who influences you, but which people give you courage. When I began, the female writer who gave me courage, among our contemporaries, was Beryl Bainbridge. I don't write like Beryl, and never have, but when I began to read her, her books were so off the wall, they were so screamingly funny in a black way, and so oblique, that I thought, If she can get away with this, so can I.

I think R. D. Laing was more responsible than any novelist was for the fact of my becoming the kind of writer I am. The spring when we were graduating, Gerald's next move, he thought, was to go to train as a teacher. So he went off to a college for an interview, and I went with him. And the couple of hours he was being shown around and interviewed and so on, I spent in the college library, and I picked up a book by Laing and Esterson, called *Sanity, Madness and the Family*. I read it cover to cover, and I felt as if my head had been blown off. It was what they call the shock of recognition. I thought, I know this. I'm glad they've told me, but I know it already. I understand this, about the corruption that can lie at the heart of human communications, the way in which people within a power structure line up, the way that a victim is selected, the way that manipulation is performed using language. When I read this, I thought, So I do know something then. And it gave me a sort of inner authority when, twelve months or so later, I started writing. Because I felt that I knew something that, for a change, wasn't about the French Revolution.

INTERVIEWER

INTERVIEWER

Can you talk more about how you create your historical characters?

MANTEL

When I'm writing a novel about historical figures, I have to be everybody. It's strenuous. I know what it's like to inhabit Cromwell, but it never occurred to me that I needed to get inside the bodies of characters like Julianne or Karina, in *An Experiment in Love* (1995). It was enough to observe them. You know the concept of the good-enough parent—well, sometimes you have to settle for the good-enough character. When the people are real, though dead, I have a different feeling toward them. I consider them my responsibility.

INTERVIEWER

E. M. Forster talked about round and flat characters.

MANTEL

My books are full of flat characters. That's absolutely fine, because you have to know what function the character has in the book. On the other hand, when you make those characters, you do feel that it's a bit like playing. You don't have the same engagement. When you're working with the main characters and the medium-size characters, and they're real people, there is an enormous drive to understand not just what really happened, but how it really felt. To arrive at the truth of them.

There are a lot of historical characters in the Cromwell books who are just names. I mean, history just leaves us their names, and I've done the rest. But there is only one completely invented character. It's the servant, Christophe, and even he has an antecedent in real life. When Cardinal Wolsey was on a diplomatic mission to France, he was being systematically robbed by a servant, a little boy, who was going up and down the stairs and each time taking out a piece of his silver or gold plate—because of course people traveled with everything in order to put on a show. He has no name, what happened to him we do not know. But his story was somewhere in the back of my mind when I invented Christophe. He is a potboy in a backstreet tavern in Calais who attaches himself to Cromwell. I thought, This boy will be useful because, in the end, when Cromwell is in the Tower, I need him to have someone to talk to. It's going to be this boy. Later I thought, I know who you are—earlier in life, you robbed Wolsey. So he is and is not a fictional character.

People say to me—and with good reason—why don't you just make things up? It's just not in my nature, if the facts are to be found. It's very perverse of me to be a novelist because I really don't like making things up. I wonder if anyone in my books is completely fictional. I think, Why invent, really?

INTERVIEWER

With the historical characters, whose internal lives have to be inhabited, do you know them well before you begin the first scene? Or do you get to know them by writing the scenes?

I start from a small core, a glimpse of someone or a little sound bite, and work from there. When I come to write what I call a big scene, especially in the Cromwell novels or any historical material, I prepare for it. Whatever I've done before on that scene, I put aside. I read all my notes, all my drafts, and all the source material it's derived from, then I take a deep breath, and I do it. It's like walking onstage—with the accompanying stage fright.

INTERVIEWER

At what point did you feel you'd found an entry to the internal life of Cromwell?

MANTEL

I think there were two points, really. When I began to read material he himself generated, that is to say, his letters. There is one particular letter, written long before he entered the history books, as it were, when he sat as a member of Parliament in the early 1520s—so a clear six, seven years before he becomes a player at court. Now, parliaments in those days were called for a matter of weeks, and usually only when the king wanted to raise a tax. It wasn't until Cromwell that Parliament was kept in session almost constantly and used to reshape the country. But this session was meant to raise taxes for a war in France. And Cromwell made a very remarkable speech in it.

INTERVIEWER

It was recorded in the letter?

No, but among his papers. Parliamentary proceedings were not recorded, so one cannot be one hundred percent sure that the speech was delivered, but it probably was. There's no reason for thinking it wasn't. He told the king, Don't have this war, you can't afford it. It was couched in the most sycophantic language, in which one must address a Tudor monarch, but basically it said, If you do this, we'll go bankrupt. What's obvious is that he's unafraid to say it and also that he's got a grip on economics as opposed to finance. He can see a wider context. He can see that there are no circumstances in which England can afford to go on these European adventures. And then there's a little letter, afterward, to a friend, which says, I've just endured a parliament for the space of seventeen whole weeks, and he gives a big, big list, going down the page, of what they discussed, and he says, at the end, "We have done as our predecessors have been wont to do, that is, as well as we might, and left where we began." This letter is always quoted by historians, and what they usually make of it is, Would you look at this, the bitter cynicism of the man before he's even started. This is Cromwell in embryo. So it's taken with deadly seriousness. And I thought it was funny. I caught on to him. I could hear his voice.

But that's the public man. The private man is a different thing, and he began when the book began, when I picked up my pen and wrote the first pages about the boy being beaten up by his father. When I'd written two paragraphs, I thought, Where am I? And obviously I was behind his eyes, and at that point all the decisions about the book were made, about how to tell the story.

INTERVIEWER

Though you're extremely hesitant to tamper with history, and though of 159 characters in the books there's only one created out of whole cloth, you must have invented most of Cromwell's private life.

MANTEL

That's part of the bargain. Otherwise you're just a pseudo historian.

INTERVIEWER

Did his letters speak about his marriage?

MANTEL

No. There's one letter to his wife that's about six lines long.

INTERVIEWER

So we know nothing.

MANTEL

We have the household books. We have names. We have inventories, so we know the things they had. We have the names of the people who live there, we've got what they spend their money on, the possessions that lie about them. That's as good as it's going to get.

What I think is a crucial passage in *Wolf Hall* is also the most interesting, as an example of what a novelist does, as opposed to a historian. When Cardinal Wolsey fell from power, he was thrown out of his London palace. He and his household had to go find somewhere to live, and they went to his house at Esher. There they walked into an unoccupied house, which he didn't use much, it was not ready, they had nothing, and they had to start housekeeping. All of this is documented. A couple of days after Wolsey's arrival at Esher, Cromwell was seen to be standing in a window holding a prayer book and crying. When approached, he said that he was crying over his misfortunes—with the cardinal down, he was going to be destroyed, and he had lost everything that he'd worked for. "All the days of my life," he said. Every historian and every biographer who touches on Cromwell reports this episode, and what they usually make of it, rather strangely, is that it's some kind of cynical display put on for the benefit of the onlookers. Why he would be doing this no one ever explains, but that's the usual take on it. Or, even if they don't put such a dire construction on it, what they say is, Well, he tells us himself what's happening. He's crying because of the destruction of his career.

But the account of that incident begins quite clearly on All Hallows' Day. Rather, it begins the evening before, on All Hallows' Eve. It seems I'm the only writer who has ever noticed that it's the day of the dead. This is a man who, in the last three years, has lost his wife and two daughters. He's now lost his patron and his career is about to be destroyed. Once you realize what day it is, everything changes. A man may cry for more than one thing at once, and when you ask him why, he may not tell you. This appears to me to be the kind of thing that a novelist notices and that historians manage to ignore, generation after generation. Their minds don't make the jump because to them it's just another dateline—it could be May the twenty-fifth. That strikes me as a really powerful example of how evidence is lying all around us and we just don't see it.

How did you decide to put the dialogue in contemporary English?

Well, it's contemporary English inflected with Tudor English. Just as with *A Place of Greater Safety*, if I could get contemporary dialogue, I wanted to use it, and blend it into my own dialogue. Only there the contemporary source would be in French, so the questions weren't quite the same. I needed to write so that I could quote a passage of early Tudor English intact and smooth my invented dialogue in and out of it, so that one tapers into the other and no one can see the join. The decisions about language are taken around that necessity. I spend time working on individual words, but I spend more time making sure that the thought processes are congruent with the era, so that the metaphors are ones by which sixteenth-century people could live. They can't talk about evolution, they can't talk about their egos. The metaphors they build must be drawn from, say, their religious worldview.

That's more important than worrying about every word. Sometimes there just isn't a Tudor word for what you want, and then you have to think hard—if no word, could they have had the thought? *Boredom*, for example, that doesn't seem right. Were they never bored? But *tedium*, they know. And somehow *ennui* seems fine. Sometimes words play tricks, change their meaning. *Let* doesn't mean "allow," it means "forbid." They call a doll a "baby," often as not. They call a clever man "witty." It doesn't mean he makes jokes. So you can't be slavishly literal. You can try to be authentic.

Of course, I'm very concerned about not pretending they're like us. That's the whole fascination—they're just not. It's the gap that's so interesting. And then there are other ways in which they *are* like us.

INTERVIEWER

The marriage fascinates me especially.

MANTEL

The marriage ... ?

INTERVIEWER

It strikes me as daringly modern. You've given Cromwell a fond companionate marriage that resonates with contemporary readers.

MANTEL

I think it would have been a very typical one, though. That's what I set it up to be—typical rather than special. Here was a man who was good with women. His relationships with women at court were possibly extremely self-serving, but he kept them on his side. And he had women friends, which is possibly a bit unusual for the time.

INTERVIEWER

You don't see many male-female friendships in Shakespeare.

MANTEL

Why would you? Friendship on the whole is not the stuff of drama, is it?

INTERVIEWER

Male friendship is certainly all over drama. And prose fiction.

MANTEL

The thing you've got to understand about sixteenth-century life is that male friendship is much more important than your marriage. My take on this Cromwell marriage is that it's not a love match, it's a business arrangement. Though they come to love each other, it's not a great romance. They're not together very much. He's virtually a stranger to his younger daughter. So far, so typical. I think the reason I decided to make it a good marriage, rather than a bad marriage, is that after her death, he remained within her family network. Her family continued to live with him. We know a lot more about the marriage of Ralph Sadler, Cromwell's...uh, PA. That was an unlikely marriage because it was a love match. This is something that's possible in this era. Look at poor Henry himself—he's the one who's really ahead of his time, he's such a romantic.

INTERVIEWER

Some romantic.

MANTEL

He wants a wife he can talk to. A lot of the court-iers, they simply don't understand this, so when his fourth wife, Anne of Cleves, comes along, nobody understands why it's such a disaster. They think, He's a king, after all. He has to breed. Why does he need to talk to her? Why does it matter that she doesn't share his cultural pursuits, and so on? The fact that there was such general incomprehension shows that these people are living in changing times. Some haven't changed yet. The Duke of Norfolk's marriage was a debacle, but there's a letter of 1537 in which he says to Cromwell that he's just had a conversation with his daughter, who's about twenty. She has a very good wit, he writes. I never commoned with her before in any matter. I paraphrase. He's saying he's never had a conversation with his own daughter. He sounds startled. He's not entirely pleased that she's got a very good wit because he wants to boss her around, and she's not having it.

INTERVIEWER

Do you find yourself judging your characters?

MANTEL

I try not to. For me the question is, Can I live with you, or can I not? I'm fascinated by really clever people, and I think Cromwell had a brilliant mind—I know he did—and a rare kind of mind in that he saw the big picture and all the details as well. It was through his grasp of detail that he managed to achieve the things he did. When he said, We're going to survey the Church property, we're going to find out where the money is, he did it in six months, and that's with sixteenth-century communications. It should have taken ten years. But he knew how to mobilize others to work for him, how to give precise instructions, how to plan. He had a big-scale vision of a different sort of country from the one he started off in, and he had the practical sense to start bringing it about.

What sort of characters can't you live with?

I'm not really interested in people who start off possessing power—royal people, for example. It doesn't mean I won't ever write about them, but I find all that less intrinsically interesting than the climb. People ask, Are you not going to write about Henry's daughter, Elizabeth I? I have such an antipathy to her, I know it's a no-go. You have to select your subjects with the same care as a biographer, because you're going to spend a long time with them. There has to be a spark of liking.

(2015)

Claudia Rankine

THE ART OF POETRY NO. 102

Interviewed by David L. Ulin

Claudia Rankine was born in 1963, in Jamaica, and immigrated to the United States as a child. She attended Williams College and received an M.F.A. in poetry from Columbia University. Since early in her career, she has crossed the lines of genre, creating books as unified projects rather than loose collections, peeling back the surface of the moment to get at the complexities underneath. She is the author of five books—*Nothing in Nature Is Private* (1995), *The End of the Alphabet* (1998), *Plot* (2001), *Don't Let Me Be Lonely* (2004), and *Citizen* (2014)—and has collaborated on a series of videos with her husband, the filmmaker John Lucas, some of which infiltrate her writing in the form of transcriptions and images.

I met Rankine over three Fridays in July at her home in Claremont, California. It was a tumultuous period: our first conversation took place the week of the police shootings of black citizens in Baton

Rouge, Louisiana, and in the suburbs of Saint Paul, Minnesota, and the ambush killing of five police officers during a rally in Dallas, Texas; the third, the afternoon after Donald Trump's speech accepting the Republican nomination for president. These public topics wove through our discussions, explicitly and implicitly, as they often do in Rankine's work. Long a professor at Pomona College, Rankine was preparing to move across the country for a new job, at Yale University; in her dining room, the sideboard was covered with piles of books on race and whiteness, for a course she was developing.

Rankine has won numerous prizes, including a National Book Critics Circle Award and a Los Angeles Times Book Prize for *Citizen*, which was also a finalist for the National Book Award. Just a few months after we spoke, she was awarded a MacArthur Fellowship, which she plans to use to found the Racial Imaginary Institute. (The name comes from a book of essays she coedited last year.) In conversation, she is thoughtful and focused, speaking softly, with an edge of urgency. "How do you get the work to hold the resonance of its history?" she wonders. It's a question that occupies the heart of all her books. That the history to which she refers is both personal and collective is, of course, the point.

INTERVIEWER

You've spent the past two years on an extended speaking tour for *Citizen*. The book came out in 2014, during the protests in Ferguson. Recently, we've seen police shootings of African American men in Baton Rouge and suburban Saint Paul and five police officers killed during a rally in Dallas. What's your sense of where we are?

CLAUDIA RANKINE

If we go back to the killing of Michael Brown in Ferguson, there was a feeling, at least for white people, that suddenly they were seeing into black lives and how these lives played out in encounters with the police and the justice system. People were shocked. Then we saw the lack of indictment. In a number of other deaths, we saw that videotaping doesn't affect the course of justice, which we knew from the beating of Rodney King. Then we saw what happened in Baton Rouge, we saw what happened in Minnesota. Now you get to Dallas, and we have created somebody like a Timothy McVeigh, a veteran who is clearly triggered by what he's been seeing in the news. In McVeigh's case, it was Waco, Texas, and with Micah Johnson, it was the killings of African Americans, the videos of these deaths. He's not interested in Black Lives Matter protests. He's interested in retaliation.

INTERVIEWER

Citizen addresses these issues directly. It is literature as an act of public engagement. And yet, poetry—all writing—begins as a private act between the writer and her material. What is the relationship, for you, between these two modes?

RANKINE

The relationship between public engagement and private thought are inseparable for me. I worked on *Citizen* on and off for almost ten years. I wrote the first piece in response to Hurricane Katrina. I was profoundly moved by the events in New Orleans as they unfolded. John and I taped the CNN coverage of the storm without any real sense of what we intended to do with the material. I didn't think, obviously, that I was working on *Citizen*.

But for me, there is no push and pull. There's no private world that doesn't include the dynamics of my political and social world. When I am working privately, my process includes a sense of what is happening in the world. Today, for example, I feel incredibly drained. And probably you do, too.

INTERVIEWER

You make work in private, but once it goes public, readers make it their own. They define the work—and, by extension, you—in terms of who they are, what they want or believe.

RANKINE

In the case of *Citizen*, I willingly moved toward that engagement. It felt like the first time I could actively be involved in a public discussion about race, in a discussion that, to me, is essential to our well-being as a country. It wasn't simply about publicizing the book, it was about having a conversation. It was also an opportunity for me to learn what others really thought and felt. The responses were various. One man said he was moved by a reading I gave and wanted to do something to help me. I said I personally had a privileged life, which I do, and that I didn't need his help. What I needed was for him—this was a white gentleman—to understand the urgency of the situation for *him* and to help himself in an

America that was so racially divided. It wasn't about him coming from his own position of privilege—of white privilege—to take black people on as a burden, but rather to understand that we are all part of the same broken structures. He said, I can take what you're saying, but you're going to shut down everybody else in this audience. And all of a sudden I was like, What? I thought you wanted to help me! To remove him from the role of "white savior" was to attack him in his own imagination. A white woman, a professor, told me that what I was calling racism was really bias against overweight black women. You might think they were just a defensive man and a crazy professor, but again and again I was coming up against what was being framed as understanding and realizing that it was not that.

INTERVIEWER

And yet, both of those people would likely describe themselves as well-intentioned, even allies of yours.

RANKINE

They came and they engaged. I have a lot more patience and curiosity than I used to for following those arguments, for seeing where they will go. Often somebody will be interrupted by another member of the audience, who will jump in to shut that person down. This either comes out of an intent to protect me or else they're just impatient with a line of thinking they don't agree with. I don't know. But one of the things I do know is that you're not going to change anybody's mind by shutting them down.

You talked about some of this in your keynote speech at the Association of Writers and Writing Programs, especially the expectation that poetry should be relatable to a white audience. That's a fallacy, and it starts with the audience, not with the poets or the poetry. It renders our relationship with language defensive—"I'm putting up a shield of language as a way of protecting *you* from all the things *I* don't want to engage with."

RANKINE

That's what makes writing challenging and interesting. How do you get the work to arrive at readers in a way that allows them to stay with it and not immediately dismiss it? It's something I think about, because I know I'm also writing for people who don't always hold my positions. It's not that I think white people are my only audience. It's that I think of America as my audience, and inside that space are white people as well as people of color. Some white people still believe that white privilege and white mobility are the universal position. If a writer has a different experience of the world, the work is no longer seen as transcendent or universal. So as I'm moving around in a piece, I am hearing all those voices in opposition.

INTERVIEWER

The voices of the audience?

RANKINE

Voices I have encountered, yes. For me, working on a piece is like playing chess. You're moving the language around to say to somebody, Yes, I know you're possibly thinking this, I know this is a possible move for you. I'm going to include it here so you don't think that I haven't been listening. An example would be the Serena Williams essay in *Citizen*. That essay was dependent on the fact that a reader could go to YouTube and look up the moments I referred to in her life. I didn't want anyone who disagreed with my take on events or remembered them differently not to have a chance to access the moments for themselves. It happened, in an interview in Boston, that a gentleman said to me, I am a real tennis fan and I don't remember any of these things happening. The actual footage was easily obtainable by searching YouTube. I could have talked about the stress of racism on a body differently, but I needed examples that were available to the reader as raw data. I didn't want anyone to take my word for anything.

INTERVIEWER

"If you don't believe me, look it up."

RANKINE

That's not a bad way to work, or to be in the work. I spend a lot of time looking things up, doing research. I am always curious what I missed because I was looking right when I should have been looking left. I think it's important for *Citizen* that many of the moments in it are researchable. Without that, its credibility as a mirroring text would be lost. It took longer to collect incidents of microaggressions from friends and colleagues than it would have to simply use my own experiences, but it was essential to me that it be a collective and researchable document.

You call the Williams piece an essay. How did it develop?

In *Citizen*, there are episodic pieces structured around microaggressions, which are set in conversation with more scandalous and murderous accounts, such as the pieces addressing Hurricane Katrina, Trayvon Martin, or stop-and-frisk in New York. But my challenge as a writer in the Williams essay was, How do you show the effect of all this injustice on a human body? On an actual somebody? And how is that somebody read by the public? I didn't want it to be a traditional lyric because I wasn't trying to create an internalized consciousness for Serena Williams. I was talking about an invisible accumulation of stress in the body, so I had to show how it worked over time. I needed a form that would allow me to do that, and so I ended up with the essay.

That said, it's a lyric essay, not an essay essay, because it was written to fit into *Citizen*.

A lyric essay in the sense that it can abandon the strict logic of argument for something more intuitive or emotional?

Yes, and it utilizes many of the techniques of poetry—repetition, metaphor, elision, for example. I love finding the lyric in nontraditional spaces. Often when I teach my poetry workshop, I will take essays or passages from fiction or a scene from a film and list them among the poems to study. The "Time Passes" section in the middle of *To the Lighthouse* is an example of a lyric impulse. Others might be a passage from James Baldwin or Homi Bhabha or an image by Glenn Ligon or a song by Coltrane.

INTERVIEWER

Let's talk about how this works in *Citizen*. On the one hand, we've got Serena in a lyric essay. Then there are the passages at the beginning, those short pieces written in the second person—the girl who doesn't want to sit next to the woman on the plane because she's African American, the coworker who mistakes her for someone else and then refers to it as "*our* mistake." Those, too, are lyric moments. Traditionally, we associate the lyric with autobiography, but here the second person opens up the writing so that it becomes a collective experience.

RANKINE

When I first sit down to write, these movements are all intuitive. Just this morning, for example, I was listening to the recording of the shooting of Philando Castile in Minnesota, and the little girl, the four-year-old in the backseat of the car, says, "It's okay, Mommy, I'm right here with you." I wrote it down. That will be the beginning of something. Every time I watch that video, my eyes tear up, my throat closes. I hear that little girl, and I am transported to a place beyond my intellect. I'm no longer thinking about the policemen—I'm experiencing that child and her utterance. When a moment enters me that profoundly, I know I can wait to write because I'll forever be in dialogue with the moment. That part of the process I don't interfere with. I will be surprised and ready to begin when her voice makes its way into a piece.

And you might sit on that line for ...

Months. Or a week. Or a day more. Or years. Once it's on the page, I feel like *that's* when the writer shows up. Right now her voice just accompanies me. In terms of *Citizen*, the initial drafts were in the first person. But I didn't think it was effective, nor did I think it was structurally honest, because many of the accounts were not actually my experiences. Even though I employed the first person in *Don't Let Me Be Lonely* to weave together disparate situations, in this book I wanted the opposite. I wanted the disparate moments in *Citizen* to open out to everyone rather than narrowing inside a single point of view. Only when I employed the second person did the text become a field activated by the reader, whoever that reader is. That's what you want—for the text to be as alive and mutable as possible.

Much of *Citizen* is about the black body. This is part of what Serena represents, and something similar plays out across the other narratives. There's the man, for instance, who knows he is going to be pulled over, so he opens his briefcase on the passenger seat. That anxiety builds up in the body.

The key is that the anxiety, the stress, isn't a narrative. It's what interrupts the narrative, what stalls mobility. It's an invisible sensation that requires adjustment by the body, beyond the space of words. As a poet, I want to use language to enter that space of feeling. I'm less interested in stories. That's one reason I write poetry. Often when people are speaking with me, I feel what they are saying is the journey to how they are feeling. I mean, it's not that I'm *not* interested in what they're saying, but I feel like what they're saying is a performance. In many conversations I realize that the thing that's being said is really not the point at all, there's this subterranean exchange of contexts, emotions, and unspoken signals. I think a lot about how white dominance is part of this invisible and unmarked dynamic.

Sometimes, what is being said is at a perpendicular angle to what is really going on.

Exactly. The question is, How do you get to an authentic emotional place? I'm often listening not for what is being told to me but for what resides behind the narrative. What is the feeling for the thing that's being told to me? One of the reasons I work in book-length projects, instead of individual poems, is because I don't trust the authenticity of any given moment by itself.

The individual poem falls prey to the same narrative contrivance—

Of the novel, yes. Its trajectory is on an arc of time. Instead, I feel that what happens formally in *Citizen*, *Don't Let Me Be Lonely*, and *Plot* is an obsessive circling of the subject. Many positions are inhabited relative to a line of inquiry. It's like one of those mirrored rooms where the spectator sees the same thing repeated in different variations and from different angles.

INTERVIEWER

So in *Citizen*, those second-person vignettes form a series of slightly different but similar interactions. And part of the effect is that we feel it in the body.

RANKINE

Didn't feel it the first time? Here it is again. We don't get there by saying it once. It's not about telling the story, it's about creating the feeling of *knowing* the story through the accumulation of the recurring moment.

INTERVIEWER

Immersion as opposed to narrative.

RANKINE

That's why, in this case, narrative is irrelevant in a certain sense. It could be these ten stories or it could be ten other stories. I tried to pick situations and moments that many people share, as opposed to some idiosyncratic occurrence that might have happened only to me. For example, many black people have been in a situation where they've been called by the name of the other black person—at the office, at the party, in the room. The stories are many and the emotion is one.

The one that sticks with me is when the second-person narrator is jokingly called a "nappy-headed ho" by a friend, because it's a failed attempt at intimacy. The speaker is reaching for connection in some way.

When I heard that story, I found it fascinating. It's a matter of perception, of course, but as my friend was speaking, I thought that person wished to belittle her because they felt ignored. It could be because she was late, simply that. Some people go ballistic about being kept waiting. I also thought the "nappy-headed" utterance could be an attempt to say, I was anxious to see you. Why were you not anxious to see me? But because whiteness sees itself in a place of dominance, suddenly the racial dynamic comes into play. One benefit of white privilege is that whiteness has an arsenal of racialized insults at the ready. Like, *I* was anxious to see you and I'm *white* so I will put you in your *black* place. I didn't say any of this when my friend was telling me the story, but it struck me that maybe this woman liked her. You know, *liked* her. When I listen to people, I'm constantly thinking, Why do you remember this moment over everything else? And what exactly was the moment trying to say to you? As people of color, we can hear, we can feel, when the language is weaponized against us.

These small moments, they stick with you.

They're what stabilize and destabilize us. As a writer, I'm trying to draw those small moments *into* the larger moments. For the Hurricane Katrina piece, I was interested in *what got said around* the abandonment of all those people. We know the storms came, that people were abandoned, some of them drowned, they were left in the stadium without food or water. But when you have somebody like Barbara Bush touring a Houston relocation site for Katrina victims and saying, "And so many of the people in the arena here, you know, were underprivileged anyway, so this is working very well for them," those are the moments I find gut-wrenching. You have a woman saying, "You know, I didn't want to turn on the lights, everything was so black, I didn't want to shine a light on that." I mean, somebody *actually* said that. Or Wolf Blitzer said, "These people ... are so poor and they are so black." He *actually* said that. I can't forget this. I made a structure to hold the utterance because I *couldn't* forget. In these moments, black people are not seen as people. The same way you do not shoot somebody with a four-year-old child in the backseat unless you don't see people.

Darren Wilson—the officer who shot Michael Brown—volunteered that when he saw Brown what he saw was a "demon." He also said, "When I grabbed him, the only way I can describe it is I felt like a five-year-old holding onto Hulk Hogan." I don't think he could have been any plainer in expressing what was in his imagination. Projections of his imagination were being laid upon the body of this eighteen-year-old. But nobody investigates that. Nobody says, Hey, let's take Michael Brown out of this situation. Nobody asks, Why are you a policeman, if stereotypes, bias, and projections are informing you when you go into situations with people of color? Not long ago I was at the Ohio Reformatory for Women. Eighty percent of the inmates were white. Where and when do we see that reality represented? These women do not exist. Whiteness cannot support evidence against its own privilege, so these women are invisible.

INTERVIEWER

How much of your thinking about these questions goes back to the theorist Judith Butler? You've long been interested in her work.

RANKINE

Years ago, I went to hear Butler give a lecture. I'd always read her work, and I was very excited to see her speak in person. Her talk reiterated much of what I had read in her books, but then someone in the audience asked, Why are words so hurtful? The entire audience was ripped into attention. Everybody wanted to hear that answer. The response was something like, Because we are addressable. And the way we demonstrate our addressability is by being open to the person in front of us. So we arrive, we are available to them, we expose ourselves, and we give them the space to address us. And in that moment of vulnerability and exposure, we are not defended against whatever comes.

This has informed so much of my thinking, in life and in writing. I'm working on a theatrical staging of *Citizen* right now and I've been exploring that vulnerability of address whenever the characters interact.

INTERVIEWER

So although I've never met Serena Williams, I have an opinion about her, she is addressable to me.

RANKINE

There's an illusion—and I think it *is* an illusion—that we have access to her body, that we are free to say what we want about her, as if it will never reach her, or other black women. All the racism around black women's bodies has landed in the person of Serena Williams, even though, on a certain level, it has nothing to do with her.

INTERVIEWER

Does that ever give you pause? You had not met her when you wrote *Citizen*.

RANKINE

I had not met her when I wrote *Citizen*. But in a certain way, I could say I didn't write about Serena Williams. What I wrote about was the public's response to Serena Williams, the things that have been said about Serena Williams, and the way she has been treated unfairly inside the sport of tennis. In that sense, I don't think I've ever actually written about her.

INTERVIEWER

How addressable are you?

RANKINE

I was in London doing a taped program for the BBC. During the Q and A, there was a white gentleman, apparently quite well-known across the water, who raised his hand and said to me, I really liked your book, but I liked you better in your book than I like you here. It wasn't a question. I said to him, Well, I think the real question is, What did you want me to perform for you? What performance were you expecting that you're not receiving right now? He didn't answer. I would have liked for him to answer. You can never quite access the image in people's minds that you are being compared with. People often say to me, I expected you to be angry. Why aren't you angry? Or they've read the book and feel the book isn't angry, but it says what they feel, so they're curious how one can say exactly what they feel without saying it in a way that's angry. This is coming from African Americans as well as white readers. I think people forget that white people are just people, and that we're all together inside a system that scripts and constructs not just behavior but the imagination.

INTERVIEWER

The imagination first, don't you think? The imagination dictates the behavior.

RANKINE

Right. Ours is a structural and institutional problem. It's complicated because of the vast amount of privilege white people are allotted inside the system, but nonetheless we are a society, and if people are walking around feeling fearful based on the imagination, an imagination put in place by a white-supremacist understanding of the world, that's a problem for everyone.

The End of the Alphabet deals with many of these issues. This is a book about someone going through or having gone through trauma, deep pain, or dislocation. We never know exactly what the dislocation is, but the source isn't important, what's important is the experience. It highlights the tension between narrative and moment as overtly as any of your books.

RANKINE

When I set out to write that book, I specifically wanted to address the question, How do you write about the feeling of devastation that we all share? You meet people and you know they've had some kind of traumatic loss, something destructive in their lives. You intuit that without knowing their story. You don't have to know anything about them, you just know. I thought, Why can't I write a book that is less concerned with narrative but centralizes this feeling beyond it? The narrative could have been twenty years ago, it could have been the Holocaust, it could have been anything, but the feeling of past trauma is communicated by whoever is standing in front of you—that's what stays real.

INTERVIEWER

It's like muscle memory.

RANKINE

It's like a muscle memory that is not private. That's the other thing that's interesting to me—it's not private, it's shared.

How do you mean?

In the sense that I can feel it. I know that sounds kind of out-there, but I feel, when I meet somebody and they have had a kind of trauma—I don't have words for it, but I feel like I know that person in the room. When you arrive at the moment where they tell you what they've experienced, it's just the words being put to the feeling. But you already knew—you knew it by their eyes, you knew it by something. I wanted to write a book that was beyond what usually gets communicated in language.

So the title refers to these limitations of language?

Yes. Beyond the narrative, beyond the storytelling, beyond the anecdotes is another world of feeling so buried and dark and crippling that it needs its own genre. Poetry! We have Robert Lowell's attempt to do that in "For the Union Dead," but that is what you might call a psychoanalytic reading. Then you have somebody like César Vallejo, who will write a poem that says, I feel miserable today as César Vallejo, and nothing can account for the misery of César Vallejo. I am paraphrasing. It's that unmarked and unnameable place I was interested in entering in *The End of the Alphabet*. The book doesn't have an arc, it just is. How many ways can you articulate the sense of nothing?

As we were saying earlier, your work often moves between voices and tenses—first person, third person, present, past—as if to blur the specifics of the self.

RANKINE

I think this is because from the beginning, even in *Nothing in Nature Is Private*, as a black person in the United States, I was always myself and a black person in the United States, you know? I was simultaneously myself personally and also myself historically—

INTERVIEWER

Your interior self.

RANKINE

My interior self, but also myself as Claudia, who moved from Jamaica, grew up with my parents, the little dramas in my life. And then, I was also the Claudia who understood that part of the way in which she lives in this country is determined by the color of her skin. What is possible for me, what is open to me, what gets said to me, what doors close when I'm approaching—all of that.

INTERVIEWER

Does the fact that you were born in Jamaica, that you came to the United States as an immigrant, complicate those things?

RANKINE

It brings in other layers to consider. When you come to this country as an immigrant with your parents— you know, that's also crucial, because you're seeing the world through their lens initially—it affects everything. I remember my mother telling me, You can't trust these white people, I don't care if so-and-so invited you over to their house, you're not going. She had spent her entire life in Jamaica. This was her first time out of the country, and she was very suspicious of the motives of white people. We lived on Harper Avenue in the Bronx. I went to Cardinal Spellman High School, which at the time required uniforms. When I started, they had scoop-neck frocks, but there were these older, cooler uniforms that had bands that connected to the skirt. There was a family at the end of the block whose daughter had gone there, so her mother said to my mother, Your daughter is going to Spellman, my daughter graduated and I have some uniforms. Would you like them? I did want them, because they were the old ones, but my mother said, No, thanks. Later, I asked, Why didn't you take them? And she said, Why didn't she come to my house and knock on the door and give them to me? Why is she taking them out of the back of her car and acting like we don't live two doors down? For her, that was a form of insult—polite people would have said hello and had a conversation before handing over the uniforms. I always regretted not getting those uniforms. They seemed so much chicer.

Your parents came to New York for economic opportunity?

Yes. They worked in hospitals. He was an orderly and she was a nurse's aide initially. It's a cliché, but he worked two jobs, so he was doing nine A.M. to five P.M. and then, I think, ten P.M. to six A.M. or some such. I don't know how, but he ended up buying buildings in the Bronx and becoming a landlord. By the time I started high school, we owned our own home at the very northern end of the Bronx. When he bought the house, it was like *A Raisin in the Sun*. Within two years, it went from a completely white neighborhood to a completely black neighborhood. You could see it happen—every day I came home from school, there would be another white family moving out. I don't think that, as a child, I knew the language around white flight, but certainly I knew the transition was happening. I could see it.

INTERVIEWER

How much do you think this contributed to your sensibility, your way of thinking about the world?

RANKINE

I've always been interested in justice, but this might have had something to do with the dynamic inside our household, because my father—he was a piece of work. I think my sense of injustice started then.

INTERVIEWER

He's no longer living?

RANKINE

No, he passed away. But he was frustrated. Who wouldn't be if you were working two jobs, if you were a black man in the United States? It was the 1970s, and, as I think is often the case, a lot of his stress got taken out once he got home.

Is this when you began to think as a writer?

In the sense of being interested in the dynamics of charged situations, of trying to figure out how language—because in his case it really was language, if you stayed silent you were usually okay—became a trigger. I think I never lost that. But it is also tied to having come here as an immigrant and a young child and being put in a situation where you have to pay attention—vigilance, that's how I would describe it. You have to have a sense of vigilance even in your private spaces. I didn't start writing until I got to college, but from the beginning I was trying to see how I could write in ways that were...not greater than me, but that were not autobiographical, let's put it that way. You have to remember that I was in graduate school during the Language poetry movement, but that I also came out of an orientation that was based on autobiography, so these two modes started to come into conversation during that period.

INTERVIEWER
You were at Williams as an undergraduate and Columbia as a graduate student.

RANKINE
Yes. I studied as an undergraduate with the phenomenal Louise Glück. Louise could probably trace her roots as a poet back to Lowell and Berryman. Much of what I was reading in college was part of that tradition, but Louise was also trying to push the mythological up against the autobiographical.

She complicated the confessional impulse. She was not interested in excess. That was useful for me. In graduate school, I read Charles Bernstein, Lyn Hejinian, and Gertrude Stein. I thought about the limits of autobiography. As a black person, it's difficult *not* to understand that you are part of a larger political and social dynamic, but those writers made me pay closer attention to the materiality of the language itself. For white people, part of their privilege is that their positionality is never under threat, so the language appears to have more mobility, if you don't care about its investments.

My question was, How do you keep the intimacy of the language that is afforded the first person in the meditative, introspective lyric, and yet make it democratic and aware of its political investments? That's why, in *The End of the Alphabet*, I put aside narrative, and it's one of the reasons I wrote the book as a book rather than as individual poems. I was no longer interested in writing poems that built toward a story or that accounted for time in any linear way. I was seeing how far I could get simply with the ordering of words.

INTERVIEWER

What about the expectation of confession? You write, in *Don't Let Me Be Lonely*, "Because Oprah has trained Americans to say anything anywhere...no longer does my editor see confession as intimate and full of silences."

RANKINE

The autobiographical impulse grew out of a push against the modernist universalizing of the "I"—no one wanted to be Auden or Eliot anymore. Lowell,

James Wright, Amiri Baraka, and Adrienne Rich—
they all rejected their early work for a more authentic
and accountable use of the first person. For Lowell,
just saying "I" was enough. For Baraka, saying "I"
as a black man meant even more. These poets were
saying, I don't want to be the universal "I." I want to
stand in the truth of my particular positioning. The
same is true of Adrienne Rich. One of the things for
me about reading Rich as a college student was that she
was overtly and clearly addressing the female body,
female identity, and female possibility, and I remember thinking, This is very close to what I would say
about these things—but not exactly. And that was
it. The next semester I signed up for writing classes.

INTERVIEWER

So your decision to write began with a connection to
Rich, but also a disconnection, or distinction?

RANKINE

Right. In order to have it say what I needed, I was
going to have to do it myself. Now it seems full of
hubris, but it wasn't like that at all. It was pragmatic.
You know, black women are nothing if not pragmatic, because their whole existence in this country has been about negotiating a life without the
fantasy of external support. It was Malcolm X who
said, "The most disrespected person in America is
the black woman. The most unprotected person in
America is the black woman. The most neglected
person in America is the black woman." If anyone
had taught Audre Lorde, Sonia Sanchez, or Nikki
Giovanni in my college literature classes, I might
have begun in a different place.

In any case, it felt as if Rich had opened up a line of inquiry I needed for my own development as a person, beginning with feminism. She and James Baldwin together—because I was reading Baldwin at the time—began to give me language to speak.

INTERVIEWER

So Baldwin had a similar impact, as an essayist?

RANKINE

I think so, because inside the African American writing community, the same kind of drama was going on. You had Du Bois's notion of what should be presented to the white world and how you should do that, and on the other hand, you had people like Langston Hughes who were not writing for any one gaze, who could write across class lines.

INTERVIEWER

And could appropriate so-called low forms, such as the blues.

RANKINE

Exactly. Baldwin comes out of that tradition as well. We see the same thing with Jean Toomer. He's somebody who refused to perform blackness and because of that couldn't write after *Cane*, which is a masterpiece. The implications of who was going to read his work, and who he'd have to be for that audience, crippled his production. I think it's something all those writers had to think about.

INTERVIEWER

This brings to mind Rich's notion that silence is poison.

That is probably the most important aspect of Rich's work for me, the idea of silence as a poison. I think that's where I started with *Citizen*, with the sense that you should speak out because if you don't, it's going to harm you.

INTERVIEWER

And yet, we now live in a culture that has embraced confession uncritically, for its own sake—as a first-person gloss on *everything*.

RANKINE

A first-person accounting. Facebook, Instagram, Snapchat—all of it is about, I am here, I'm eating this, I'm standing in front of this, I'm seeing this, I'm with this person. It's all right if that's how someone finds their way to a public voice and a sense of community. The question for me is how to retain the intimacy of autobiography and still speak to the generalities of existence. In my books, there isn't one answer. For *Don't Let Me Be Lonely*, the use of the first person was very necessary.

INTERVIEWER

Although it's a mistake to assume that this first-person narrator is you.

RANKINE

Some people had trouble with that idea, that the first person could be a structural position unconnected to any particular self.

And then they felt it as a kind of—

Betrayal.

Because you had deceived them?

In their opinion. The text does say that the "I" is a construct. At no point does it say, This is nonfiction. In *Don't Let Me Be Lonely*, because it contains so many disparate narratives and travels across such a range, I needed an engine that pulled everything together while still allowing things to shift like a gear shift, and that was how the first person was intended to function.

Like *Citizen*, *Don't Let Me Be Lonely* takes on a wide array of narratives. There's the political narrative, there are several overlapping personal narratives, there's the question of loneliness, there's an extended meditation on death.

There were stories told to me by friends that I wanted to include. I had a friend whose sister had lost her children. There were stories of people dying that I heard twice removed. I was in their company but as the partner or friend of somebody else who was visiting. The first person let me maneuver seamlessly through these different lives.

INTERVIEWER

Throughout the book, you appropriate images or bits of information, such as a list of pharmaceutical companies or the Google search bar. That device seems to have its roots in *Plot*, where you use language to describe what might otherwise be images—the paintings the protagonist makes, for one.

RANKINE

I've always been very interested in the visual. The visual is capable of doing things text can't do. It never occurred to me in *Plot* to use actual images, although as I was working, I wondered, What does she do, this character I've created? And I thought, She's a painter! So I decided I could put the space for her work in the book. I'm not sure if that idea made it to the final version of the text. Looking back, it does feel like with each book I wrote, I was taking baby steps toward an inevitable relationship on the page with the visual, but each time it felt risky. By that, I mean unconventional.

INTERVIEWER

What caused the shift, the decision to integrate actual images—and not only images but also screen grabs, bits of data—into the body of the text?

RANKINE

You begin to see things as possible by reading other peoples' work. A big influence on me was Charles Bernstein. I remember reading works of his that were just lists, and I had this fantasy that if I had a house with a foyer, where you walked in and had to move through it to get to the main rooms, I would have a recording of Bernstein reading his poem "In Particular" playing on a loop. I carried that desire, that image, around in my head for a long time, and I'm sure it allowed for the use of images, because as Bernstein was listing these people—"An Indian fellow gliding on three-wheeled bike / An Armenian rowing to Amenia / An Irish lad with scythe" and so on—I was seeing them.

INTERVIEWER

Your books, taken together, trace their own sort of movement. In *Nothing in Nature Is Private*, you're feeling out the territory, with a variety of poetic forms and subjects. Despair or dislocation becomes a theme in *The End of the Alphabet*, although we don't know exactly what the crisis point is. In *Plot*, the crisis sharpens, revolving around life and birth—the narrative center is a woman reluctant to give birth to a child who is already growing inside her. Then, *Don't Let Me Be Lonely* pushes that internal despair to some kind of political engagement, and *Citizen* traces the desolation of public life.

RANKINE

That's accurate, I think, although this shouldn't suggest I knew what I was doing. I think that *Plot* is the most autobiographical because it's a book I wrote before I was pregnant, almost as a way to think about what it means to be an artist and to be a mother. We see that in *To the Lighthouse*, and I was also interested in Bergman's films, which sometimes show a reluctance toward parenting on the part of the male characters, based on a reluctance to replicate their own childhoods. So all those things were floating around.

Perhaps the most surprising turn in *Plot* comes at the end, which is written from the point of view of the child. It becomes a reconciliation, or conciliation in any case. "One has to be born," the child says. You shift persons here, not just grammatically—the actual protagonist becomes someone else.

RANKINE

My favorite part of *Plot* is all the definitions of *plot*, the idea that the thing that buries you is also the narrative of your life. It is important that the story include the product of the story. So let's say I was talking about my mother and myself, which I wasn't or maybe I was, who knows, but let's say I was, then the child's voice functions as a recuperative gesture to the struggle that preceded it, which is not to say the child won't have the same struggle—

INTERVIEWER

Or that the mother will be redeemed.

RANKINE

Right, just that the life is not the thing to be refused.

INTERVIEWER

All of that is only seen in retrospect, anyway, at which point the details appear inevitable. We read it in terms of cause and effect, whereas we all know this is not the condition of being alive.

RANKINE

Yes. There have been devastating moments, and there will be more devastating moments, but there will also be a life. I gave a reading in New York not long ago and somebody, a young black man, said, I read *Citizen* and I want to know why there aren't any hopeful moments in the book. And I said, The book is full of people living their lives, and even if it focuses on the interruptions to those lives, around the interruptions there are still lives. That, I think, is important to remember. So that's why bringing in the voice of the child represents a restorative moment. That was the intent of the afterword.

INTERVIEWER

The End of the Alphabet is your densest book. Then there's a real shift toward transparency between *Plot* and *Don't Let Me Be Lonely*. How conscious were you of that?

RANKINE

One of the things I wanted in *Don't Let Me Be Lonely* was for the language to be transparent. I didn't want people to have to stop to think, I don't know what she means by that. I wanted it to feel simple, accessible, even conversational. As a writer, this was the challenge—How do you get the ideas of, say, Butler or Lauren Berlant or Derrida or all the reading you've done, all the thinking you've done, inside seven sentences that say, I saw this thing and it made me sad? And how do you do it in a way that the research material is not effaced, that trace elements are still present? That seems always to be the challenge—to create transparency and access without losing complexity.

What about the shift, or expansion, of poetic form to include, or even become, prose?

RANKINE

When I was working on *Don't Let Me Be Lonely*, I started working in paragraphs. I was still utilizing repetition, metaphor, all of the poetic techniques and devices available to me. They were just applied to the sentence, not the line, the paragraph, not the stanza. But when I handed the book in, my then publisher said, This is not a poetry book. And it wasn't just them. I remember a male poet who came to my house—I was living at that time on 116th Street—we went for a walk in Riverside Park and he said to me, As your friend, I want you to know that *Don't Let Me Be Lonely* is garbage. It's not good. I'm telling you this as your friend.

INTERVIEWER

This was based purely on the form?

RANKINE

The form. It's not poetry, I don't know what this is, but it's not very good. I had to get a new publisher. This turned out to be a good thing because it forced me to say, You know, you could be right, but if it's going down, I'm going with it because it's what I mean. In those moments you just say, Whatever. Thank you very much for reading. That is what I've got. And not only is it what I've got, it's what I mean.

I also got a letter from an editor who had been a fan of *Plot* and asked to see new work. I sent the new work and he replied, I don't know what you think you're doing, but I can't publish this. Again, I thought, Okay then—I didn't send it to you, you asked for it. So that's how *Don't Let Me Be Lonely* began its public life. After Graywolf took it, many of those people who criticized it came around. The editor who had rejected the pieces for his journal sent me a nice letter saying something to the effect of, I was cleaning out my office before classes started, and I came across your poems. I read them again, and boy was I wrong. Which was very kind of him to have done.

INTERVIEWER

The moment of thinking, This is what I've got, and not only that, but this is what I want, this is what I mean—it seems essential, transformative.

RANKINE

People often ask the question, When do you know that you're finished? And I think that's when I know, when I've said what I mean. It might have taken me ten years or five years or two weeks, but that's what I mean. For now.

(2016)